From Raccoon Plain to Pakachoag Hill

A History of South Worcester, Massachusetts, highlighting the growth and dispersal of an English Enclave

David K. Jones
David M. Mickelson

Published 2016 by
Glade Street Press
southworc@gmail.com

ISBN-10: 0-692-64935-2

ISBN-13: 978-0-692-64935-0

Design and layout by
Carolyn Daughtry Krill
and
David Mickelson

Cover drawing from Inside Facts about Whittall Rugs and Carpets, a pamphlet by Frank A. Cox, 23 p., 1915.

Contents

List of Illustrations

Acknowledgments

A book like this demands research, and for that librarians are particularly important. We wish to thank several that were particularly helpful. At the Robert H. Goddard Library at Clark University, Beverly Presley and Fordyce Williams scanned several items from collections that could not be lent. At Worcester Public Library, Joy Henning willingly aided us in the search of the Whittall files and other parts of the Worcester Collection. At the Worcester Historical Museum, Robyn Conroy was very helpful in allowing us to view their map and photo collections and in getting permissions to use them. Evan Thornberry at the Norman B. Leventhal Map Center at the Boston Public Library scanned several fragile documents for us. Marie Dvorzak and Toby Lathrop, of the University of Wisconsin Library System, were very helpful in obtaining items on interlibrary loan and assisting with primary searches for fairly obscure maps and publications. Carolyn Daughtry Krill was a major contributor to the appearance of the book.

We would also like to thank Ronald Charette and Patricia Reardon, both South Worcester history buffs, and enthusiastic supporters of the South Worcester Neighborhood Center, for reviewing a draft of the manuscript. Their thoughtful comments are appreciated and helped to improve the manuscript. Bob Townsend, Paula Buonomo, The Rev. Nancy Strong, and Amy Mickelson kindly helped with photos. William A. Newman, co-author of "Boston's Back Bay", provided inspiration and advice on book writing and railroads. Melvyn Thompson, author of "Woven in Kidderminster" was an inspiration to pursue the history of Whittall and the other English carpet makers that worked for him.

Finally, we thank our families for their support and interest in the project and assistance in obtaining photos and other information. Our cousin Lucy Roe provided much information about family history and the Kidderminster, U.K.–Worcester, U.S.A. connection. Vin Mickelson read, edited, and commented on the manuscript, took several photos that we used, and helped find a number of obscure references as we made use of at the excellent library at the Wisconsin Historical Society. Karen Jones, Don Jones, Margaret (Jones) Bishop, and Rebecca (Jones) Francis reviewed portions of the manuscript and provided much needed encouragement throughout. We appreciate all of the help.

Preface

The United States is justly proud of its tradition as a nation of immigrants, and the field of study that deals with it is immense and varied. And yet, the literature as it relates to English immigration is relatively sparse. Some reasons given for this are the scarcity of records of early emigration from that country, and records that lumped English, Scots, Welsh, and Protestant Irish together as "British".[1] And, some students of the subject seem not to have seen English immigrants as "foreign" enough for study, perhaps taking their cue from Alexis de Tocqueville, who quipped that Americans were simply "that portion of the English people charged with exploiting the forests of the new world."[2] There may be yet another, subtler reason for the paucity of Anglo/American immigration studies. Although there were exceptions, the great majority of English immigrants came to the United States after careful deliberation and with clear-headed choice — not pushed from England by persecution or starvation, but "pulled" to the United States by the promise of opportunity — for the chance to own some land, for lower taxes, to become prosperous, and to become free of class restraints. The ringing sonnet on the statue of liberty — *Give me your tired, your poor, Your huddled masses yearning to breathe free, The wretched refuse of your teeming shore* — doesn't reflect the typical English immigration experience. In short, they weren't underdogs, and therefore, not an interesting subject for study. That's unfortunate, because their stories are not without interest or adventure. And, they made at least two important contributions to the growth of the United States: They helped settle and develop the American West, and, they were essential to the development of America's textile industry in the northeast.

Where enough immigrants were attracted to certain locations or employment opportunities, they often formed their own distinct communities where they lived among their kind. By definition, an "enclave" is any small, distinct area or group enclosed or isolated within a larger one. Many English enclaves sprung up around the United States during the nineteenth century, and they varied widely in the occupations and traditional habits they brought with them. In Elmira, NY for example, Yorkshire quarry miners celebrated their traditional "Rushbearing" festival, and Sheffield cutlery workers in Connecticut formed their own church congregations. In the Midwest, English farmers and miners established libraries and musical societies that emphasized English culture. Other enclaves had English-style pubs, cricket clubs, self-help societies, unions, and fraternal organizations like the St. George's Society. Initially, the early American textile mills drew their workers from the local farm communities, but before long, English textile workers found their way to them. And English textile manufacturers often brought their labor forces with them when they built their mills in America. Their dominance in the Frankford area of Philadelphia attracted so many immigrant workers that it became known as "Little Britain."[3] Soon, nearly every textile firm, whether American or English built, included some English immigrants, and they became a significant part of the workforce where their special skills were needed, or, as was often the case, where their reputation as steady and reliable workers gave them preference. American owners sometimes used recruiting agents that operated in English textile towns, but word of mouth and letters from immigrant kin usually brought all the skilled workers they needed. In 1840, Lowell, Massachusetts had 10 textile mills employing more than 40,000 workers, mostly young local women. Thirty years later, an American female weaver complained that, "great numbers of skilled English operatives are on their way to compete with us for bread…"[4] So many of them came to the neighboring city of Lawrence that, by 1860, they had their own newspaper and the city was called "the Bradford of

America."[5] This phenomenon was repeated in various degrees in many of the hundreds of textile mills that made up the new industrial landscape of the northeastern United States.

One of the most intriguing enclaves was created by Harrison Benn, who learned his trade in the family business of Joseph Benn & Co. of Bradford, Yorkshire. In 1904, in order to escape heavy British import tariffs on wool, he relocated ("outsourced" as we say now) the business to Greystone Village, in northern Rhode Island. He relocated a good piece of Yorkshire, as well. Benn recruited about 1,000 Yorkshire workers to work in his mill and surrounded it with "an idealized version of a Yorkshire village."[6] Streets were laid out for Bradford-style tenements and boarding houses, a social club, an auditorium, and shops. Eventually, the village added a cooperative store, a church, a pub, a cricket field, "and other activities specific to Yorkshire culture."[7] Benn's experiment was unusual in that he consciously created an enclave aimed at preserving a small piece of England in America. Typically, enclaves grew spontaneously, without such planning.

In their early stages, these enclaves fostered a sense of community and comfort to English immigrants as they settled into their new world. Although this new world shared a common language and system of law with the old, its customs differed and required adjustment. But their assimilation wasn't anywhere near as difficult as those non-English immigrants who had to struggle against the barriers of poverty, language, custom, and laws right from the start. Ethnic historians agree that these barriers actually strengthen and extend the survival of ethnicity. Without them, English enclaves assimilated quietly into the mainstream culture and disappeared quickly. For this reason, Charlotte Erickson's study of the English experience in America calls them "the Invisible Immigrants." While they lasted, English enclaves fostered native pride and the retention of English customs. However, these manifestations of "Englishness" survived only as long as there were enough first generation immigrants to foster and refresh them. Even Benn's conscious effort to transplant an English culture in miniature expired after a generation. As wages stagnated there, some families put upward mobility before communal identity and left for better jobs elsewhere. This was the pattern of the more typical English enclaves, as most second-generation descendants became Americans and merged into the mainstream and found jobs and/or married outside their communities. By the third generation, descendants were scattered and were generally unconcerned with their heritage.

This book tells the little known story of English immigrants who were pulled to America by the promise of opportunity and found it in South Worcester, Massachusetts. Their enclave owed its start to an English immigrant named Matthew J. Whittall, who built a carpet mill there in 1890, on the Middle River. Through the prosperous times of the late 1890s and the early 1900s, they held on to their English heritage as best they could as they moved to the new American suburbia and raised American-born children. This book places South Worcester in the broader context of the City and the Nation as a whole through two World Wars, the Depression, and the postwar growth of the middle class. The 1950s saw their American grandchildren, including the authors, move away and break their last connections with the community.

Notes:

1. The numbers of Scotch, Irish, and Welsh are said to have been a small part of the total. Accordingly, and where possible, we extrapolated them out from totals provided and used the specific designation of "English" to the remainder.

2. Barkan, *Immigrants in American History*, p.21.

3. Farley, *Making Arms in the Machine Age*, p.10.

4. Blewett, *The Yankee Yorkshireman*, p. 72.

5. *The Lawrence Journal* (1871–77).

6. Blewett, *The Yankee Yorkshireman*, p. 60.

7. Ibid., p. 64.

— Chapter 1 —
Pakachoag Hill

In late September 1674, a small group representing the Puritan government of the Massachusetts Bay Colony arrived at the Nipmuck village of
Sachem Horowaninit, on Pakachoag Hill in what is now South Worcester
(fig. 1-1). The principals were Daniel Gookin, Indian Superintendent, and
his friend and companion, the Reverend John Eliot, Missionary.[1] Pakachoag
was the last stop on their journey through Nipmuck country; their purpose,
wrote Gookin, was "to confirm their souls in the christian religion, and to
settle teachers in every town, and to establish civil government among them,
as in other praying towns."

Praying towns had originated earlier from a Colonial law passed in
1646 mandating "the Propagation of the Gospel amongst the Indians."
Eliot, then a minister at Roxbury, had learned the Native language and was
uniquely prepared and eager to take up the task. After an initial period of
trial and error, he gained a significant following of "Praying Indians" but felt
their conversion would remain tenuous while they lived "so unfixed, con-
fused and ungoverned a life, uncivilized and un-subdued to labor and order."
So, he concluded, they must live in fixed permanent settlements where they
could be monitored, instructed, and mentored—away from their villages,
their ancient traditions, and their familiar old ways.

In 1651, Eliot moved his praying Indians to Natick and established
the first of these praying towns. Gookin, a Captain of the Cambridge militia,
and Speaker in the Massachusetts House of Deputies, assisted him from the

start. Like Eliot, he was a student of the Indians and argued that "our best endeavours should be put forth to reduce them from barbarism to civility." The Natick experiment proved successful and won support for their theory that once Christianized, the Natives could be civilized and assimilated.

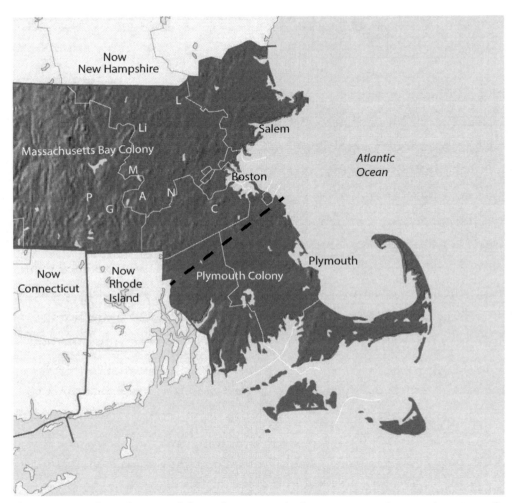

Figure 1-1. Map of eastern Massachusetts and adjacent states showing location of Plymouth and Massachusetts Bay Colonies. Also shown are the locations of circa 1660 praying towns: A, Ashland; C, Canton; G, Grafton; L, Lowell; Li, Littleton; M, Marlborough; N, Natick. P is the location of Pakachoag Praying Town in the southern part of what is now the city of Worcester and in the northern part of the town of Auburn. (Base map from http://mapsof.net/map/massachusetts-relief-map)

By 1660, six more praying towns had been settled at Lowell, Marlboro, Littletown, Canton, Ashland, and Grafton (fig. 1-1). The experimental phase was over, and they were now central to a more comprehensive colonial Indian policy. Land wanted for new colonial settlements would be purchased from or "donated" by the Indians, a small portion of which would then be granted back to them for a town "on condition of their subjection to the yoke of Christ."[2] Here, the Indians would accept the Gospel, submit to English law and jurisdiction, and adopt English culture. This was the established policy when, less than a decade later, colonial expansion began moving deeper into the interior. Gookin and Eliot, who started as partners in a missionary endeavor, had come full circle with the new policy and now were partners in its implementation.

In 1668, Gookin was sent by the General Court to examine the area called Quinsigamond and "make a true report whether the place be capable to make a village." After reporting to the court that there was, in fact, "meadow enough", plans for a settlement began. Soon after, Gookin claimed that the Indians about the area "began to hearken unto the gospel", and he and Eliot went there to "encourage and exhort them to proceed in the ways of God." The following year, July 1674, Gookin returned again, this time with a deed for the purchase of their land. Horowaninit, called by the English "Sagamore John", was among the leaders who signed or witnessed the deed, giving the Colony eight square miles of land in exchange for "twelve pounds lawful money."[3]

By September 28, Gookin and Eliot were back to perform the ceremony that would make Pakachoag a Praying Town. "Pakachoog", wrote Gookin, "is seated upon a fertile hill and is denominated from a delicate spring of water called ' pleasant water,' that is there" (fig. 1-2). This fertility helped sustain a better than average sized village of about 20 families and 100 people. It was the largest of the three villages of related bands called Nipmuck, or "Fresh Water People" in the area. As a semi-nomadic people, their villages acted as base camps, where they grew corn and other crops, and from which they traveled to seasonal hunting, trapping, fishing, and gathering places.

Gookin later described the ceremony at Pakachoag. They arrived there about noon, having made the journey from Manchage (Oxford) about 10 miles distant, and after a brief rest at Horowaninit's wigwam, the inhabitants of the village were gathered. Eliot preached and psalms were sung, which

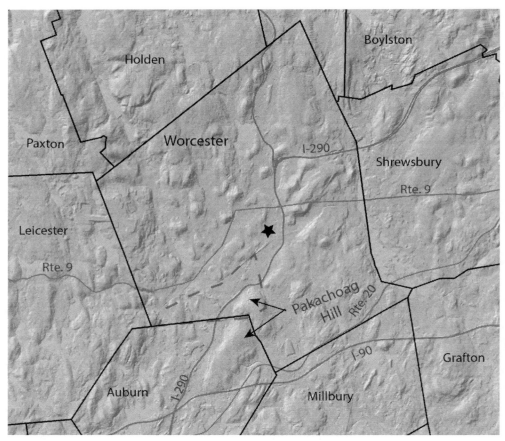

Figure 1-2. Map of the city of Worcester and surrounding towns. The star indicates the location of City Hall. Major highways are shown. Pakachoag Hill is shown in the southern part of the City of Worcester and the town of Auburn. The dashed line surrounds the South Worcester neighborhood. Area is about 12 miles across. (Base map from Office of Geographic Information (MassGIS), Commonwealth of Massachusetts, MassIT.)

"they attended reverently." Then Gookin "opened a Court" to establish their new civil government. Horowaninit was appointed "ruler of this town", and "clothed with authority of the English government". He also confirmed a new constable, a "good and sober man" named Matoonas. In closing, Gookin admonished the new citizens of the Bay Colony "to be diligent and faithful for God, zealous against sin, and careful in sanctifying the Sabbath". "Then was the whole duty concluded with prayer."

Gookin and Eliot stayed that evening at Pakachoag, and left for their homes near Boston the following morning. It isn't known if they stopped by the new English village of Quinsigamond, but it might be supposed they did. It was only a few miles distant, a few houses had already been started there, and Gookin had more than a passing interest in its progress. He was, after all, the driving force behind the settlement and also a would-be land-owner. A list of the first 30 proprietors and their house-lots included Daniel Gookin, with 50 acres and his son, Samuel, 25 acres. Perhaps they planned to live there, or maybe these were only investments. We will never know because just ten months after the ceremony at Pakachoag, the Nipmucks and Puritans were locked in a deadly and destructive war. Before it was over both villages, Quinsigamond and Packachoag, were ravaged and abandoned.

Apparently, neither Gookin nor Horowaninit had seen the war coming. It had its origins among an alliance of tribes of the Plymouth Colony led by Metacom, who was called by the English "King Philip". Tensions between Metacom and the Puritans had been simmering for years, as colonial policy toward the Natives shifted from peaceful coexistence to subjugation.

After war erupted in the Spring of 1675, the Bay Colony Puritans rushed to support their counterparts at Plymouth, while Metacom sought allies for his cause. Horowaninit was soon faced with a desperate choice. He could side with Metacom in a fight for the centuries old traditional life he had been born to, or side with the Puritans and fight for a strange new way of life he hadn't begun to comprehend. Under pressure from Metacom's emmisaries and from his own "Constable" Matoonas, he chose Metacom. By mid July, Pakachoag Nipmucks led by Matoonas were raiding the English settlements at Brookfield and Mendon.

Once fully ignited, King Philip's War spread like wildfire throughout New England, uniting the Colonies in an epic struggle against their Native inhabitants. At first, the intensity of Indian resolve shocked the English and set them back on their heels. During the first eight months, Indian raids wrought havoc on English frontier settlements, and it appeared they might actually be pushed back to the coast. But even as they celebrated their victories, Indian fortunes were shifting. By the summer of 1676, they had exhausted their food supplies and were suffering from hunger and disease, and as disillusionment set in, Metacom's alliance disintegrated. Horowaninit was among the first to see the hopelessness of their cause, and he surrendered over 160 of his followers to the authorities at Boston. Soon after, in August, Metacom was killed, quartered and beheaded, and the war was over.

King Philip's War devastated the Native populations of New England. Thousands were killed in battle or died from hunger and disease, and many survivors sought refuge among the Mohegan in Connecticut and Abenaki to the north. Survivors who were captured or surrendered were often executed or sold into slavery, but thanks mostly to the efforts of Gookin and Eliot, others were spared and shown a measure of English mercy. These were placed among colonial families as servants; the rest were removed to four designated villages where they could be kept under constant observation.

The Pakachoag Nipmucks shared their measure of all the various fates suffered among Metacoms followers. Horowaninit was spared, but only because he surrendered Matoonas and helped execute him. His ultimate fate is uncertain, but the children he surrendered were sold into servitude; Gookin himself took two of them, a boy and a girl. Other Pakachoag survivors were sent to the established camps at Natick or Hassanamesit (Grafton). No longer a threat, these Nipmucks and their descendants were left to eke out a living as best they could, and were gradually forgotten by the dominant English society.

Ironically, this neglect gave them back some measure of freedom. The Natick camp was gradually abandoned as Nipmucks moved to other reservation communities such as Hassanamesit, or to their own traditional homelands. Among them was Samuel Bowman, a Nipmuck who left Natick after 1719 to live on Pakachoag Hill. He and his family lived there in a semi-traditional manner, supplemented by hiring his labor to local farmers. His granddaughter Hepsibeth, who was born there in 1761, represented the last stages of cultural transformation. As a young girl, she and her widowed mother supported themselves in the manner of most 18th century New England Natives: cultivating small gardens, gathering wild food, and serving in English households. As a young adult, Hepsibeth married a widower named Jeffrey Hemenway and assumed the life of a typical low-income housewife; raising children and taking in laundry and ironing to supplement the family income. About 30 years later, after Jeffrey died, she moved to a small rental on Mechanic Street where she supported herself and a crowd of dependents, first as a laundress, later as a cook, and in 1847 as a "wedding cake maker", much sought after by wealthy families and highly respected in the community.

When Hepsibeth died in 1848, she was by no means the "last of the Nipmucks." She was just one among those who, with perseverance, pride, and great courage had successfully bridged the gap between two cultures. Many of their descendants still live in Worcester, though most are unrecognized as such. One of them is named Thomas Doughton, a Holy Cross College Professor who is working to preserve the "delicate spring of water" that is still there on Pakachoag Hill.

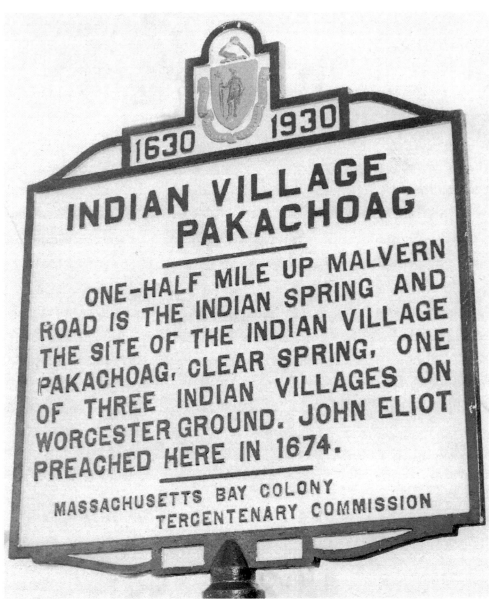

Figure 1-3. An historical marker stands near the site of the Pakachoag Praying Town at the corner of Southbridge Street and Malvern Road, South Worcester. (From the collections of the Worcester Historical Museum, Worcester, Massachusetts.)

Notes:

1. The Reverend John Eliot is well known as the "Apostle to the Indians" for his missionary work among them, and for his translation of the Bible and a grammar of the Native language called "The Indian Grammar Begun". Daniel Gookin is an equally fascinating and important figure, but not nearly as well known. He emigrated first to Virginia in 1641, then to Maryland, where he had acquired several large plantations. His non-conformist beliefs lured him to the Puritan Massachusetts Bay Colony in 1644 where he began his life-long career in service to the Puritan government. This was interspersed with several returns to London and service there for Oliver Cromwell. After Charles II was restored to the crown, Gookin escaped to Massachusetts with two of the judges who had condemned Charles I, and where, it is believed, he protected them against Royal revenge. For the rest of his life, Gookin resisted British efforts to limit the colony's independence through a combination of persuasive argument and thinly veiled disobedience. In his capacity as Indian Superintendent, Gookin traveled extensively among the Indians and probably understood them better than anyone, including Eliot. His two books about them, "Historical Collections of the Indians of New England" and "The Doings and Sufferings of the Christian Indians," are invaluable primary accounts. In the aftermath of King Philip's War, Gookin worked tirelessly with Eliot to protect and give fair treatment to the surviving Natives. In 1681 he was elected Major General of the military forces and held that position until his death March 19 1687.

2. The Puritans asserted their rights to the land as (1) given by a patent from the King, and (2) granted by God. John Winthrop, Governor of the Massachusetts Bay Colony, quoted God's instructions to "replenish the earth and subdue the land." Therefore, Winthrop argued, "that which lies common and hath never been replenished or subdued is free to any that will possesse and improve it". With this construction, land deemed not economically productive by the Puritans was theirs to take, and Indian land rights were legitimate only if approved and "granted" by the General Court.

3. Like most Native Americans, the Nipmuck did not share or at first understand the European concept of land "ownership". Horowaninit would have considered the territory described in the deed as a place his people collectively used and inhabited. He probably thought he had agreed to share that use with the English, in return for which he gained some trade advantages and a strong ally.

— Chapter 2 —
Puritan Legacy

The Puritans' victory in King Philip's War settled once and for all which culture would dominate and carry the future, but it came at a great price. Thousands died, families were uprooted and left grieving, and homes, farms and crops were destroyed. The whole line of interior frontier settlements was abandoned and pushed back more than 20 miles toward the coast, and the colony's economy, based largely on fur and agricultural exports was dangerously weakened. Yet the Bay Colony responded quickly, and by the spring of 1677 resettlement plans for most of the towns were well underway. But prospects for the resettlement of Quinsigamond were dismal. The war had cleared the Nipmucks who might have acted as a protective barrier had their Praying Towns had time to mature, but now the area was open to Indian attacks from the north, and still very much a frontier. It wasn't until 1684 that enough families were willing to risk settling there. This time the plantation would be called Worcester. Daniel Gookin (now Major General), and his planning committee chose the name in a not so subtle gesture of defiance. It honors the Puritan victory over Royalists supporting Charles II in Worcester, England, in 1651; the same Charles II, now restored to the crown and in the final stages of his battle with the Puritans in New England.

While Worcester, Massachusetts was in its beginning, the Bay Colony was nearing its end. In fact, the settlements of Quinsigamond (1673), and Worcester (1684), are like bookends for the twilight years of the Puritan experiment in Massachusetts. In the decade between, the war-weakened colony was in spiritual decline and dying from within, and at the same time, they were fighting a legal battle with the Crown they could not win. To understand this, we have to go back to the beginning.

The Massachusetts Bay Colony was originally organized as a commercial enterprise by English investors with a charter from the Crown. But before it was launched, a Cambridge-educated Puritan named John Winthrop joined the venture, got elected its governor, and then took the charter and its governing authority with him to America. With this dazzling coup, the Puritans had secured their "city on a hill." Winthrop and the first Puritan settlers sailed to America in the spring of 1630, and during this voyage he laid out his famous vision for the colony. It would be, first and foremost, a covenant with God to live as one body, in strict accordance with His will.

They had taken a "commission" he said, "to improve our lives to do more service to the Lord, and work out our salvation under the power and purity of his holy ordinances." Winthrop said that they were not there to "seek out great things for ourselves", and warned: "if we shall be seduced and worship other Gods, *our pleasures and profits*, and serve them, it is propounded unto us this day, we shall surely perish out of the good Land whither we pass over this vast Sea to possess it."

It seems one of the great ironies of history that this spiritually centered "city" would become so commercially successful. But these Puritans were not misguided misfits. They were intelligent, educated, and possessed of a variety of vital skills, and were bound together in a common purpose under a strong leader. Governor John Winthrop (fig. 2-2) had all the leadership qualities so often touted in modern leadership guides. He had a vision for his community, and set goals to fulfill it; results were closely monitored, and impediments along the way were eliminated. He could do all this because his government was essentially theocratic, its franchise limited to like-minded and carefully vetted church members, and it was virtually independent of the Crown.

This drawing is designed to illustrate the relative positions of home-lots. The number on the map corresponding with the one set against the name below will indicate the location occupied by that person.

1	Ephraim Curtis.	11	Bridget Usher.	21	Thomas Hall.
2	Thomas Brown.	12	Ephraim Curtis heirs.	22	Peter Goulding.
3	Daniel Turell.	13	Daniel Henchman.	23	James Butler.
4	Samuel Daniel.	14	Daniel Gookin.	24	Thomas Allerton.
5-29	John Wing.	15	Digory Serjent.	25	Isaac George.
6	George Danson.	16	Charles Williams.	26	William Weeks.
7	Samuel Simpson.	17	George Ripley.	27	Isaac Bull.
8	Adam Winthrop.	18	William Paine.	28	George Rosbury.
9	Mr. Peirpoint.	19	James Holmes.	30	John Wing's Mills.
10	Hezekiah Usher.	20	Alexander Bogell.		

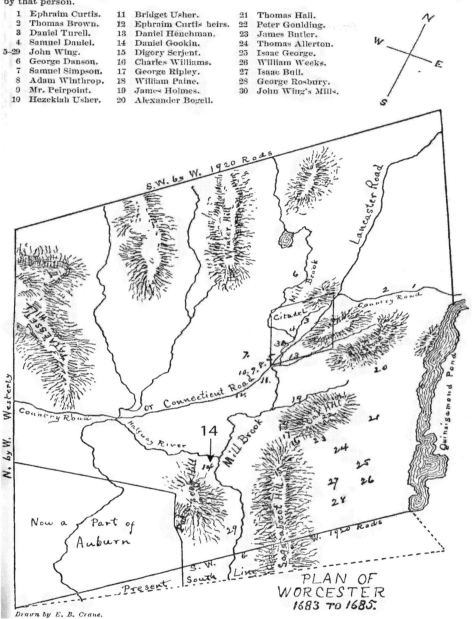

Drawn by E. B. Crane.

Figure 2-1. Map of Worcester portraying the location of farms in 1683–1685, at the time Worcester was named. Daniel Gookin's farm is number 14, on the north side of Pakachoag Hill (arrow). Map was made by EB. Crane at the time of the 200th Anniversary of the Naming of Worcester. (From Hoar, 1884, p. 115.)

During the early years of struggle and adjustment, sheer necessity was met by unified purpose, and if toiling for God seemed more worthy than toiling for "pleasure and profits," toil they did. They put aside all comfort, cherished work, and despised idleness. And the Puritan work ethic was born.

Figure 2-2. Portrait of John Winthrop, Governor of the Massachusetts Bay Colony intermittently between 1630 and 1648. From Burton, A. H., 1899, A History of the United States, p. 52. (http://commons.wikimedia.org/wiki/File:John_winthrop_illustration.3.jpg)

Within two years they built a self-sufficient economy based on furs, lumber, fisheries, and ship-building and developed a trade system with England, other European ports, and other colonies. For more than a decade, wave after wave of Puritans came, and as their numbers grew, so did the number of towns that lined the coast of New England like links in a chain; each one granted to family groups who bound themselves together by covenants that reinforced the basic aspirations of the colony "to live as one body." Each of these new towns was meticulously planned in advance and settled with an agreed upon government, its leadership, and church, and its minister. As the community matured, new laws were passed to encode and solidify the objectives of the covenant. In 1636, the General Court established the College of Harvard for the training of ministers and school teachers, and in 1647, grammar schools were mandated for every town. Although aimed in part to maintain religious and moral orthodoxy, they were also intended to develop a literate community of informed citizens. Other laws were designed to restrict, rather than enable, individual expression. In 1649, it was ordered that "whosoever shall profane the Lords day by doing any servile work or such like abuses shall forfeit for every such default ten shillings or be whipped."

By the mid-17th century, the Puritan experiment in Massachusetts had reached its zenith. A first hint of decline came in 1649 with the death of John Winthrop; its founder, driver, and guiding force. Over the next two decades, a prosperous and powerful merchant class emerged along the coast that ignored his warning against the seductions of "pleasure and profits," and paraded their wealth in fancy clothes and stylish homes. As their eyes turned to these "other Gods," church membership and attendance declined. Alarmed Puritan ministers railed against their commercialism and backsliding, demanded repentance, and warned of God's punishment. Now, all disasters—earthquakes, fires, plagues, and storms—were seen as signs of God's displeasure and their sermons became jeremiads: "Righteousness Rained from Heaven," "Days of Humiliation," "Times of Affliction," and "The Day of Trouble is Near." Boston Minister Cotton Mather best captured what had happened to the "city on a hill" when he said, "Religion begat prosperity, and the daughter devoured the mother."

Meanwhile, an expanding population was moving deeper into the interior, powered by newcomers from England and a younger generation hungry for land and less interested in covenants. The settlement at Quinsigamond is a vivid example. In 1673, while Daniel Gookin was planning the community, he learned that the General Court had already granted choice lots to the Church of Malden and several individuals.[1] Although this false start was resolved, it was a serious breach of the covenant oriented town-building process that had bound the colony in a cohesive network.

King Philip's War was the most drastic sign yet of God's anger. Surely, the Indians were unleashed by God to punish them, but why? State and

Church combined in a search for answers. In November 1675, the General Court made a thorough inquiry into the sins of the colony, published them, and made laws to restrict them. Yet the question remained; how can we return to God's grace? The church answered this one: They had come to New England with a covenant from God, and had failed it. Of course they were being punished, *but God is merciful.* The way to redemption is through a renewal of the covenant, to be undertaken as a special act in every town and every church. This hopeful concept of reformation and reconciliation helped carry the Colony through the war.

But the fires of war hadn't yet cooled when more trouble came from across the sea. In June 1676, Edward Randolph landed at Boston on a mission for the crown. His stated purpose was to investigate land disputes between the Bay Colony, Maine, and New Hampshire. But his real purpose was to investigate the Bay colony itself. For more than a decade, Charles II had been hearing complaints that Massachusetts was disloyal to the crown and breaking English laws. In 1664 he had sent a commission to the colony to measure the loyalty of its leaders and reassert royal authority. The commission was met with stubborn resistance and accomplished nothing. In a huff, one of the Commissioners later summed up the prevailing colonial attitude. "They of this colony say that Charles I granted them a charter as a warrant against himself and successors, and so long as they pay the fifth of all gold and silver ore they are not obliged to the King but by civility."

Twelve years later, Edward Randolph was received with the same arrogance, more hostility, and even less cooperation. When he returned to England, the vindictive emissary wrote two scathing reports. The first one falsely claimed that the people of the colony were "well affected to his Majesty and his government", but the magistrates "keep the country in subjugation and slavery, backed with the authority of a pretended charter." The second report gave a detailed list of colonial violations: they had formed their own commonwealth, denied appeals from England, they coined their own money; and they violated the Acts of Trade and Navigation. These and more were listed, all of them true. Randolph's reports had the desired effect.[2]

The royal government was outraged and demanded a new charter limiting colonial autonomy. It would take a while; there were legal issues to be resolved, but the royal course was fixed. The issue played out for eight more years while the General Court of Massachusetts appealed, delayed, and reluctantly made changes to fix the offending violations. But they would not—in fact, *could* not concede their self-government, "… for it would offend God." Minister Increase Mather agreed. Submitting, he said, "would be inconsistent with the main ends of their fathers' coming to New England." If we resist, the colony might suffer, but "better suffer than sin and if they suffer because they dare not comply with the wills of men against the will of God, they suffer in a good cause, and they will be counted martyrs in the next generations and at the great day." In the end, martyrdom prevailed. In 1684, England vacated the charter and ended colonial self-rule. Edward Randolph, the "evil genius" himself, carried the news to New England.[3]

Winthrop's "city on a hill" lasted fewer than 55 years—less than the average life span of a Puritan man. Regardless of how one views the Puritans, we can marvel at their energy and lasting impact. Consider that within that brief span of time, they overcame centuries-old Native cultures, and forced them to change or die. They took their land, and changed it to suit their needs. Then by their own design, they changed themselves. They had already decided what they wanted to be on the way to New England, and then went about becoming it. In this they weren't entirely successful—human nature and outside forces prevented it—but the goals they aspired to, the results they achieved, and the institutions they established survived in some form long after their government. Much of what they became, we inherited, and we still aspire to many of their goals. Puritan self-governance ended the same year Worcester, Massachusetts was born, but *Puritanism* bled into Worcester and helped shape its future.

The belief that an educated citizenry is essential to good citizenship produced the College of Harvard just six years after the birth of the colony, and then produced a system of universal education. It was a unique concept, with no precedent in England or elsewhere, and it survived to become an American institution. Two hundred years later, a system that once turned out good Puritan citizens was turning out good Americans citizens. In 1898, the Superintendent of Worcester Public Schools boasted, "It may be affirmed without danger of contradiction that no city in America can claim to rival Worcester in the number and variety of its general educational institutions. Of all these institutions, the public schools… have been the chief instrument in promoting the intelligence of the people, and we must depend upon them in the future to insure to every home the priceless blessings of an advancing Christian civilization."[4]

In 1690, Cotton Mather, the Boston minister, said "The People of New England are a People of God." More than 200 years later, Protestant minister A. Z. Conrad wrote: "The influence of the churches in Worcester is prodigious. They are the prime movers in every social reform. They inculcate the doctrines and principles of civic righteousness. They are the great conservators of moral health. They are the first to protest against lawlessness. They encourage and enjoin every public and private virtue, and condemn every vicious tendency. Worcester people are a church-going people. As compared with other cities of its size, our city is reverential and respectful in its attitude toward religion. As a result, its moral tone is high."[5]

Church and State strictly enforced the "Moral Ideal" of Puritan society. There was no room for dissent or backsliding, and this intolerance gave rise to traits that in a later, more diverse and secular society gradually softened into the "high moral tone" of an "advancing Christian civilization" encouraged by church and state in 1890's Worcester. But a moral superiority still echoes in that tone. In an 1891 article about a new wave of "foreigners",

Light Magazine sniffed: "To produce some of the alleged humanity that reaches our shores, it would seem that an original and special creation were necessary. However, they are here, and here to stay. We must make them over into American citizens… to make them thus, our schools must be taught by God fearing, country loving teachers."[6] Thus, foreigners became Americans, and the "Ideal" of American exceptionalism lives on today.

"Puritanism is the haunting fear that someone, somewhere, might be happy." This popular characterization is an exaggeration with a basis in fact. Puritans were human, and they liked to drink, make love, play, and be merry—but all in their time. The law designed to protect the Sabbath is now remembered for the excesses it engendered. These too, have softened but as every living resident of Worcester knows, vestigial blue laws prohibiting the sale of alcohol, commerce, or certain activities on Sunday have endured to the present day. Another restraint, the sheer necessity for constant labor, left little time for fun. The Puritans worked hard for long hours because they had to. Idleness was the enemy of survival. Over time, hard work became an "Ethic" and a model for society. In 1907, William A. Lytle, president of Worcester Board of Trade, said: "The Worcester of to-day, like the Worcester of early days, is made up of a conservative, industrious, persevering and hard-working people. Our success as a city has not been one of mushroom growth in population, and sudden riches, but rather the kind that is sure to come to either an individual or a community that is enterprising, honest and industrious."

Today, we do not credit enough the spirit of independence the Puritans brought with them, and which bred American independence. That is not to say they sought to establish a free state, but they did seek freedom *from* a State. They found it in New England and held on to the last. In his speech celebrating the 200th anniversary of the naming of Worcester, John Frisbie Hoar credits that independent spirit to England, the "cruel nurse" of the

Puritans, where "our fathers drew from her bosom the courage with which they resisted her."

> "Strong mother of a lion line,
>
> Be proud of those strong sons of thine,
>
> Who wrenched their rights from thee."

When a new wave of English immigrants came to South Worcester in the late 19th century, these English Puritan traits were still alive.

Notes:

1. Ephraim Curtis, of Sudbury, was one of these "Sooners." In 1673 he settled on 500 acres of the Quinsigamond Plantation. According to George Frisbie Hoar, "He is entitled to rank as the first settler of Worcester and represents an element which has not received full justice from New England history, the brave and adventuresome frontiersman."

2. Randolph downplayed the ravages of King Philip's War. He made no case for sending aid to the distressed Colony, and the Puritans didn't ask for any. They did accept a shipload of supplies collected and donated by church members in Dublin.

3. Randolph was universally hated, and mocked by New England quipsters as the Devil.

4. Clarence F. Carroll, Superintendent of Public Schools, quoted in Rice, F.P., 1899, *The Worcester of Eighteen Hundred and Ninety-Eight*, p. 283.

5. Conrad, A.Z. (Reverend), "Protestant Churches" in Rice, F.P., 1899, *The Worcester of Eighteen Hundred and Ninety-Eight*, p.165.

6. Light, A Journal of Worcester and Her Neighbors, 1890, v. 4, no. 2, p. 50.

— Chapter 3 —
Jonas and Gershom Rice and the First Permanent Settlement, 1713–1769

On the first day of April 1713, Mrs. Elizabeth (Haines) Balcom of Sudbury, Massachusetts sent a letter to her daughter, Elizabeth Rice, who lived in Groton, Connecticut. They hadn't seen each other since Elizabeth and her husband Gershom Rice moved to Groton shortly after the birth of their first son, Gershom Jr. That was in 1696, and since then, about 15 years had passed and five more grandchildren had been born in Groton. Abbreviated here, (but uncorrected) the letter is a window into its time.[1]

Mostly, she writes about their health, and hers: "Dear and loving children after kind love presented to you all hoping that these same lines will find you better than you were when you wrote[.] I have had a very ill time my selfe many sorts of pains that I faint of blood and now that faintness at my stomach remaineth at times[.]"

Raised a Puritan, she hoped that these 'afflictions' that "… the Lord is sending amongst us… may be for gods glory and our good." Yet, she sends with the letter some healing herbs for her grandchildren, with instructions for their use: "for Elizabeth and mathyas [Mathias] also the child here is garlick boyl in milk and he should eat and drink all and I wold have you get some wormwood and tansy and spearemint and steep them and… lay them on his Stomach…and for Elizabeth I have sent saffron and wild margoram flowers and she may pound them and mixe them with a little sugar…"

At the end of the letter, there is the hint of a future reunion "… If she (Elizabeth) is able to come down when you come I should bee glad to see one more of the children before I dye. I have sent you seeds and herbs and flowers and garlic for the child and so rests your mother which loves you well and it is hard to be parted I should bee glad to you bee hear and soe I rest."

Mrs. Balcom must have known as she wrote this that Gershom Rice and his brother Jonas had recently sold their lands in Groton, and purchased land in nearby Worcester, where they planned to settle. Indeed, shortly after it was written, Gershom and his family moved to Marlboro, where Jonas and most of his other siblings lived, and where they could finalize their plans. For Mrs. Balcom, we can assume there was a least one reunion at her home in nearby Sudbury. She lived until the year 1715; time enough for her daughter and "one more of the children" to "come down" to Sudbury for a visit.

Gershom and Jonas Rice were second-generation members of a family of 13 siblings, all born and raised in Marlboro between the years 1654 and 1679, when it was still a Puritan town. In their youth, the Bay Colony Charter was revoked and replaced by the Dominion of New England; they were young still when its hated Royal governor, Sir Edmund Andros, was jailed and sent back to England, and when the current government was installed, October 7, 1691. On that date, Marlboro became a town in the Colony of Massachusetts, Province of Massachusetts Bay.

The Rice family was large even for those times when families averaged seven children per family. Gershom, born 1667, and Jonas, 1672, were the fifth and seventh sons of Puritans Thomas Rice and Mary (King), who emigrated from England, married in America, and raised eight boys and five girls. Ironically, it was this productivity that ultimately made dispersal of the family necessary. Throughout New England, high birth rates and low mortality rates had tripled the population between 1660 and 1700. As a result, land resources in the older towns were getting scarce and young men like the Rices had to look elsewhere for farmlands of their own.[2]

When the second settlement of Worcester began in 1684, Gershom and Jonas were still young, unmarried, and supporting the family farm in Marlboro. When Gershom married Elizabeth Balcom, about 1696, the best lands in Worcester were taken, and so they moved to Groton. And, when Jonas married Mary Stone, in about 1701, the Worcester settlement was on the verge of collapse. In 1702, the European war known as Queen Anne's War in North America, stoked new raids along the frontier by Indian allies of New France, and later that year, the Provincial Government declared Worcester too remote for protection. As a result, the town was abandoned, except for one stubborn holdout named Digory Sargent. As historian Lincoln Kinnicutt put it, "He was the last inhabitant to desert the second attempt to form a settlement and he was obliged to, when he was killed and scalped by the Indians in 1703."[3]

With Worcester out of the picture, Gershom and Jonas bought more land in Groton (1704 and 1709) then sold it when the outlook for peace suddenly re-opened prospects for re-settlement in Worcester. In December 1711, Jonas bought 60 acres of land in Worcester, and in May 1712, Gershom bought a 60-acre tract nearby. One year later, Queen Anne's War formally ended with the Treaty of Utrecht, and the Rice brothers made their move. On October 13, 1713, Gershom, Jonas, and a well-placed patron named Col. Adam Winthrop, addressed a petition to the General Court stating their desire to "… endeavor and enter upon a new settlement of the place from which they had been driven by the war." The claim that they had been driven out of the earlier settlement by the war was misleading, perhaps to enhance their status in the petition. Neither Gershom nor Jonas actually inhabited Worcester during the second settlement as many historians have since claimed. The petition was approved, and it marks the beginning of the first permanent settlement of Worcester.

Jonas Rice was the town's first permanent settler (fig. 3-1). He moved there with his family in the fall of 1713, and Gershom followed with his family in the spring of 1715. In short order, they were joined by more settlers, many of them Rice family siblings: brothers James, Ephraim Sr., Elisha, and Josiah; sister Grace came with her husband Nathaniel Moore, and sister, Sarah, with her husband Peter King.

Author William A. Emerson paints a rather romantic view of these early days of the settlement: "[A]fter the Indians ceased to trouble the settlement, the best energies of the inhabitants were given to the work of subduing the wilderness… the lonely and solemn woods… at last broken by the ringing tones of the axe and the sound of falling timber; then came the time for burning the dry trunks and branches, the planting of barley and corn, the building of houses and barns, walls, fields, and roads, and in the course of time, when the stumpage had become sufficiently decayed, removing the charred stumps and roots by the use of oxen and heavy chains, then leveling the land, removing the stones, and at last introducing the plough; after this followed the various processes of planting, the setting out of fruit trees and vines, until the wilderness was made to blossom as the rose."[4]

Historians are fond of saying that Jonas lived "alone" in this "wilderness" until Gershom arrived.[5] But it's more likely that he had help from one or more of his brothers with the building of his house, barn, outbuildings and fences, and also with the first plantings. During this time, he had their company and protection, along with their help. And when Gershom came with his family, the cycle of building and planting was repeated; brother helping brother, and neighbor helping neighbor. It is also unlikely that Jonas settled in a "wilderness", if defined as an uncultivated area previously uninhabited and unimproved by human beings. From the accounts of Daniel Gookin, we know that Nipmucks cultivated fertile places like Sagatabscot and Pakachoag Hills. Other areas were routinely cleared by fires set by the Indians to remove undergrowth and promote grasses that attracted deer and other game. In his earliest description of Worcester (then "Quinsigamond") Gookin said there was "meadow enough" and early descriptions of land divisions for the first permanent settlers bear that out.

Figure 3-1. Historical marker on Grafton Street commemorating Jonas Rice. (Photo by Vin Mickelson.)

JONAS RICE

ON THE SLOPE OF THE HILL ONE-HALF MILE WEST STOOD THE HOUSE OF JONAS RICE, THE FIRST PERMANENT DWELLING IN WORCESTER, BUILT IN 1713. HE SERVED AS SCHOOLMASTER AND HIS SON, ADONIJAH, WAS THE FIRST WHITE CHILD BORN IN WORCESTER.

MASSACHUSETTS BAY COLONY
TERCENTENARY COMMISSION

Not all of the settlers had large farms outside the town center like Jonas and Gershom. Most had smaller house and planting lots in the village, near the common, where they communally raised their livestock. They built a garrison near Main Street and the common, and slept there during the first year, going out during the day to plant their crops and build their first homes. Indians still prowled occasionally, hoping for unguarded opportunities, so three more garrisons were added. By 1718, the infant village contained about 58 dwellings, 200 inhabitants, a gristmill, and two saw mills; one year later, Capt. Moses Rice added a tavern to the mix.

By spring of 1721, Jonas and Gershom thought their village ready to be incorporated as a town and they sent a petition to that effect to the General Court. This was granted, and Worcester was incorporated on June 22, 1722. This marks the time when Gershom and Jonas truly became the

"Fathers of Worcester" as they have since been called—not just because they were first to settle there, but because they played key roles nurturing, managing, and guiding the town for the next two decades: Gershom was a town Selectman six of the years between 1724 and 1746 and town treasurer between 1736 and 1739; Jonas was a Selectman nine years between 1722 and 1740 and most years between 1722 and 1753. He was also Deacon of the first church from 1748 to 1753.

Gershom Rice called the first town meeting on September 1722, for the election of town officials: Selectmen, Constables, Tax Assessors, Town Clerk and Treasurer. We are familiar with these offices today; others, important then, are now quaint: Tythingmen, to watch over a dozen or so families each and to keep them in order. A carryover from the Puritan era, they kept the lid on undesirable behavior, like tippling, Sabbath breaking, idleness, irreligion, and "rude practices." Hog reeves made sure that wandering hogs were yoked and fitted with nose rings to keep them from rooting into neighboring gardens. (Pig sties weren't common until the early 1800s—until then hogs wandered freely until rounded up for slaughter.) Fence Viewers made sure the allotted portions of common lots were properly fenced "hog tight and horse high". Surveyors of Highways had the authority to call fit and able men together for compulsory work on roads and bridges. Town meetings took place on a regular basis thereafter, all carefully recorded. Among the first priorities were bounties for crows, rattlesnakes and wolves, the building of fences, bridges and roads to connect farms to each other and to market; a tax for "reclaiming disorderly beasts", and standards for weights and measures—all the tasks necessary for the making of a farm community.

While busy with these civic necessities, the new town leaders were not neglecting their religious responsibilities. If their government was no longer Puritan, the Puritan religion was still a central part of their lives, and public worship was still required by law. So, there were no complaints when each family was assessed £10 for the support of public worship at the second town meeting. The first worship services were held in the house of Gershom and ElizabethRice and in the house of his brother James, until a meeting-house was built 1719 on the site of the present City Hall. Then, two events converged that would put serious strains on the peace and cohesiveness of the community for several years. One was an internal affair, the kind of thing that could have happened in any Puritan-based town where religious opinions were strong; a schism, or break in the community over the selection of the first town minister. A faction led by Benjamin Flagg contested the Rev. Andrew Gardner, who was brought in by the Rice brothers, and Gardner was ultimately removed in October 1722. Infighting continued for another three years during which the town had no minister and had to settle for occasional itinerant preachers. The schism was finally healed October 1725 when Rev. Isaac Burr was installed pastor. Rev. Thaddeus Maccarty succeeded him on June 10, 1747, and his ministry covered a 37-year span that included the Revolutionary War. During his ministry a new meetinghouse was erected in 1763 on Worcester Common, known as the "Old South Church".

In the midst of this infighting, the homogenous settlement of English Puritans of Worcester got their first taste of diversity, when a group of Presbyterians came to settle. These people, known in America as "Scotch-Irish", were descendants of colonists from Scotland who settled in about 1609 on land in Northern Ireland, Province of Ulster that had been taken by England. They called themselves Ulster Scots, lived in their settlement, the Ulster Plantation, and never thought of themselves as Irish. Like the Puritans, they were dissenters, and by the 1690s they were at odds with the state Church of Ireland. In the spring of 1718, Governor Shute of Massachusetts invited them to New England, where they could bolster the settlements on the frontier; and so, the first significant post-English Puritan immigration to New England began. When the first of these settlers arrived in Boston, some were sent straight away to Worcester, and by some accounts, nearly doubled its population before the year's end.

Surprisingly, they got along reasonably well at first. They worshiped under their own minister in one of the garrisons, while the infighting over a Town minister wore on. Some of the newcomers served as lookouts during an Indian scare called Lovell's War in 1722, and some served as town officers along with the Rice brothers. But when Rev. Burr was finally installed in 1725, the Scotch-Irish were expected to worship under his ministry and contribute to his support. As an inducement, the town offered to occasionally share the pulpit with a Presbyterian minister, and with this understanding, Scotch-Irish and English worshiped together, and shared some of the best pews. But over the next 11 years no Presbyterian took the pulpit, and in 1736, the Scotch-Irish made a formal appeal to the Town for relief from the tax. The response was negative, and demeaning: The "request is unreasonable" they replied; it stems from "irregular views and motives…" and is "unworthy of us to countenance." Suddenly, the Scotch-Irish found themselves being referred to in the pejorative as "Irish", and some began moving to New Hampshire, and elsewhere. Others, in 1740, started to build a meeting house of their own, only to see it destroyed by some "unruly" members of the town. More families left Worcester, but others had set their roots too deep.

Among the deeply rooted, was James McClellan, who in August 1718, purchased 75 acres of land from Gershom Rice. The land was at "Bogachoge" (Pakachoag), in the south part of the town. With this and other purchases, McClellan established a large farm between Pakachoag Hill and the Leicester line. Other families like McClellan's stayed, and assimilated. Another century would pass before Worcester would again face the challenges posed by a diverse immigrant culture.

At the town meeting of April 1726, selectmen allotted 40 acres of land for a school and appointed "Mr. Jonas Rice to be the schoolmaster and teach such children & youth as the inhabitants shall sent [sic] to him to read and write as the law directs." They were referring to a law passed in 1647 that required every township of "50 households to maintain a common school, and each town of 100 families should keep a grammar school". That law was still on the books, and there was a fine for failure to comply. Accordingly, Jonas had offered his services, and the children who were able (if any) went to "school" at his home on Sagatabscot Hill. But after his term expired, it was announced, "that the town will not have a school." On December 12, 1727, the Selectmen of Worcester were called before the General Court to explain themselves. Their answer is unrecorded, but perhaps it went something like this: We have been busy building a new town from scratch, converting meadow into farm, guarding against Indians, establishing a meetinghouse and ministry, and dealing with an influx of outsiders. Or, maybe they just promised to comply with the law straight away. In any case, Benjamin Flagg was promptly employed as schoolmaster and the Court dismissed the fine.

This shaky start was just the beginning of a school dilemma that plagued Worcester for rest of 18th century. The town had a widely dispersed farm population that was too remote from the town center for a single town school. To solve this, five school quarters were formed in 1731, one in the town center and one each in the north, south, east and west, and the selectmen were instructed to "provide a suitable number of school dames… for the teaching of small children to read". These neighborhood schools were likely the homes of the "school dames" who taught there, as there were yet no schools. This arrangement was replaced in August 1732 by a "moving school", with one teacher, Richard Rogers, who moved from one section of town to another, teaching at selected homes.

In 1738, the first schoolhouse was built near the Court House at Lincoln square, but the tug of war between the town and the quarter districts continued. The "aristocrats" of the town center, now growing in influence, wanted a full time writing school and a grammar school, while farmers in the "skirts" wanted 3 month moving schools, and no tax for a grammar school they wouldn't use. For the year 1740, £100 was allocated for schools—£50 for a grammar school & £50 divided among the quarters or skirts for a "writing master". From that time on, financial support for schools was allocated annually in a variety of ways that walked a line between the demands of the town and fairness to the skirts. In 1744, for instance, the town paid James Varney £3 2s 6d for keeping a school on "Baggachoage" (Pakachoag) in the south quarter. The following year, they allowed inhabitants living remote from "ye house" the benefit of sums "as they are assessed" to support a suitable school "… as best manner they may be able". Finally, a committee was appointed to fix places for four schoolhouses on the out quarters of the town. Their proposal, approved in 1749, included a school for the south quarter on "ye hill between N. Moore jr. [sic] and Wm elder's" near Pakachoag Hill. Nothing happened with this proposal, and no schoolhouses were built in the outskirts until the year 1800.

Ten years after it became a town, Worcester was a typical inland farming village, relatively isolated, uncomplicated by class distinctions or extremes of wealth or poverty, and still centered on family and church. Then it was thrust in a new direction. In April 1731, the General Court of Massachusetts made Worcester the shire town, or capital, of the newly formed County of Worcester. The decision to bypass four towns that were older, more established and more populous seems strange, but it was a practical one based solely on Worcester's central location among them. As shire town, Worcester became an important place where county courts would meet, and all county business would be conducted. A courthouse was built at Lincoln Square, and the town center along North Main Street spread from it with the homes of judges, lawyers, and clerks. Worcester became a hub for stagecoach lines, taverns and inns, and merchants opened retail stores stocked with foreign imports.

By the mid-18th century Worcester had taken on a dual personality, with stark differences between the town center and its outskirts. The center was now commercially vibrant, and something of a destination point. On court days especially, it bustled with commerce and entertainment. Court days were held each quarter and often combined with market fair days, attracting visitors from the entire county who came to shop, watch court proceedings, horse races or wrestling matches, or the "frequent exhibitions" of discipline at the stocks, pillory, and whipping post on the top of Court Hill.[6]

The professional classes were now well established, and a class hierarchy was taking shape. It was a place where ambitious men seeking wealth and power could find it, especially in commerce, politics, and land speculation, and the atmosphere here was more cosmopolitan, secular, and more politically and intellectually engaged. It was an environment that attracted and suited the young John Adams (later second President of the United States), who came here in 1756 to teach at the new Latin Grammar School. Socially, Adams mixed easily with Worcester's emerging elite class, and enjoyed his evenings among them, discussing philosophy, theology and politics.[7] But he was bored with teaching, and the "dullards" he taught there. Then a prominent Worcester lawyer named James Putnam invited him to attend during Court Week while he and other lawyers pleaded their cases before the Court of Common Pleas. Greatly impressed, Adams took up and completed the study of law under Putnam and left to practice in Boston in 1758, at the age of 23.

Men of wealth and influence, as typified by the Chandler family, now dominated town offices. John Chandler Sr. served in various town offices and the General Court between the years 1732 and 1753, and he was judge of probate 1731 to 1740. His son, John Jr., served variously as town treasurer, town clerk, selectman, and judge of probate over the period 1753 to 1775. His importance extended even into the meetinghouse; as one of the largest contributors to the new one built in 1763, he was given the first choice of a pew.

In the outskirts, life went on much as it always had. The work was still hard, and the workdays still long, but the land had long since been broken to the plow, and fenced. And, finally, the Indian scares were over and they could work their fields in peace. According to Worcester County historian Duane Hurd, "To be industrious, orderly, decently religious, with education enough, seems to have been their notion of a good life."[8]

In the earliest town meetings, when yeomen selectmen like the Rice family decided things, priority was given to making roads between the farms so neighboring farmers could help each other get started, and that interdependence remained. It was the rare New England farm that achieved total self-sufficiency, so they developed a cooperative network of farms for this purpose. Together, they shared activities like barn raising, the use of scarce oxen for plowing, and looms for weaving; they shared days for meat butchering and specialized skills like blacksmithing, weaving, and shoemaking. Before there was a market, they exchanged or sold their surplus and specialized products to each other and achieved a comfortable living for their families. Now, they had a central market in the town center where a growing population of non-farmers needed their goods.

Most of the farms raised corn, principally, and root vegetables such as carrots, turnips, and parsnips; leaf crops like lettuce and cabbage, and onions, beans, pumpkins, squash, and peas. Almost every farm grew flax for the making of linen clothing, many grew barley, and a few grew wheat where conditions permitted. Most farms kept some sheep for wool and the average per farm was 10. Hogs were raised for meat, chickens for meat and eggs, and goats for milk, cheese, and butter; every farm had some of each, but cattle, oxen, and horses were still scarce. Fruit trees, mostly apple, were grown for food and hard cider, the primary drink for every member of the family, regardless of age.

The word "bountiful" might best describe Worcester farms at mid-18th century. There wasn't much poverty, or wealth for that matter, except for the land.[9] And, herein lies the age-old problem faced by the agricultural society: Land was the farmer's "bank", and his family's future. Some, like Gershom Rice, had enough to bequeath to their heirs or sell as a down payment for more land. Others had too many heirs and not enough land, and the cycle repeated itself—young men moving and looking elsewhere for land or employment. This was happening throughout New England, not just Worcester, but here a variety of new opportunities opened with the growth of the professional and merchant population in the center. These were the service jobs to be filled by artisans, coopers, carpenters, joiners, tailors, weavers, shoemakers, etc. that supported the center elites. These became a lure for young men from other towns, and increasingly, we see these "landless laborers" moving in and out of Worcester, looking for opportunity. Some found it and stayed, others were "warned out", and moved on.[10]

By the year 1763, Worcester had grown to a population of 1,478. The Seven Year War (French and Indian War) between British America and New France ended that year, giving Britain and its American subjects victory and possession of the eastern half of North America. There were no battlefields in Worcester, but more than 450 Worcester men went off to fight, including elites like Col. John Chandler, and yeomen like Adonijah Rice, first-born son of Jonas. Otherwise, exposure to the war was mainly limited to occasions when Generals like Lord Jeffrey Amherst passed through, or militia bands set up tents and serenaded the town.

As previously noted, 1763 was also the year the new meetinghouse was built on the common. In 1863, at the 100th-year anniversary of this event, Rev. Leonard Bacon reminisced about those who attended the opening day: [11] "They dressed according to their means and their several stations in society … some walking in family processions from one house to another along the village street, others on horseback from their farms… many a wife riding behind her husband on the pillion, many a damsel behind her father or brother, probably none in any wheeled carriage other than a farmer's wagon. They met for their Thanksgiving at the call of a proclamation which ended with 'God Save the King'." This was a time when Worcester and all of New England was mostly English, and mostly loyal to the Crown they had recently fought for. Two years later, in 1765, the Stamp Act was passed, beginning the unrest that preceded the Revolution.

Jonas Rice lived his adult life on his original homestead on Sagatabscot Hill, now Union Hill.[12] He died in 1753 at age 81, and was buried on Worcester Common. To protect his gravestone from vandalism, the original was eventually moved to the Worcester Historical Museum, where it is on display. A reproduction is on the Common today (fig. 3-2).

In April 1736, Gershom Rice sold his first Worcester house near the corner of Grafton Street and Wall Street (fig. 3-3) and moved to the farm laid out for him on Pakachoag Hill, in the south part of town (now north part of Auburn). He lived there until he died, December 19, 1768, at the ripe old age of 101 years, 7 months, and 10 days. His wife, Elizabeth, had died in 1752, at age 80. According to Gershom's obituary he "retained his reason and understanding in a very good degree to the last." That is fortunate, because at that time there were no insurance policies or public support for the aged and infirmed. These were family affairs.

In the year 1748, Gershom's son, Gershom Rice Jr., had bonded himself to the care of his aging parents, in a signed agreement. It provides another interesting window into the times:

> "Know all men by these Presents that I Gershom Rice
> Junr. of Worcester… am holden & personly Bound
> and obliged… to Faithfully during ye natural life of
> his aged father and mother to deliver to them or one
> of them yearly… one hundred and twenty pound of
> good beef two hundred forty pound of good pork
> four barrels of good Sider nine bushels of Indian corn
> three bushels of Rye Two bushels of wheet Two bush-
> els of malt one bushel of Saltt, thirty five pounds of
> butter seven bushels of apples four quarters of mutton,
> Twelve pounds of sugare four ounces of pepper two

ounces of allspice forty pounds of cheese and suitable
and desent clothing of all sorts and all other neces-
sarys of life not afore mentioned and nursing in sickness and necessary phisians and also convenient house
Rooms and a horse to ride to ye place of worship and
also to afford them… a decent Christian Burial at
death…"

The duties of his son and heir having been formalized and agreed to,
Gershom Rice "enjoyed a long and almost uninterrupted state of bodily
health" for another 20 years.[13]

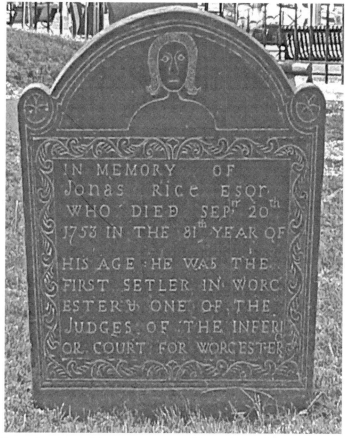

Figure 3-2. Reproduction of the gravestone of Jonas Rice that is on Worcester Common. The original is in the Worcester Historical Museum. (Photo by the authors.)

Figure 3-3. Gershom Rice House on Grafton Road, May 5, 1903. (Courtesy, American Antiquarian Society, Photographs of Seventeenth and Eighteenth Century Structures in Massachusetts taken 1887–1945 by Harriette Merrifield Forbes, Image 408027-0809.)

Notes:

1. Proceedings of the Worcester Society of Antiquity, Vol. 19 p. 337, has the complete text of Mrs. Balcom's letter, and another enclosed with it to her "Deare and Loving grandson" Gershom Rice Jr. In it she says "… all my bowles yearn to you all and to thee in particular…"

2. A majority of the Rice siblings lived past their 70s, and many beyond. Gershom: 101, Thomas: 94, Peter: 97, Mary: 80, Frances: 96, Jonas: 81, Grace: 94.

3. Kinnicutt, Historical Notes, p.2.

4. Emerson, Incidents, Early Days of the Settlement.

5. Descendant George M. Rice, at the dedication of a memorial to Jonas Rice says he lived with his family "alone in the depths of the primeval forest surrounded by savage beasts and still more savage men."

6. Howland, *Heart of the Commonwealth*, p. 22.

7. In a letter to a friend dated October 12, 1755, Adams wrote of Worcester, "Be not surprised that I am turned politician. This whole town is immersed in politics."

8. Hurd, *History of Worcester*, Vol. 2, p. 1511.

9. According to Lincoln, p. 263, "… those who by infirmity or misfortune were destitute were inconsiderable. There was a general equality of the pecuniary condition resulting from industry, frugality and temperance, which either prevented indigence, or relieved its wants. Those who needed aid were sustained by the charity of their neighbors."

10. In colonial times, newcomers could be "warned out" or coerced out of a town that feared they could not provide for themselves and might become a town burden.

11. Bacon, Historical Discourse.

12. There is a site marker for the Jonas Rice house at the corner Heywood and Vale Streets.

13. Full text is in Proceedings of the Worcester Society of Antiquity, Vol. 19.

— Chapter 4 —
Worcester in the Revolution

Shortly before noon, April 19, 1775, an express rider raced into Worcester on an exhausted white horse, shouting: "To arms, to arms, the war has begun!" The rider, twenty-three year old Israel Bissell, had just come from Watertown with a hastily written letter from General Joseph Palmer:

"Wednesday morning near 10 of the clock—Watertown

> To all the friends of American liberty be it known that this morning before break of day, a brigade, consisting of about 1,000 to 1,200 men landed at Phip's Farm at Cambridge and marched to Lexington, where they found a company of our colony militia in arms, upon whom they fired without any provocation and killed six men and wounded four others. By an express from Boston, we find another brigade are now upon their march from Boston supposed to be about 1,000. The Bearer, Israel Bissell, is charged to alarm the country quite to Connecticut and all persons are desired to furnish him with fresh horses as they may be needed. I have spoken with several persons who have seen the dead and wounded. Pray let the delegates from this colony to Connecticut see this.
>
> J. Palmer, one of the Committee of Safety."[1]

Ten years earlier, revolution would have been unthinkable for the citizens of Worcester and elsewhere in Massachusetts. They had recently fought alongside British troops in the war with France, celebrated their common victory, and felt a glowing pride in their British citizenship. Finally, after seven long years of raids and threats of raids, they enjoyed a time of peace, prosperity, and general contentment. But the war had nearly doubled Britain's national debt, and its leaders began looking to the colonies for new sources of revenue. In 1764, while Parliament debated a stamp tax, Samuel Adams of Boston raised the earliest objection to taxation without representation: "This we apprehend annihilates our Charter Right to govern & tax ourselves — It strikes our British Privileges, which as we have never forfeited them, we hold in common with our Fellow Subjects who are Natives of Britain: If Taxes are laid upon us in any shape without our having a legal Representation where they are laid, are we not reduced from the Character of free Subjects to the miserable State of tributary Slaves."[2] A member of Parliament who knew the American character, predicted the consequences: "The [Americans] I believe are as truly loyal as any subjects the king has, but a people jealous of their liberties and who will vindicate them if ever they should be violated."[3] In spite of these warnings, the Stamp Act passed in March 1765, sending these loyal subjects on their path to vindication.

Colonial resistance to the stamp tax was so effective that Parliament was forced to repeal it within a year. But at the same time, Parliament affirmed its right to legislate for the colonies "in any matters whatsoever," and followed up in 1767 with a series of measures aimed at asserting it. Collectively known as the Townshend Acts, they set off a series of actions and reactions that escalated tensions in all the major colonial cities, especially Boston, where British troops were stationed in 1768, and the Boston Massacre followed in March 1770.

So far, these events left Worcester and the rest of rural Massachusetts relatively undisturbed. At the time, Worcester was still an isolated agricultural

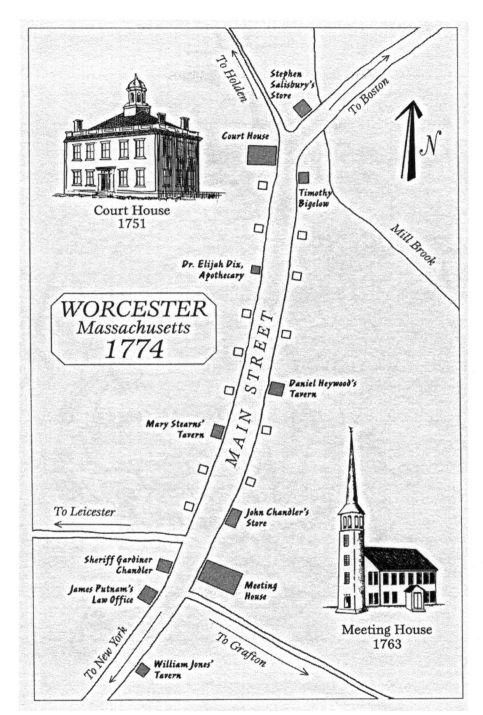

Figure 4-1. Map of Worcester 1774. (From Raphael, 2002, The First American Revolution, p. xii.) (with author permission)

town (fig. 4-1) of fewer than 1900 inhabitants.[4] The vast majority of people lived on farms of 50–100 acres in an agrarian "middle class" life style that was modest and challenging, yet fulfilling. Adding to their sense of well-being was their status as citizens. As property owners they could vote, participate in town meetings, and hold public office. But their politics focused on the parochial issues of the farm, and they served their public obligations accordingly—as fence viewers and hog reeves and the like—leaving the leadership roles to the wealthy elites in town who hankered for them. As a result, members of that class, like John Chandler and his stepson Timothy Paine, held all the levers of power in public office as well as the courts.

Until now, the common farmer had no quarrel with this deferential political system, or with the elites they placed in office. According to historian Ray Rafael, "The wealthy, who were literate and learned, could record deeds, take minutes at meetings, and guide ordinary folk through the legal system and an increasingly complex world of affairs… It was of little import to them that John Chandler voted with the governor on matters of no local interest [or] that the men who moderated or recorded their town meetings possessed more than their share of worldly possessions."[5] Their quarrel began when they came to believe that the ruling class was a threat to their rights.

In the fall of 1772, Samuel Adams and his Committee of Correspondence in Boston pondered ways to rouse the citizens of rural Massachusetts. They decided to reach out, "reduce them to reason and make them our friends."[6] By the end of the year, they had reached out to every town in the Colony with a remarkable political treatise known as the Boston Pamphlet. In clear language, it listed each of their Charter rights and British infringements on them. A letter went with each pamphlet, inviting a response: "Great Pains has been taken to persuade the British Administration to think that the good People of this Province in general are quiet and undisturbed at the late Measures… This renders it more the more necessary that the sense of the People be explicitly declared." During spring and early summer of 1773 the responses came in, and they exceeded every hope and expectation. The people of rural Massachusetts were awake, disturbed, and friends of the cause.

In Worcester, the Pamphlet was read aloud at the regular town meeting in March 1773, and five men, including a young blacksmith named Timothy Bigelow, were chosen to draft a response. Bigelow was one of those natural born leaders who seems to come from nowhere at the right time. He grew up on his father's farm in the south part of Worcester known as Pakachoag, and now owned a blacksmith shop and a small lot in town where he lived with his wife, Anna, and their children. Although he had left the farm, his work, civic duties and his militia training kept him in touch with the farmers, where his sympathies remained.[7] His education was elementary, but his intelligence, conviction, and natural political skills made him a formidable adversary of the elites he would challenge. In this first challenge, his response to the Pamphlet aimed at balance, mixing sentiments of "fond affection" for Great Britain and its sovereign with censures of British actions in Boston. It was strong enough to satisfy local radicals and balanced enough to get past the elites. This would be the last time a level of tolerance and restraint prevailed.

Shortly after the town meeting, Bigelow and others formed a Committee of Correspondence to stay in touch with radicals in Boston and elsewhere. The first of these Committees had been organized at Boston in November 1772, and now there were more than 80 in Massachusetts alone. Their members were the eyes and ears of the radicals, who remained alert for any British designs on their rights and coordinated responses to them. When costumed patriots dumped British tea in Boston Harbor onDecember 16, 1773, the news spread quickly through the countryside and raised patriot fervor to new heights. The patriots of Worcester were no exception. John Adams wrote: "The spirit of Liberty is very high in the Country and is universal. Worcester is aroused. Last week, a monument to Liberty was erected there in the heart of the Town within a few yards of Coll Chandlers door."[8]

On December 27, Timothy Bigelow and his Committee of Correspondence met with other local patriots and organized the American Political Society, a political action club whose mission was to oppose "the machinations of some designing persons in this province, who are grasping at power, and the property of their neighbors." This was clearly aimed at the elites and their power.

Within a year, membership in the APS had grown to 71, giving them a sure majority vote and complete control of the agenda and outcome at the next town meetings in March, April, and May 1774. Angry and frustrated, loyalists led by attorney James Putnam, a John Adams mentor, called for a special town meeting to reassess previous votes and consider shutting down the Committee of Correspondence. Once again they were outnumbered and outvoted by the patriots, so 52 Loyalist "Protesters" signed a scathing dissent and had it published in the Boston newspapers. In it, they ridiculed their patriot opponents for "discoursing on matters they do not understand," and declared them "enemies to our King and Country, violators of all law and civil liberty, the malevolent disturbers of the peace of society, subverters of the established constitution, and enemies of mankind."[9] The harmless fissure that once separated Worcester by class was now a chasm separating patriots and loyalists. It would never be bridged.

For the patriots of Massachusetts, the last leg on their road to revolution started in the summer of 1774. In June, their Committees of Correspondence spread the news of Britain's most punitive measure yet, the Massachusetts Government Act, revoking the Colony's 1691 charter and disenfranchising its citizens.[10] Above all of the so-called "Intolerable Acts" this one realized their darkest suspicions and justified their only option—a complete break from the mother country. In Worcester and elsewhere in the colony, vindication came with startling speed and pent-up fury.

By early July 1774, the American Political Society was in full readiness mode, providing each member with gunpowder, flints, and muskets, and drilling the militia under Timothy Bigelow. At the same time, they planned a dramatic showdown with their local adversaries. At the town meeting on August 24, in full public view, they forced each of the protesting Loyalists to strike their signatures from the dissent recorded in the town record. Next, they forced Clark Chandler, the town clerk, to scratch out each line of the dissent, and for good measure, made him dip his fingers in ink and drag them over the first page.

A few days later, they went after the lawyer, Timothy Paine. Once respected and admired, and a moderate among the Loyalists, he had been recently appointed by the king to serve on the new Council. On August 27, before an estimated crowd of 1,500–3,000 men from around the county, Paine was forced to write his resignation and then read it, hat in hand, over and over again. On the day before Paine's public humiliation, Timothy Bigelow was in Boston representing Worcester in a multi-county meeting of patriots at Faneuil Hall, and was one of a five-man committee charged with drafting the resolutions. They resolved that "Every officer belonging to the courts" was to be considered a "traitor cloaked with the pretext of law," and that each county should shut down their last bastions of British authority — their courts.

Reaction to the resolution was explosive. On the morning of September 6, 1774, more than 4,600 patriots from greater Worcester County assembled in formation on both sides of Worcester's Main Street, and then 25 court officials were made to march between them, hats in hand, as they repeated their renunciations of office, 30 or more times each. "With this ritualistic act of submission, all British authority vanished from Worcester County, never to return."[11] Scenes like this were repeated in every Massachusetts shire town except Boston, the only one still under British control seven months later, when the "shot heard 'round the world" was fired at Lexington.

When the alarm came, Worcester patriots were ready to go to war with a "minutes notice." That same day, a company of Minutemen marched to Concord under their chosen leader, Captain Timothy Bigelow. Over the course of the war, 400 men went off to the fight, leaving women, children and the elderly to tend homes and farms as best they could. Regardless of who served or stayed at home, the long War of the Revolution touched every Worcester family. When it was finally over, Worcester celebrated the peace on May 7, 1783 "with the ringing of bells, the discharge of 13 cannon, and the display of the American flag. In the evening there was a ball, where the ladies made a brilliant appearance, and heartily joined their expressions of joy on this happy occasion." [12]

Of course, not everyone shared the joy. James Putnam never wavered from his Loyalist beliefs. In February 1775, he was forced to flee to Boston after his cattle were stolen, his gristmill burned, and being "threatened with bodily harm." While there, he was commissioned Captain of a company of loyalists who served with the British army. In 1778, he was one of 308 loyalists named in an act of the Massachusetts Legislature that banished them from America and confiscated their estates. He later moved to Nova Scotia, Canada, where he served as Judge of the Supreme Court and member of the council. He died there October 23, 1789. He would never understand or condone the Revolution, or the people who accomplished it. In a letter to his American brother, he wrote: "I want to see you and my friends, if I have any, but I don't wish to live in your country, under your government, I think I have found a better. No thanks to the Devils who have robbed me of my property. I do not wish to live with or see such infernals." [13]

John Chandler and two of his sons, Rufus and William, were also named in the Act of Banishment. They went to London, where John died in 1800. His wife, Mary, remained in Worcester with six of their minor children to preserve her dower, which would otherwise have been confiscated. It was all they had left after his property, valued at £36,190, was confiscated and auctioned off. Clark Chandler, John's third son and the former town clerk, fled Worcester in 1775 but returned the same year and surrendered himself. He was charged with aiding the enemy and imprisoned, but later paroled. After a brief stay in Lancaster, he returned to Worcester and owned a store on the corner of Main and Front streets. He died in 1804. Rufus Chandler died in London 1833, but his brother William made his way back to Worcester where he died 1793. In all, 10 children of the broken family of John and Mary Chandler grew to maturity, married, and took up life in America. None of them ventured into politics.[14]

If not "joyous," the fates of the Paine family were much kinder than those of their Chandler relatives. Timothy Paine escaped banishment, and remained in Worcester until his death, in July 1793. Apparently, his forced recantation and the humiliation he endured while making it sufficiently appeased the patriots. After the war, Timothy served as representative to the general court 1788–89, and in 1789 was an unsuccessful candidate for congress. In 1778, he completed construction of a home on his estate on the Great Road to Boston, now Lincoln Street. His son, Dr. William Paine, was a signer of the Loyalist Protest of June 1774 earning him the epithet "Tory Doctor" and a place on the Banishment Act of 1778. He sailed for England and served with the British forces as apothecary, then physician, until 1782. With the conclusion of peace, he was placed on half pay and moved to Saint John, in Canada, where he became increasingly frustrated: "I am most discouraged, and find it absolutely impossible for me with all the Industry, & economy I am master of, to live upon my half pay & profession."

In 1787, Paine returned to Massachusetts, first at Salem, and then to the family home at Worcester after his father died in 1793. Old animosities were either forgotten or forgiven, for he was soon restored to prosperity and distinction. He became an honorary member of the Massachusetts Medical Society, a fellow of the American Academy of Arts and Sciences, and a founding member of the American Antiquarian Society. On July 14, 1812 he became an American citizen, and he died at the age of 82, on April, 19, 1833.[15] The Timothy Paine house at 140 Lincoln Street is one of the oldest surviving homes in Worcester. In one of those ironic turns of history, it is now owned by the Timothy Bigelow Chapter of the Daughters of the American Revolution.

Timothy Bigelow gave his all to the patriot cause and became its tragic hero. His minutemen arrived at Concord too late to catch the British, and within a week the militia was re-organized, and Captain Bigelow was commissioned a Major. In September, he took part in Benedict Arnold's exhausting and fateful expedition up the Kennebec River and over the mountains to Canada for an attack on Quebec. The attack ended in disaster, and Bigelow was captured and held prisoner-of-war until August 1776, when he was exchanged. After a brief return to Worcester, he re-entered the service and participated in the battles of Saratoga, Valley Forge, Monmouth, Stoney Point, Verplank's Point, and Yorktown. After 7 years of war, Bigelow returned to Worcester, not as a hero, but as a broken man. Unable to rebuild his once profitable blacksmith business, he fell into debt and was sent to debtors' prison. According to the records of the Worcester County Jail, he was committed there February 15, 1790, and discharged April 1, 1790 "by Death."[16] He was 51 years old, and was survived by his wife and five children. More than seventy years after his death, a monument to Timothy Bigelow was erected on the Worcester Common as the gift of his grandson, Colonel Timothy Bigelow Lawrence. It was dedicated April 19, 1861 (fig. 4-2).

Not every participant in those turbulent times held the strong convictions of Loyalists like Putnam and Patriots like Bigelow, or suffered their consequences. There were those, particularly within the growing merchant and service sector of the population, who were caught in the middle. Neither farmer nor elite, they were the entrepreneurs of their time, and it was important to be on the right side. Nathan Patch was one who would now be

Figure 4-2. Monument on Worcester Common dedicated to Timothy Bigelow. "Revolutionary War hero Col. Timothy Bigelow, was a blacksmith born on August 12, 1739 on a farm on Pakachoag Hill in what is now Auburn, Mass." (Photo by the authors.)

called a "self-made man." He moved to Worcester from Ipswich in 1772, right into the eye of the revolutionary storm. He was already on his way to wealth through land investments, and when it came time to take sides, he joined the 52 Loyalist Protestors. Two years later, it was clear he had chosen the wrong side. On September 5, 1774, the day before the dramatic gathering on the common, Nathan Patch and 42 other Protesters were assembled at the Kings Arms Tavern. They had been ordered there by Worcester's Committee of Correspondence, who informed them," satisfaction would be demanded of them by the town." One by one they signed a prepared apology that said in part: "We acknowledge we have cast cruel aspersions upon the town of Worcester... for which we are sorry, and take this opportunity publicly to manifest it."[17] Whether their signatures represented a change of heart or a practical need, we will never know. We do know that Nathan Patch went on to serve the American army as a soldier and supplier. After the war, he bought and sold lands in Worcester, Vermont, and the West, and became one of the richest men in town. When he died in 1805, he left extensive tracts of lands in Massachusetts and Vermont to his sons, Joseph, who also was a Revolutionary War soldier, and Henry, who was not. Neither seems to have shared their father's quest for wealth, as they both lived out their lives as yeoman farmers in Worcester.

In 1836, 52 acres of the Henry Patch farm on the northerly side of Packachoag Hill was sold to Father James Fitton, the site of the future College of the Holy Cross.[18]

Notes:

1. Berthelson, *An Alarm from Lexington.*

2. Miller, *Sam Adams*, p. 45.

3. Debate in parliament On February 2, 1765. See Miner, *Colonel Isaac Barré*, p. 16.

4. Lovell, *Worcester in the War of Revolution*, population data, p. 9.

5. Rafael, *The First American Revolution*, p.19.

6. Rafael, *Founders*, p. 109-110.

7. Bigelow served public office as surveyor of highways (1761), hog reave (1763), tything man (1766), fence viewer (1771), see Raphael, *Founders*, p. 111.

8. 8. Letter to James Warren quoted from Raphael, *Founders*, p. 130.9. Rafael, *Founders*, p.133.

9. Rafael, *Founders*, p.133.

10. Lord North said the purpose of the act was "to take the executive power from the hands of the democratic part of government," which it did. It also removed democratic input from the selection of local judges, sheriffs, and juries. But the worst blow, aimed at the heart of town democracy, limited town meetings to one per year, and then only after the governor approved agendas.

11. Raphael, *Founders*, p. 145.

12. Lovell, *Worcester in the Revolution* quoted from the *Massachusetts Spy*, May 8, 1783, p. 106-107.

13. Putnam, *A History of the Putnam Family Volume I.*

14. Sturgis, *A Sketch of the Chandler Family.*

15. Janzen, *Paine, William.*

16. Colvin, *Worcester Hero of the Revolution.*

17. Breen, *American Insurgents*, p. 212.

18. Kuzniewski, *Thy Honored Name*, p. 23.

— Chapter 5 —
Pre-Industrial Worcester: The Blackstone Canal and the Decline of Farming

After of the Revolutionary War, the farmers who won it faced the same issue as the one that spawned it—increased taxes as a result of war debts. This time, they had representation, but it favored the merchant class. "Two-thirds of the state tax assessment was based on ownership of land, leaving wealthy merchants off the hook while requiring tillers of the soil to pay with money they did not have."[1] At the same time, merchants were suing farmers for debts. Between 1784 and 1786 suits by retailers for debt collection involved 32.8% of farmers in Worcester County.[2] By 1785, there were 86 imprisoned debtors in Worcester, most of them war veterans like Timothy Bigelow, in debt to merchants like the Salisburys, who never served, and former Loyalists like the Paines and Chandlers who had served against them.[3]

In late summer of 1786, desperate farmers tried to stop debtor trials by shutting down the courts, sparking an armed protest known as Shay's Rebellion. It was short-lived, and was crushed by the Massachusetts State Militia the following February. It failed because a new coalition of merchants, lawyers, and former Loyalists had joined forces with government officials in putting it down. But the farmers had made their point, and a chastened state legislature later enacted relief measures and pardoned their leaders. Within a year, peace and prosperity had returned to the countryside.

At the beginning of the 19th century, Worcester wasn't much different than the other small towns in the county. Its economy was agrarian, with a mix of domestic trades and crafts, and once again, rural politics prevailed. Town records have the familiar ring of Puritan times; along with the widening of roads and repairs of bridges, Tythingmen were still elected to monitor their neighbors' morals, farm animals were allowed to roam the town center, and bounties were assessed for crows. Figures 5-1 and 5-2 show maps of the city as it was in 1790.

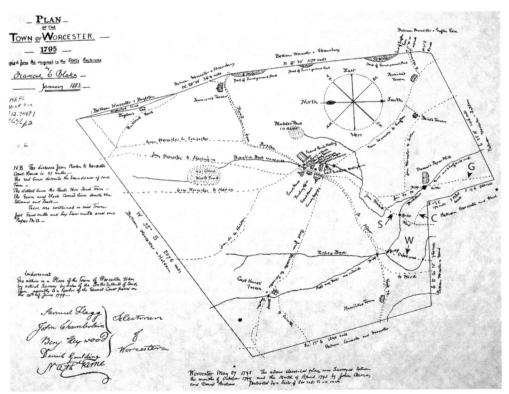

Figure 5-1. Reproduction of map entitled "Plan of the Town of Worcester – 1795 – Copied from the original in the State Archives by Francis E. Blake, January, 1883". Note that north is to the left. Added labels indicate approximate location of modern streets: C, College St.; G, Greenwood St.; S, Southbridge St.; W, Webster St. (From the collections of the Worcester Public Library.)

The first progressive action by town government was taken only after years of prodding by the State and infighting between the town's center and rural representatives. In 1800, Worcester finally built ten schoolhouses—two in the center district, and eight in the outlying districts, at costs ranging from $247 to $270 each. They were small, one-room wooden structures

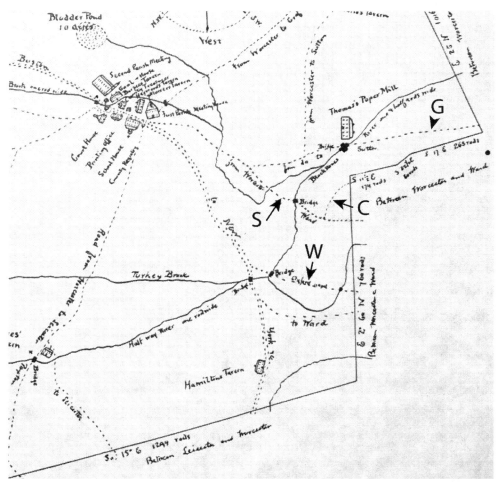

Figure 5-2. Expanded view of South Worcester from the map shown on Figure 5-1. Reproduction of map entitled "Plan of the Town of Worcester – 1795 – Copied from the original in the State Archives by Francis E. Blake, January, 1883". Note that north is to the left. Added labels indicate approximate location of modern streets: C, College St.; G, Greenwood St.; S, Southbridge St.; W, Webster St. (From the collections of the Worcester Public Library.)

"fitted with the plainest possible benches and desks, poorly heated in winter, and always poorly lighted."[4] Nevertheless, public education finally moved beyond the town center and into the countryside.

During the next 25 years, the influence of farmers over town affairs slipped away. The first signs of a "new order" appeared during Shay's Rebellion, when merchants and professionals in the town center joined with government forces to defeat them. As Kenneth Moynihan wrote, "The men who would shape the new era and profit from it would not, for the most part, be the artisans and farmers... Instead they would be men of commerce, like Salisbury, and men of the law, like Lincoln, who had moved to Worcester during the Revolutionary turmoil..."[5] Gradually, the conservative inertia of the countryside gave way to the commercial ambitions and civil aspirations of the center. In 1816, the town voted to restrain horses, mules, cattle and swine from going at large, and three years later the office of Tythingman was discontinued. In 1818, a committee reported that costs for the support of the poor had increased "to an alarming degree" and proposed they be "collected into one establishment" where it would be cheaper to keep them, and where they would be "diverted from the miseries to which a life of idleness leaves them exposed."[6] Later that year the town bought the Jennison farm, near the Shrewsbury border, where the poor could live under one roof and "labor in such a way... that no one may be permitted to lead an idle life."[7] By 1824, the "men who would shape the new era" were the dominant town leaders, and they proclaimed that the "character, population and resources of town" justified building a Town Hall for their civic business.[8] Later that year, the French Revolutionary War hero, Marquis de Lafayette, visited Worcester, where "he was happy to observe such decided proofs of industry, sobriety, and prosperity."[9] What these "proofs" were is unrecorded, but during his visit he was entertained by Levi Lincoln and others of his class, who likely talked about the Blackstone Canal and the inevitable progress it would bring.

"Boosters" like Lincoln and the Salisbury brothers had always believed that Worcester, a center of government, could also become a center of commerce, but until now, the realities of geography trumped their ambitions. Worcester was without navigable rivers to the sea, and its roads were primitive and limited.[10] At a time when most of the Nation's goods were imported from Great Britain, this made the export and import of products prohibitively expensive. As a Blackstone River historian wrote, "Incredibly, it was cheaper for a Boston merchant to ship goods overseas to Liverpool, England, than to haul them 40 miles overland to Worcester."[11] The Blackstone Canal offered a solution, and although merchants of Providence, Rhode Island, launched the project, Worcester businessmen invested heavily in it, and became its agents and managers. In a letter dated May 14, 1822, the City of Worcester made its case for the canal. Noting the many manufacturing shops that now lined the banks of the Blackstone between Providence and Worcester, the letter said, "We cannot doubt also that this extensive tract of territory will be greatly benefited by opening a water communication—as it will probably reduce the expense of transportation to Providence, Boston, New York, and many other places, from one-half to one fourth of what it now is. It will probably open a market for many products, which we cannot now send abroad, by reason of expense of transportation, and will enable us to carry on, with success, many branches of industry, which cannot now be pursued."[12]

Excavation for the canal commenced in Rhode Island in 1824, and the first canal boat arrived in Worcester from Providence on October 7, 1828, loaded with salt and bags of grain (fig. 5-3). As it moored at the Central Street basin (fig. 5-4), cheering crowds greeted the Lady Carrington, and from its deck a Worcester selectman named Piney Merrick addressed them. In the florid oratory of his time, he pointed out what the mere promise of the canal had already accomplished; "… the great impetus to the tide of population… the enlargement of all parts of our village… the well built mansions and shops and manufactories" and the rise in property values along the route. "Ask the owners for the prices for which they will part with [their lands], and you will find

On Oct. 7, 1828, the LADY CARRINGTON entered Worcester from Providence; the first boat to travel the Blackstone Canal, which ran through Union St and across the lower end of Front St, where it was spanned by a bridge. On this bridge, a large crowd collected to cheer as the boat came in. The canal was operated for about twenty years and cost $750,000.00

Figure 5-3. The Lady Carrington arrives in Worcester. (From the collections of the Worcester Historical Museum.)

that feet are now deemed as valuable as acres once were." "I will not speak of our future hopes" Merrick said, but then he did: "We rejoice in this day… in the conviction that this expanded field of enterprise will be diligently harvested by the energetic exertions of our population. Let then the products of the verdant hills and teeming vallies [sic] around us be wafted to market on this new and easy pathway."[13] For a while, his hopes were realized. Farm

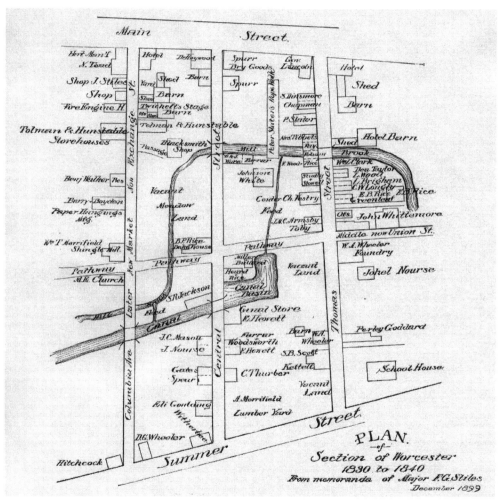

Figure 5-4. Map showing the location of the northern end of the Blackstone Canal in downtown Worcester. (From the collections of the Worcester Historical Museum.)

produce and home manufactured goods like cloth, shingles and chairs, wafted from Worcester in canal boats that returned from Providence with staples like flour, grains, and molasses, and raw materials like coal, cotton and dyes.

Revenues from the canal increased over the next four years, but peaked in 1832, and then began a steady decline. High water in spring, low water in late summer, and the constant need for maintenance on boats and canal caused cancelled or delayed scheduled runs, and were costly. Sabotage and legal actions by angry mill owners over water rights added to the financial woes of the Canal's investors, who began looking for a way out. And then came the railroads.

Looking to re-capture trade they had lost to the Canal, Boston investors chartered the Boston to Worcester Railroad in 1831. It opened service July 6, 1835, and the following year, business more than doubled; "… passenger cars were well patronized, and there was more freight than the company was prepared to care for."[14] Other railroads soon followed. The Western Railroad, from Worcester to Springfield, opened in 1839, the Norwich & Worcester in 1840, and the Providence & Worcester in 1847. The coming of the railroads made the canal irrelevant. On April 22, 1846, the canal company sold the rights and privileges of the Massachusetts portion of the canal to the Providence & Worcester Railroad Company. Locks, boats and water rights went up for sale three years later. At the inauguration celebration of the Providence & Worcester Railroad Company, a toast was made: "To the two unions of Providence & Worcester; the first as weak as water, the last as strong as steel."[15] Nevertheless, the Canal can't be written off as a failure. In its heyday, and even before, it ignited population and economic growth up and down its path, and helped make Worcester the commercial center its boosters wanted it to be.

The impact of the canal is clearly evident in a superb map of Worcester in 1833, by H.S. Stebbins (fig. 5-5, 5-6, and 5-7). Here is Worcester, at the height of its canal days and at the edge of a new era. It will be our guide for the rest of this chapter.

60

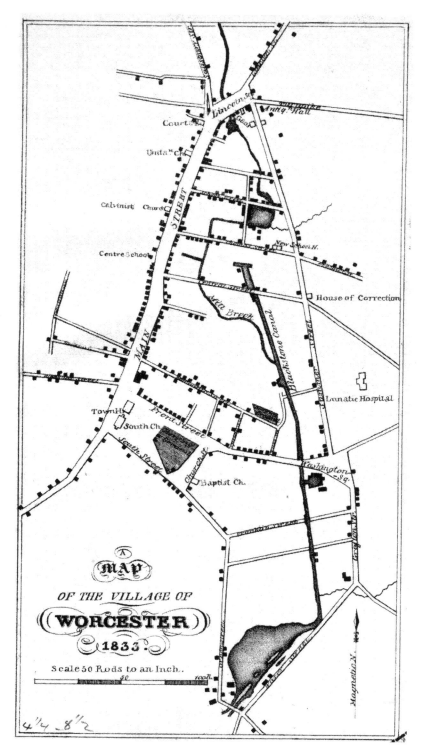

Figure 5-5. Inset map showing the Village of Worcester, 1833. Taken from Stebbins, H., 1833. (From Harvard University Library, online publications: http://vc.lib.harvard.edu/vc/deliver/~maps/009504409)

An inset on the map highlights the town center, where the impact of the canal is most apparent (fig 5-5). Before the canal, Main Street stood alone as the commercial center. By 1833, the center has spread east along several streets that lead to the commercial activity around the canal, and link Main Street to its new borders formed by Summer and Grafton streets. Main Street, Lincoln Square and the Common are dense with homes, shops, offices, and public buildings. Until recently, the homes of the affluent stood alongside those of the laboring classes, but wealthy individuals (like Levi Lincoln) had begun building separate neighborhoods for themselves on the west side of town. These are accessed by several new streets that were (or soon would be) named Pearl, Elm, Chestnut, Walnut, and Highland. The social separation we see beginning here will be characteristic of Worcester well into the 20th century, and is still visible today.

Public buildings owned by the town include the "Centre" School on Main Street (a primary and female school), a brick schoolhouse on Thomas Street (a Grammar and boys school), and a separate "African School" near Pine Meadow, built in 1831 for the town's twenty or so "coloured" children.[16] The Town Hall, built on the Common in 1825, "is a neat brick building of fine architectural proportions" as befits the men of commerce who do the town's business. A large hall on the first floor was used for town meetings and other public functions, two large halls on the second floor could be rented, and the basement was used to store fire apparatus.[17] Other public buildings served the growing needs of Worcester County. The third and greatly enlarged County Court House opened in 1803 on Main Street near Lincoln Square. On the eastern side of town, the County built a House of Corrections on Summer Street in 1817, and further south, a Lunatic Asylum for the care of the mentally ill opened January 1833. (By the end of the year, its trustees reported it was already in a crowded condition!)

Old South Church stands on the Common next to the Town Hall. It was no longer used for town meetings, nor was it the sole custodian of religious expression. Behind it and the "Burying Ground" is a Baptist Church, and on Main Street there is a Calvinist and a Unitarian Church. (After 1811, when Massachusetts passed the Religious Freedom Act, Worcester stopped taxing its citizens for church support, leaving each church to tax its own congregations.) The Antiquarian Hall, at the corner of Summer and Lincoln Streets, was erected in 1820 to house the collections of the American Antiquarian Society, beginning with the extensive library of its founder and benefactor, Isaiah Thomas, the famous Patriot, printer, and newspaper owner. The stone "Gaol" nearby on Lincoln Street is the sad place where Timothy Bigelow spent his last days.[18]

The Worcester Register of 1829 gives us an approximate breakdown of the commercial makeup of the town. Then, there were more than a dozen merchants selling goods from England and the West Indies, and nearly twice as many selling local products like boots and shoes, hats, clocks, and watches. In the trades, there were eleven carpenters, eight masons and brick makers, seven blacksmiths, seven coach, harness and saddle makers, five stone cutters, three printers, one or two each of cabinet makers and metal smiths, and a scattering of others. In the professional classes, there were sixteen (!) lawyers, four physicians and two dentists. There were also four barbers, three drug stores, two groceries, and two bakers. Of the sixteen taverns listed in the Register, most were in the center, and a few were on stage roads leading from it. Washington Square, having been recently farmland, is beginning its commercial transformation. On its southern edge, a distillery "offers for sale New England Rum, molasses, cider brandy and high wines," and farther south, is the brewery of S. Burt & Co., which in 1830 sent 1000 barrels of "double ale" down the canal for sale.[19, 20]

Among the buildings on the Stebbins map are the offices of four banks, three newspapers, and a fire insurance company. Those who work there are members of a growing business-oriented community that is shaping the town in their own image. In 1829, their representatives passed laws against smoking pipes or cigars, and "playing ball, drive whoops or fire crackers on any streets in town."[21] Clearly, they had come a long way from those not so distant days when farm animals roamed freely about the town.

Outside the village margins, the Stebbins map depicts a countryside that is still rural, with borders measured from stakes to trees or piles of stones (fig. 6). But it's not untouched by change, the most obvious being the Blackstone Canal, which cuts through the southern midsection of town to the Millbury border. Overland access to the outside world has also improved; a radial network of roads connects the Shire town to its county neighbors, and beyond, via three toll roads added after the Massachusetts Turnpike act was passed in 1796. The first stage line opened in 1783, and coaches were by the 1830s carrying passengers and mail on nearly every one of these roads. In September 1836, stage lines reported 122 departures and arrivals per week between Worcester and fifteen destinations in Connecticut, Rhode Island, and Massachusetts. More change is evident on the larger streams that run through Worcester and drain the Upper Blackstone Valley. At the turn of the century, they powered only the occasional grist or saw mill; by the 1830s there were some machine shops and factories. Even with dams, there were no streams in Worcester that could power a large factory or textile mill, but some could power the shops that made machines and tools for textile manufacturing. This adaptation may have given rise to Worcester's later prominence in machine manufacturing. By 1832, there were at least seven machine shops making carding, spinning, weaving, and shearing machines for the textile industry.[22] Some of these were conveniently near small "factories" where cotton was spun, wool was "fulled" (cleaned) and finished cloth was sheared. Other manufactures included the Washburn & Goddard Wire and Wood Screw factory, two iron foundries, a lead pipe factory, and two paper mills. With the notable exception of Washburn & Goddard's, which was on the Mill River near North Pond, most of this industrial growth was in the southern half of Worcester, where Tatnuck Brook and Kettle Brook join near

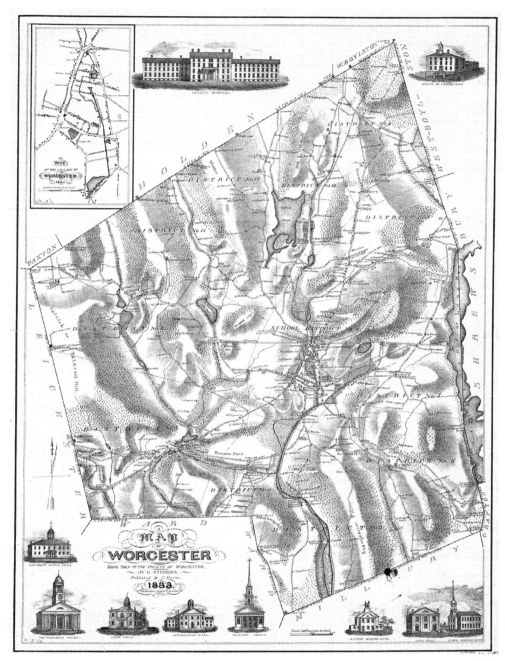

Figure 5-6. Map of the City of Worcester from 1833. Taken from Stebbins, H., 1883. (Same source as figure 5-5.)

Curtis Pond to become the Middle River, which flows east to the Blackstone River. Villages were beginning to form around these mill sites, which will be identified on later maps as Tatnuck, New Worcester, South Worcester and Quinsigamond. Eventually, these villages took on their own unique identities as characterized by their diverse manufacturing and ethnic populations. The rest of this chapter will focus on the early formation of the Village of South Worcester (fig. 5-7).

In 1824, Luther White and Jubal Boyden purchased land with a dam privilege on the Middle River and opened one of Worcester's earliest machine shops, where they made machines for processing wool.[23] In 1827, they leased an adjacent building to the partnership of Hatch & Gunn, who made wool broadcloth, the first in Worcester. (This is the "woolen factory" on figure 5-7, near the White & Boyden machine shop.) The limits of water power were shown the following year, when Hatch & Gunn sued White & Boyden for failure to provide sufficient use of power from the water wheel shared by both firms.[24] On the Middle River west of White & Boyden's was Thomas Sutton's lead pipe factory, which opened in 1831 using the first iron water wheel in the Country. East of White & Boyden is the abandoned twine factory of Peter Slater. Slater, who died in 1831, was a most interesting early South Worcester resident. As a boy, he learned rope-making as an apprentice in Boston, and later became an active participant in the Boston Tea Party and the Revolutionary War.[25]

By 1833, the schools of Worcester were organized into twelve districts. Their boundaries are outlined on the Stebbins map with dotted lines, but these cannot be seen in figure 5-6. District one was the town center, surrounded by districts two through twelve in (mostly) a clockwise fashion. The one-room schoolhouses built for these districts in 1800 are identified within the map. South Worcester was district four. As a distinct district, South Worcester began its own identity within the broader area once referred to as "Boggachoag" for the hill that dominates it. The district is bordered on the

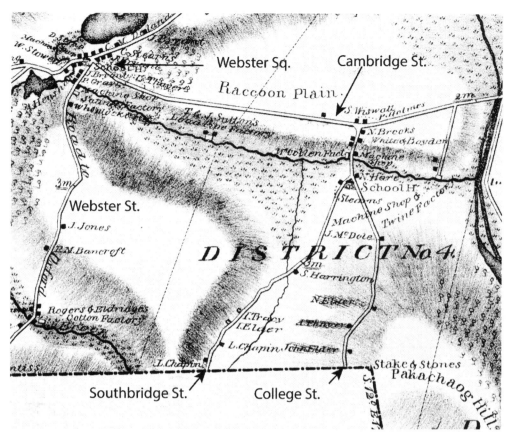

Figure 5-7. South Worcester portion of the map of the City of Worcester from 1833. Taken from Stebbins, H., 1833. Major modern streets in South Worcester and the location of Webster Square have been labelled. (Same source as figure 5-5.)

south by the town of Ward, and its northern border encompasses a broad, level area called Raccoon Plain.[26] The Middle River runs easterly across the district, cutting in it half, and the only east-west road was not yet called Cambridge Street; on figure 5-7 it is merely called "the Road across Raccoon Plain." The "Road to Ward" (Southbridge Street) extends south from Raccoon Plain and meets the "Road over Boggachoag Hill" (College Street) a bit south of the Middle River. At the junction of these two roads sits the then thirty-three year old South Worcester Schoolhouse.[27]

Along with the district reorganization, schools and teachers were placed under the jurisdiction of a school committee composed of representatives from each district. Otis Corbett, the representative for South Worcester, wrote this report for the year 1833: "I have found in this school several very fine female scholars attending to History, Arithmetick, Geography and Eng. Grammar, the males of the same age comparatively dull and sluggish in their progress."[28] Perhaps the "sluggishness" of the males is due to the fact that these sons of farmers saw no practical use for their schooling. They could not have known then that farming in this area was on its way out.

Before the Revolution, the farms of six families dominated the area that became district four. From north to south on figure 5-7 they were: the Nathaniel Brooks farm, on the road to Raccoon Plain; the Nathan White farm that skirted the western edge of Pakachoag Hill between the Brooks farm and modern Tracy Place; and the Thaddeus Chapin farm that extended south from White's farm into Ward. West of these farms, between the Road to Ward and the Road to Oxford (Webster Street) were the farms of William and James Trowbridge, and William Elder. With the exception of the Elders, who were Scotch-Irish, these families were descendants of English Puritan settlers, and there were many marriage ties between them. In 1833, six descendants of these families—Luther White, Nathaniel Brooks (2nd), John Elder Jr., Nathan Elder, James Elder, and Lewis Chapin—still lived in district four.

Also living in the district were eight families who had moved here within the last decade. Like their established neighbors, most were descendants of Puritan families and shared a farming heritage; unlike them, they didn't inherit the family farm, so they came here looking for land or other employment. For better or worse, they arrived when a rapidly growing population was putting land into commercial use and driving up land values. Although this hastened the end of subsistence farming in Worcester, it also opened new opportunities for employment in the trades or in commerce. By 1850, all the farms in district four had been sold off or were greatly reduced in size and function. A few owners moved from Worcester to continue farming elsewhere, but most stayed and adapted to new occupations off the farm. In the next few paragraphs we look more deeply into the lives of some of these families. The information comes from Wall, *Reminiscences of Worcester* and various city directories, land and tax records. Their houses or businesses are located on figure 5-7.

Samuel Wiswall purchased his "tillage land" on Raccoon Plain in 1826. He sold it sometime after 1833, and moved to Vermont where he died in 1839. N. Hare, shown on the map near the schoolhouse, is Horatio Nelson Hare, a "Yeoman", meaning he owned his own land. He sold this farm and moved to another in Leicester, sometime before 1840. In 1830, Samuel Harrington Jr., also identified as "Yeoman," purchased part of the Nathan White farm, near where Malvern Road School now stands. Sometime before 1845, he sold this farm, but stayed in Worcester. The city directory for 1845 lists him is as a carpenter, living in the town center.

Pitt Holmes was a "Yeoman" in 1830 when he purchased land on Raccoon Plain from James White, a descendant of Nathan White. He became a carpenter in the 1840s and then a prosperous Worcester real estate developer, "buying, developing and building houses on large tracts of land." He kept at least part of his original farm as his home. The city directory for 1869 lists "Holmes, Pitt, carpenter, home Cambridge S.W."[29] Alden Thayer, Sr., came from Mendon, and was a "Yeoman" in 1830 when he purchased land from William Goss near the Elder and Chapin farms on Pakachoag Hill. In the 1850 city directory, he is listed as a "Grocer" and is living on Summer Street.

Moses Stearns, also listed as "Yeoman", pieced together a large farm from several tracts he purchased between 1832 and 1838. These included part of the farm of the late Henry Patch on the road "leading from School number four", and land adjoining the Boyden & White property, but giving them access rights for the repair of their dam. He lived there long enough to have the junction of College Hill and Southbridge Street named "Stearns Square", but on a much smaller property. In 1846, he was assessed for taxes on "2 houses, 2 cows, and 1 pig." Ten years later, the City Directory listed him as a machinist, living at 365 Southbridge Street. Thomas Tracy was in Worcester as early as 1793, when he appeared on the tax abatement list as "poor, and a family to support." He presumably found work with William Trowbridge, who in 1826 sold about one acre of land, "the same where Thomas Tracy now lives" to George and William Tracy, laborers. In 1828, George Tracy sold the property to Lewis Tracy, Tailor, "where Thomas, William & I live". The 1856 City Directory lists William Tracy, shoemaker, at Tracy Place.

J. "McDole" is a corruption of the name McDollen. On the Stebbins map (fig. 5-7), his farm is situated on the Road to Boggachoag (College Street). John McDollen was born in England about 1784, and may be of Scotch-Irish descent. He married Mary Stearns of Worcester in 1823, and bought his land in multiple purchases between 1821 and 1829, some of it from heirs of Henry Patch. He began selling off his farm in the 1850s and in 1865 he sold about 14 acres to Holy Cross College. That year, he was living on College Hill, and he was still a farmer, but his neighbors were now Holy Cross professors, wire workers, wool sorters, and machinists. According to his death certificate, he was a "boot maker" when he died in 1876, age 92.

Descendants of established families faced the same challenges as their more recent neighbors. They all remained in Worcester, and some hung on to vestigial remnants of their farms until they died. William Elder came to Worcester in about 1747 and was Scotch-Irish. He was one of the 52 Loyalist "Protesters," who were later humiliated and forced to renounce their allegiance and "make satisfaction" to the Patriot majority. Three sons were living in district four in 1833. John Elder Jr. died in 1841. His farm on Pakachoag Hill was occupied for a while by Nathaniel Elder, but by 1851, Nathaniel had a Fulton Street address, and all subsequent city directories record him as a laborer. James Elder bucked the tides of change. According to the 1876 city directory, he was still a farmer on Southbridge Street near the Auburn city line. (This would be near Tracy Place.) However, it is unlikely that the farm still provided a sustainable living at this time.[30]

Deacon Nathaniel Brooks was a descendant of Captain Samuel Brooks, who settled in Worcester about 1753. Samuel was a man of prominence and wealth, and in 1774 he, like William Elder, signed the Loyalist protest, and later had to recant. It is said that when war came, he worked and fought against the crown. The Nathaniel Brooks property on Raccoon Plain remained in the family, at least in part, well into the industrial period. After Nathaniel Brooks died in 1850, his widow, Mary Chadwick, lived there with her sons, Nathaniel Newton Brooks (Farmer) and Horace Earle Brooks (Surveyor) until her death in 1876. By this time their address was 1 Chelsea Street.[31] Lewis Chapin was a grandson of Benjamin Chapin Sr., who came to Worcester from Mendon before 1760 with sons Benjamin Jr., Eli, and Thaddeus and settled near Auburn on the west side of Pakachoag Hill. According to census data and city directories, Lewis Chapin remained a farmer at his home on 165 Southbridge Street until he died in 1874. His son Edward, a carpenter, lived at this same address, with his wife and family.[32]

By 1850, the heirs of Nathan White had sold the family farm. Nathan came from Uxbridge and settled here sometime before 1779 and his marriage to Eunice, daughter of Benjamin Chapin Sr. The city directory for 1850 lists 24 White surnames; all living in town, most in various trades or as laborers, and none were farmers. Luther White, the former partner in the White & Boyden machine shop is listed as a "Knife Grinder" living at 2 Central Street. Jubal Boyden is probably the first of that family to move from Auburn into South Worcester. His brother, Joseph Boyden, became a renowned watchmaker, but he kept the east tract of his original purchase (about where Fitton Field is today) as a small farm until he died 1882. In the 1860 census, Jubal is boarding with Joseph and family and is listed as a farmer.

In 1841, Luther White & Jubal Boyden sold their property with two factories and two dwelling houses on the west side of the Road to Ward,

(Southbridge Street) and another tract on the east side, to Joseph Boyden. Jubal and Joseph were descendants of John Boyden, a Lieutenant in the French and Indian War, who married Elizabeth, a daughter of Gershom Rice Jr. and lived on the south part of Pakachoag Hill (now Auburn) about 1740. We don't know why the White & Boyden machine shop failed while many others would succeed. But, by 1850, according to Lincoln, the principal business in Worcester was 'Mechanical" and agriculture was second. Its population had exploded during the past decade from 7,500 in 1840 to 17,000, and these newcomers weren't looking for farms.[33] Among them, were investors who knew how to make money in the buying and selling of land. In 1865, Joseph Boyden sold his land on the west side of the road to Charles S. Messenger for $30,500. It contained about 52 acres, including the site and water privilege of the White & Boyden shop. In 1870, Messenger transferred this property to the Crompton Carpet Company for $37,000. The rate of decline of agriculture differed among the districts, and a large number of older inhabitants were still farmers in 1850. With land values rising, it is remarkable how many remained farmers for the rest of their lives. But, for the students of the district four, class of 1833, farming would only be a memory.

Notes:

1. Raphael, *First American Revolution*, p. 212.

2. Ibid, p. 13.

3. Raphael says that in 1785, Clark Chandler, the former Tory Town Clerk and now a merchant, "dragged fifteen debtors into court." See *First American Revolution*, p. 217.

4. Chenoweth, *School History of Worcester*, p. 121.

5. Moynihan, *A History of Worcester*, p. 109. He is referring here to Stephen Salisbury I and Levi Lincoln Sr., who gave rise to two of Worcester's most prominent and influential families.

6. Worcester Town Records, 1818.

7. Bishop, *The Story Behind Worcester's Poor Farm*.

8. Since Puritan times, town meetings were conducted at the meetinghouse (church), which now felt "disinclined" to let this continue. Early Records of the Town of Worcester, vol. 6 p. 196.

9. Wall, *Reminiscences*, p. 246-248.

10. As Margaret Erskine (*Heart of the Commonwealth*) said of Worcester's rivers, "not one of them was worthy of the name river, and not one of them was navigable by any vessel larger than a small rowboat or canoe."

11. Doherty, *The Poison Stream*.

12. Wilson, *The Blackstone Canal*.

13. National Aegis, Address to the Citizens of Worcester Upon the Arrival of the Lady Carrington, 1828.

14. Washburn, *Industrial Worcester*, p. 52.

15. Worcester Historical Museum, *Landscape of Industry*, p. 81.

16. Worcester was one of few towns in the region with a black community.

17. Lincoln, *History of Worcester*, p. 348.

18. It was torn down in 1835 after its prisoners were transferred to the County House of Corrections.

19. Washburn, *Industrial Worcester*, p. 288. Distillery of Daniel Heywood & Co. advertisement 1827.

20. Turner and Parks, OSV Documents. Worcester Brewery of Trumbull & Ward.

21. Worcester Town Records, 1829.

22. Massachusetts Historical Reconnaissance Survey Town Report, Worcester, 1984.

23. Americas' Textile Reporter, August 7, 1902.

24. Hatch and Gunn won their case. Decisions of the Supreme Judicial Court of Massachusetts, vol. 39.

25. After the War, Slater returned to Worcester and married Zilpah Chapin. He is buried in Hope Cemetery. Jordan, *Colonial and Revolutionary Families of Pennsylvania*, p. 1146.

26. Ward was set off from Worcester in April 1778, renamed Auburn 1837.

27. One other road runs south from Raccoon Road to the Middle River. This may have been laid out for access to Slater's twine factory.

28. City Document 31, p. 328.

29. Gray, George, *The Descendants of George Holmes of Roxbury: 1594–1908.*

30. Wall, *Reminiscences of Worcester.*

31. Cutter, *New England Families.*

32. Wall, *Reminiscences of Worcester.*

33. Lincoln, *History of Worcester.*

— Chapter 6 —
Industrial Worcester: Growth, Diversity, and Reform

On the 18th of March 1848, Worcester became a city. Town leaders had applied for a city charter in 1847 after its population exceeded 10,000—the minimum required by Massachusetts—and in the short period between application and incorporation, the population had grown to 15,000. Over the next two decades, Worcester would more than double this population and rise to prominence as a major commercial and industrial center. The population trickle that brought lawyers, professionals and merchants to the Shire town after 1731 widened to a flood of opportunity seekers when railroads gave the inland city cheap and ready access to markets and raw materials. When the first (Boston & Worcester) railroad opened July 4, 1835, a thirteen year old Worcester diarist named Louisa Trumble wrote:

> "Many strangers were attracted by the novelty, & the town was crowded through the day. Great expectations are entertained that this facility will increase the business and importance of our town."[1]

Great as these expectations were, they couldn't have anticipated that several more railroads would make Worcester a transportation hub and expand its reach, or that its business and importance would be powered by manufacturing. But by 1870, Worcester was an important industrial city, with "several hundred manufacturing establishments employing more than 10,000 workers."[2] There are several reasons for this, in addition to the railroads. Limited water power merely shifted mechanical innovation toward machine and tool building, and created the diversity of manufactures that became a Worcester trademark. Enterprising and farsighted businessmen like Stephen Salisbury II and William T. Merrifield invested in mechanical entrepreneurs, either directly through loans, and/or by leasing them buildings fully equipped with power, and machines (fig. 6-1). These rental or "power factories" helped a majority of Worcester's early manufacturers get their start without a major capital investment of their own. (These are now called "Coworking Spaces" and are again becoming popular in many parts of the country.) Once freed from the rivers, manufacturers could build their shops and factories where they wanted—near raw materials and markets, or near railroads with access to both. One of these buildings that still stands in downtown Worcester is shown in figure 6-2.

Figure 6-1. This advertisement from 1883 illustrates the ready availability of steam power to the entrepreneur needing power to begin manufacturing. The 1883 Worcester City Directory, p. 642. (https://play.google.com/books/reader?id=gvc-CAAAAYAAJ&printsec=frontcover&output=reader&hl=en&pg=GBS.PA8)

Figure 6-2. One of the Salisbury "power factories" that still stands. It had rooms that were rented to entrepreneurs as they started businesses, typically using steam power. This one is at 49–51 Union St. (Photo by the authors.)

Where did all those inventive mechanics come from in the first place? According to an article in the London Times, there was such a type, and they had their roots in New England. Published in 1878 as a review of the American machinery exhibition at the Paris Universal Exposition, it says: "The New Englander is an inventive animal. We are told that his 'brain has a bias that way.' He is always restless to fix up something in a more convenient fashion than it has ever been fixed up before. The New Englander mechanizes as an old Greek sculptured, as the Venetian painted, or the modern Italian sings; a school has grown up whose dominant quality, curiously intense, widespread, and daring, is mechanical imagination."[3]

Young men with "mechanical imagination" could be found throughout New England—on farms, in metal and craft shops, or in small mills. Attracted to the "novelty" and prospect of Worcester, they found fertile ground for their inventiveness, and stayed. And later, in their wealthy and prominent retirement years, they helped others like them. The individual accomplishments of these mechanical entrepreneurs fill volumes of Worcester biographies. The most famous of them is Ichabod Washburn (1798–1868). He was born 1798 in Kingston, Massachusetts of a family with Puritan roots going back to Governor Bradford of the Mayflower. He attended public school there until the age of nine, when his widowed mother could no longer support him, and he was "put out to live"—the colloquial term for being apprenticed—to a harness maker, five miles from home. He was later apprenticed to various blacksmith shops in Leicester, Auburn, and Millbury until age 20, when he came to Worcester as a free man to work for William Hovey and "acquired a practical knowledge of all types of machinery."[4]

He started his first business, making woolen machinery, with a loan from Daniel Waldo, one of the wealthiest merchants in Worcester. By 1822, he had enough capital to buy the water rights on the Mill River at Northville and made wire and wood screws in partnership with Benjamin Goddard (fig.6-3). In a short time they had outgrown the limits of water power there, so Washburn turned to Stephen Salisbury II, who dammed the Mill River on his property (Salisbury Pond), built a factory on it (Grove Mill), and leased the fully equipped "power factory" to Washburn (fig 6-4).

At what became known as the "North Works" (fig. 6-3), Washburn focused on the wire business. Earlier, he and Goddard had developed a "drawing block" which greatly improved the production of wire. Over time, in various partnerships, the company founded by Washburn grew, and made "piano forte" wire for pianos, crinoline wire for hoop skirts, rough wire for transatlantic cable, and barbed wire, the "wire that settled the west." At the time of his death in 1868, his company had expanded to sites in Quinsigamond and South Worcester (fig. 6-5) and was the largest wire-making firm in America.[5]

Washburn's story is typical of those early mechanical entrepreneurs who shared his Puritan-inspired belief that the "sleep of the laboring man is sweet." Apprenticeships like his gave form to their work ethic and a "practical knowledge" of the tools and machines they worked with. Benefactors

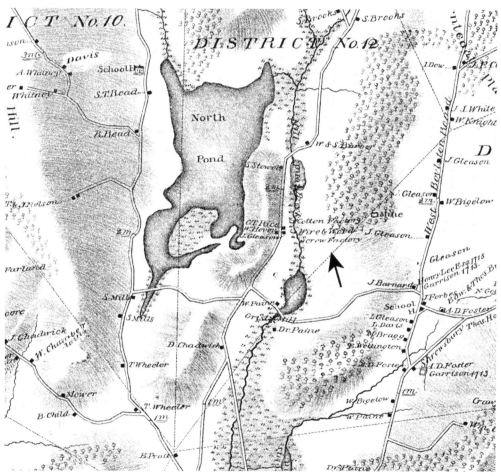

Figure 6-3. Part of map of the northern section of the City of Worcester from 1833. Arrow points to Wire & Wood Screw Factory of Washburn and Goddard. North Pond is now Indian Lake. The road just west of, and then crossing, Mill Brook is about where West Boylston St. and Goldstar Boulevard are today. Stebbins, H., 1833. (From Harvard University Library, online publications: http://vc.lib.harvard.edu/vc/deliver/~maps/009504409)

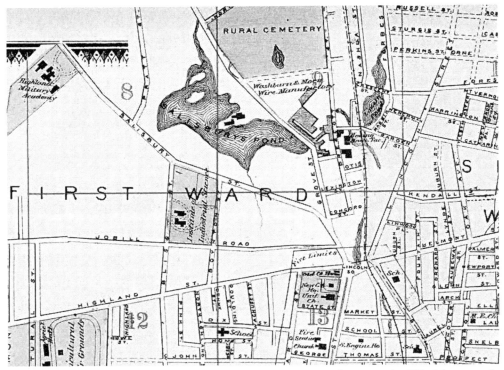

Figure 6-4. Detailed view of North Worcester in 1870 showing the Washburn and Moen Wire Company just east of Salisbury Pond and south of Rural Cemetery on Grove Street. Note also the location of the Institute of Industrial Science on Salisbury Street just south of Salisbury Pond. Beers, F. W. and Sanford, G. P., 1870. (From the collections of the Worcester Public Library.)

like Waldo, who provided capital for his first business, and Salisbury, who built and leased him a factory, typified the farsighted "venture capitalists" of their day; businessmen who saw the future and invested in it. Salisbury, for example, went on to build other mills for rent, and then built and rented homes near them to their workers.[6] Like many of his peers, Washburn in his later years gave generously to the community he helped build. Closest to his heart was the perpetuation of Worcester's mechanical tradition. To further the education and science of the mechanical arts, he originated the idea, and gave $30,000 toward the building of Mechanics Hall. And in 1865 he was a co-founder (along with John Boynton and Stephen Salisbury II) of the Worcester County Free Institute of Industrial Science, where he built his version of a power factory and gave it to the school. At his expense, he erected a machine shop, furnished it with a steam engine and machinery, and set up an endowment to fund its superintendent, staff, and financial aid for student apprentices. In 1886, the school was re-named the Worcester Polytechnic Institute.[7] Washburn was never much interested in politics and never held public office. In that regard, he was different from many of his peers who, after successful careers, gave back to their city through service in its government.

The mayors who served Worcester during the 19th century mirrored the economic and population changes that transformed it. The first was Levi Lincoln Jr. (1848–1849). He was born in Worcester, graduated from Harvard law school, and was a Supreme Court judge, Governor of Massachusetts, and a member of Congress before he became mayor. Eight of the next nine

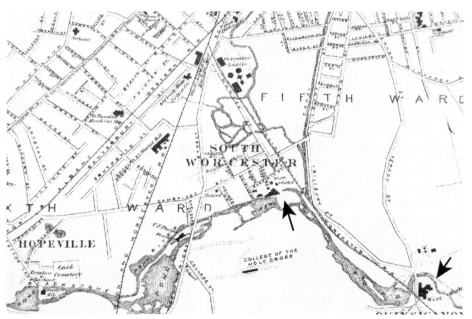

Figure 6-5. Detailed view of part of South Worcester in 1870 showing the Washburn and Moen Wire Company Central Works on Sherman St., just south of Cambridge St. and the South Works in Quinsigamond Village (see arrows). Beers, F. W. and Sanford, G. P., 1870. (From the collections of the Worcester Public Library.)

mayors (1849–1864) were also lawyers, who practiced law in the county seat and later served in public office. For the remainder of the 19th century, (1865–1900) just two of the next sixteen mayors were lawyers, while fourteen were businessmen or manufacturers, a reflection of the economic and power shift that was ongoing in Worcester. These mayors also mirror the magnet of opportunity that was Worcester, and the in-sourcing of its population. As noted, Levi Lincoln Jr. was a native of Worcester, but after him, thirteen years would pass and eight mayors would serve before another Worcester native took office, and that was his son, D. Waldo Lincoln, who served 1863–1864. For the entire period — 1848 to 1900 — only four of the twenty-five mayors (including the two Lincolns) were Worcester natives, while the rest came from elsewhere. In today's colloquialism, we would call them "carpetbaggers." Yet — whether native or outsider, lawyer or businessman — all the mayors of the 19th century were born in America, and shared an English Puritan/Yankee heritage. This would change in 1901, when an Irish Catholic named Philip J. O'Connell became the first mayor of the 20th century. His story begins about 76 years earlier, when the first Irish came to Worcester.

Before the Blackstone canal was built, Worcester was as homogeneous and Protestant as a typical English village. That ended abruptly in July 1826, when about 500 Irish canal builders came to finish the job started two years earlier in Providence, using inexperienced local laborers. These workers had been brought to America by an Irish contractor named Tobias (Tobey) Boland to build the Erie Canal, and when that was finished, to the Blackstone Valley where their skills and experience were much needed. Originally from the relatively prosperous areas of south and east Ireland, they were already acculturated to English ways, were educated, and could speak, read, and write English. But, they were members of a "papist religion" and not welcome in Protestant Worcester. At first, they weren't allowed to enter the city without a pass, or to bury their dead there, and they were accepted only conditionally as temporary workers. But a good many of them found employment in town around the wharfs, or as boatmen or in other labor, and settled in Pine Meadows (along what is now Shrewsbury Street) near Worcester's black community.

For the average Worcester citizen, the Irish settlers were a novelty, darkened by ignorance. According to one story, a townsman was watching an Irish worker name Walter Boyce, with "the greatest scrutiny and curiosity." Finally, Boyce asked the man if he "thought I had horns on." "Well" said the man, "I was led to believe so and it has been taught to us. But, I find I am entirely mistaken, for you are a fine, strong, healthy appearing race of men."[8] Ignorance gradually gave way to acceptance, tempered by ridicule for their love of whiskey and rum. By the 1840s, these "Pioneer Irish" had established a thriving community with a church, clubs, schools, and even a small symphony.[9] Boland, the Irish contractor who brought them here, found plenty of contracting opportunities in the growing city, and soon became a prominent and wealthy man.

A second wave of immigration in the mid 1840s to 1850s swelled Worcester's Irish population from 600 to 3,000. These came from western Ireland where Gaelic was still spoken and English ways were resisted. Most were uneducated, poor, and illiterate, and among them were Potato Famine victims who suffered from disease. In Worcester, they settled among the Pioneer Irish like unwelcome in-laws, and looked to their "hosts" for housing and jobs. They were consigned to the most menial work, mostly in railroad construction jobs contracted by Boland. In their work ethic and habits, they were completely unsuited to industrial Worcester and even Boland considered them indifferent workers.

Tensions began to build between the two Irish groups when Boland began recruiting French Canadians, who were then trickling into Worcester. They boiled over on Palm Sunday 1847, when hundreds of Irish appeared at a hiring fair for railroad construction jobs, already fueled by drink, and angered over what they perceived as Boland's unfair hiring preferences. After emptying the nearby saloons, they went looking for Boland and other "lace curtain" Irish men—those who called themselves Irishmen yet acted like Englishmen. Fortunately, Boland wasn't at home, but the "Palm Sunday Riot" marked the beginning of a sustained period of gang violence and destruction that nearly tore the Irish community apart. It was this state of anarchy that prompted the petition for a city charter in 1847. According to Mayor Levi Lincoln, the "most urgent, and probably, the prevailing motive" for the petition was "the organization of a vigilant and efficient police."[10] But it would be years before an "efficient police" developed, and the Irish were left to settle their own affairs. Eventually, responsible members of their community, mostly Mexican War veterans, outfitted themselves with uniforms and formed a quasi-police force called the "Jackson Guards". By 1852, they had routed the gangs and restored order.

But the experience had shaken the Yankees of Worcester and rekindled latent beliefs in the moral depravity of the Irish. Out of this grew a movement called the "Know-Nothings", an anti-Catholic, anti-immigrant society that quickly swelled to over 1,200 members and helped elect in 1854 a sympathetic mayor and others to city office. The movement fizzled quickly, but wariness remained until after the Civil War. Although the Irish were just 30% of the population, they represented 40% of Worcester's Union veterans. In the wave of patriotism that followed the war, it was hard for people to hate those who served, and the image of the Irish community improved.[11]

Fortunately, farsighted city leaders chose education and assimilation over exclusion and abandonment. Public schools remained free and open to all, in spite of the fact that the children of Irish immigrants nearly overwhelmed the system. In 1869, they exceeded native born; yet free night schools were made available to their working parents. As a result, 2nd generation Irish Americans had a better life than their parents. Acculturated and educated, young men gradually moved into middle class white collar jobs, and the lower middle class as skilled workers. And, many young Irish American women found a niche for themselves beyond domestic service, as school teachers.

When Philip O'Connell became mayor in 1901, Irish Americans were about 35% of Worcester's population—41,000, of the total, 118,425. His personal story is the story of the Irish experience in general. His parents came from Ireland in the 1840s, and his father was a veteran of the Civil War. After attending Worcester public schools, Philip attended Boston University law school and graduated Magna Cum Laude. He practiced law in Worcester until his appointment as (the first Roman Catholic) Justice of the Superior Court of Massachusetts. The Irish were only the first foreign and ethnic group who followed opportunity to Worcester. After them came French Canadians, Swedes, Finns, and Norwegians, and, after the turn of the century, Polish, Italians, Armenians, and Russian Jews. Worcester no longer trembled as they came. Instead, it took them in and made them Americans.

When the first city government took over in 1848, it inherited responsibility for 13 schoolhouses, 39 teachers and about 1,500 pupils. Also, a fire department with seven "engineers", five engines and one hook and ladder carriage, a police department consisting of a city marshal, an assistant marshal and five constables and an almshouse on 240 acres with a hospital, and over 100 miles of "highways" to be maintained. For the rest of the century, Worcester's mayors and their administrations were faced with the demands of an exploding population for more schools, for roads and road maintenance, for fire and police protection, and for water supplies, and sewage disposal. There would be many other issues along the way, but these were usually the most significant expenditures, and therefore the most controversial, pitting practical needs against inherent parsimony.

In his 1848 inaugural address, Mayor Lincoln said, "Let there be no neglect, no indifference, no remissness in attention to the first of all public objects, the education of the youth of this city."[12] To their credit, his successors made public schools the top priority for the remainder of the 19ᵗʰ century, if not always with equal enthusiasm. By 1855, the city had erected nine new schoolhouses as replacements for the aging one-room structures built in 1830, including one for South Worcester.[13] When stingy administrations balked at funding, additional school rooms were sometimes made from the coat rooms and hallways of existing buildings. In his annual report of 1869, Superintendent of Schools Albert Marble explained that "unprecedented expenditures" during the prior year were necessary because the "city is at a period of unprecedented growth, with annual population increases of 12-15% and 9,000 children to be educated." Perhaps knowing these expenditures would be controversial, he added: "We have a large rich, enterprising, and rapidly growing city, and nothing but perhaps a niggardly policy in our public affairs, can stop its growth."[14]

Next in the line of expenditures were city streets and their maintenance. Here again, financial prudence had to be overcome by necessity. When Worcester became a city there were no paved roads, and some were content to keep it that way. Mayor Knowlton's term in 1852 was especially "turbulent" because of large expenditures for paving Main & Front Streets, leveling Mowers Hill on Main Street, and for two expensive bridges and a viaduct on Southbridge Street. But in 1856, twelve new streets were laid out; similar street expansions would follow, and the needs of a growing city were met.

In 1848, Worcester was recording about 200 arrests per year, mostly for drunkenness and disturbances in the Irish settlement called "Scalpintown" on the east side, in the general area of modern Green, Gold, and Madison Streets. In 1850, the city added 7 night watchmen, but they had little desire to interfere with the troubles in that neighborhood. There were no rules governing the police force until 1856, no police uniforms until 1865, and no formal organization of the department until Marshals with military experience from the Civil War took office. In 1871, the name "watchmen" was changed to "patrolmen". The fire department grew apace with little controversy. In those days, fires were common, and having the means to fight them was popular. The most disastrous fire was the one that demolished the Merrifield "power factory" building and others nearby, in June 1854. According to the New York Times "The firemen worked hard to stay the flames. Governor Washburn (Massachusetts) took a position on one of the engines and worked until the fire was subdued." In spite of the Governor's help, a large number of manufactories were destroyed, and 1,500 employees thrown out of work. When the first Steam Fire Engine or "steamer" was purchased 1860, at a cost of $3,000, it was the pride of the city. [15]

When Worcester became city, it relied primarily on wells and springs for its general water supplies, plus a few large wells at various locations for fire fighting. A small reservoir built near Bell Pond in 1858 provided an additional, but still inadequate, supply of water. Several mayoral administrations agonized over the costs for new water sources until the matter was finally put to the citizens for a vote. In January 1864, they narrowly (582 to 564) approved a proposal to take land for a reservoir at Lynde Brook in Leicester and introduce its water to the city "at a cost not to exceed $100,000". This supply was supposed to satisfy the city's water needs for at least 50 years, but before the end of the 19th century, additional supplies would be taken from Hunts Reservoir (1876), Holden Reservoir (1883), and Kettle Brook (1898). [16]

Sewage disposal became a far more vexing problem, once the city awakened to the need for it. Worcester made do with cesspools and a few sewers until 1866, when a law was passed "to appropriate Mill Brook and other brooks therein for the purpose of sewage, drainage and the public health." But, according to Joe Doherty, "this made matters worse" because the law "made provision for 44 separate sewer lines to empty directly into Mill Brook, with no pretreatment whatsoever... By 1873, the stream was an abomination. Its foul waters ran thick with industrial poisons and raw domestic sewage." As it oozed its way through the east-side working class (Irish) neighborhoods, their complaints went unheeded, as were outcries from the town of Millbury and factory owners along the upper Blackstone. Fixing it, according to the city, would be too expensive, but at last, after a lawsuit, it conceded to at least hide the problem. "In 1884, city engineers and construction crews began the arduous work of burying Mill River. They built a stone arch roof over the old Blackstone Canal from Salisbury Pond to the southern end of the city (fig. 6-6), then buried it, effectively removing Mill River from sight and smell… within 10 years, virtually no sign of Mill Brook remained."[17] The problem of pre-treatment was left for a later time.

In her interesting case history, Trees At Risk, Evelyn Herwitz tells us how some 19th century local leaders and urban reformers made Worcester a "city of trees", in spite of a tight-fisted public and its elected officials. All around the country, leaders of recently industrialized cities were coming to understand "the bitter truth… that the price of urban prosperity was pollution, overcrowding and cholera." "As city after city shed fields for factories", there was growing remorse over the loss of their rural past. By mid-century, pastoral nostalgia evolved into a disdain for modern cities—the "city evil". But moderate reformers saw the benefits of city and country, and sought to combine both by importing nature to the city in the form of parks and tree plantings. Over the next several decades, "private citizens and local governments set out hundreds of thousands of trees. The results, at the turn of the 20th century, were "lush, canopied streets and densely shaded parks".[18]

Mayor Henry Chapin brought up the need for public parks in Worcester, in his 1850 inaugural address: "Increasing as our city is in population, the time will soon come when the necessity for more extensive public grounds will press upon us. With the exception of a common, which is by no means a large one, we are nearly destitute of them." A year later, his successor, Mayor Bacon, established the Committee on Shade Trees & Public Grounds, for maintaining the common and burial grounds and for planting and main-

Figure 6-6. Photo of the covering of the Blackstone Canal in downtown Worcester. (From the collections of the Worcester Historical Museum.)

taining shade trees along city streets. Three years later (March 1854) the city purchased 27 acres of land for $11,257.50, becoming probably the first city in the nation to buy land for use as an urban public park—now Elm Park. The public was not happy. They dismissed the park as swampland, and too far from public access, but their real problem was with government spending. Chastened, the city left the park unimproved for nearly two decades. In 1870, a "relentless visionary" named Edward Winslow Lincoln took over as head of the Commission on Shade Trees & Public Grounds and restored its purpose. By the end of 1870s, the commission was planting more than 700 street trees each year. In 1873, the city authorized $2000 for the "unemployed and destitute" to excavate the first ornamental pools at Elm Park. This was later followed with more pools, foot paths, landscaping, and the iconic cast iron bridge (1881). The park became a popular success — a "pleasure ground" for strolling, skating, feeding ducks, and, apparently, for making love. In response to the "close-fisted" policies of Mayor Clark Jillson, "Lincoln quipped that the cost of re-seeding trampled grass should be financed by marriage licenses and birth certificates, because: 'one half the courting in the City is commenced or consummated on the PUBLIC GROUNDS why should not the profit inure to this COMMISSION…'"[18]

In a speech celebrating the city's 50th anniversary, Frank P. Goulding said, "Worcester has always been a liberal city."[19] That seems an odd statement, given the near uniform first half-century of fiscally conservative governance, and a miserly Yankee electorate that discouraged government activism. What Goulding was referring to was the socially progressive side of Worcester, the side that emerged and blossomed during the "Age of Reform". As industrialization swept the Northeast, not only did it awaken yearnings for a lost rural past, but it also awakened a moral impulse for the improvement of society. In city after industrialized city, social movements like urban renewal, improved working conditions, anti-slavery, women's rights, temperance, and a host of others emerged, and most found fertile ground in Worcester. As a major transportation hub, the city was easily accessible to reform ideas and reformers, and it had the facilities — lecture halls, hotels, restaurants — to host them. Worcester became a Mecca for reform movements and conventions of all kinds, but the three most lasting and prominent were anti-slavery, women's rights, and temperance.

On the eve of the civil war, about 200 African Americans lived in Worcester. Most were descendants of 18th century slaves owned by wealthy families, like the Chandlers and Paines, and many were of mixed Nipmuck-African ancestry. In 1781, Worcester attorney Levi Lincoln Sr. won an appeals case on behalf of a slave named Quock Walker, which effectively ended the practice of slavery in Massachusetts.[20] Eventually, former slaves from around the County settled in Worcester, where they found work as laborers or servants. They were accepted and well-treated for the most part, but not as equals; a separate section was made for them in the Mechanics Street burial ground and the early school system had a separate "African school" as noted earlier. In the mid-1830s, the black populations of Worcester County lived in real fear of bounty hunters, who were kidnapping their youth for sale as slaves in the South. In September 1839, for example, a young "mulatto" named Sidney Francis was taken from Worcester and brought to Richmond, Virginia. He was later rescued, but his and other kidnappings caused public outrage and bolstered the cause of anti-slavery reform. By this time, Anti-Slavery Societies formed by William Lloyd Garrison had hundreds of members living in Worcester County, and some of the most radical lived in Worcester. Their cause was the immediate abolition of slavery, "disunion" of states from the country that tolerated it, and withdrawal from all pro-slavery religious or political organizations. Other, less radical reformers in Worcester supported the Union, and opposed the spread of slavery. Eli Thayer was a member of this group.

Thayer was born 1819 in Mendon, Massachusetts. He came to Worcester to attend the Worcester Manual Labor School (later Worcester Academy), where he later taught and became its Principal. In 1848, he founded and built the Oread Collegiate Institute, the Nation's first college for women. After teaching there for a few years, he turned to politics. During the early to mid 1850s, he was (consecutively) an Alderman in Worcester, a member of the State House of Representatives, and a Representative to the U.S Congress (fig 6-7).

While in the legislature, he originated and took out a charter for the New England Emigrant Aid Company, for the purpose of colonizing the state of Kansas with New England antislavery settlers. Amos Lawrence, of Boston, financed it, but Thayer did all the groundwork: lecturing, organizing, and fund-raising throughout New England. Ultimately, his company sent more than 2,000 New Englanders to Kansas who helped create the towns of

Figure 6-7. Portrait of Eli Thayer as he looked when a member of Congress. (Courtesy of the Library of Congress: http://www.loc.gov/pictures/item/2010649209/)

Lawrence, Manhattan, and several other towns. A bust of Thayer sits in the Kansas State House, and in Worcester, Kansas Street was named in his honor.

The first National Woman's Rights Convention was held in Worcester, in 1850. Its final resolution called for "equality before the law without distinction of sex or color." In a society deeply immersed in the concepts of fairness, it's not surprising that the rights of women entered the field of reforms. Females had been active for years in various reform movements, especially temperance and antislavery, but only as separate sub-groups for women. In 1840, a Worcester woman named Abby Kelley changed that when she became the first female elected to a high position in William Lloyd Garrison's American Anti-Slavery Society. Kelley grew up and attended public school in Worcester's Tatnuck Village, then moved to Lynn, Massachusetts in 1836 to teach school. After hearing a lecture by Garrison, she joined the Female Anti-Slavery Society of Lynn and became recognized as a dynamic public speaker and an effective organizer. Her later promotion by Garrison was an affront to some male sensibilities and caused a split, but he widened his agenda to include women's rights, and before long women filled all positions of his Society except president. Kelley married radical abolitionist and women's rights advocate Stephen Symonds Foster in 1845. Two years later, the

Fosters' bought a farm in Tatnuck where they lived and sometimes provided shelter for slaves escaping north on the Underground Railroad. (Now called the Liberty Farm, it is a designated Historical Landmark).

Whether in separate female reform groups or desegregated groups like Garrison's, a host of women had become highly skilled as organizers, public speakers, and fundraisers and were well prepared to fight for their own rights. In 1848, Kelley and a number of like-minded feminists held a women's rights convention in Seneca Falls, New York, and laid plans for the first National Convention to be held at Worcester in 1850. It was a success, with about 1,000 attending, and a major event for the newspapers and the public. As a result, the second National convention was again held in Worcester the following year, in an even larger forum. Abby Kelley was a key speaker at both events, and made this closing statement at the second convention: "I do not speak of women's rights, but of human rights, the rights of human beings. I do not come to ask [for] them, but to demand them; not to get down on my knees and beg for them, but to claim them."[21]

It might be assumed that temperance reform came from a mythological Puritan intolerance for happiness. Actually, Puritans enjoyed their hard cider, beer, wine, brandy, and gin. In early Colonial times, the manufacture of rum was New England's largest industry, and Worcester in its canal days had its own distillery, a brewery, and plenty of taverns. The fact is, temperance reform, like slavery and women's rights, grew out of a serious social disorder; Americans were drinking far too much, and far too often. Rosenzwieg quotes a study showing that Americans between 1790 and 1830 "drank more alcoholic beverages than ever before or since". It was, he says, an era when drinking "suffused all areas of life" including the workplace. Laborers and artisans alike were routinely paid in "wages and grog" and "the rum barrel was always near the work".[22] While it's true that church leaders were prominent in the temperance movements, their moral opposition was to the sin of excess and its consequences for the addicted, their families, their employers, and their communities. In this they had common cause, especially with women, manufacturers, and public officials.

The American Temperance Union was formed in 1833, and one year later there were about 5,000 state and local temperance societies. Although some reformers insisted on total abstinence, others sought responsible drinking, which was the early stance of the Temperance Union. However, some communities went further, closing taverns or cutting off the sales of alcohol. In 1835, the Town of Worcester voted by a narrow margin to "withhold their approbation for License to sell ardent Spirits from all Retailers and Innholders."[23] In protest, angry tavern owners and hotel proprietors closed their doors for a few days, to the distress of business travelers and visitors. After a one-year dry period, liquor sales were approved until 1855 when the City prohibited the sale of liquor by popular vote. In the meantime, "new workplace bans on drinking had a more direct impact on popular customs."[24]

Beginning in about 1830, a number of machine shops and factories "had banned drinking during work hours and had stopped employing intemperate workmen." Coinciding with the spread of these bans, workplace reforms had shortened the workday from twelve to ten hours, and drinking became a leisure after hours activity, enjoyed mostly in the kitchens of Irish working class homes. It was impossible to control drinking under these circumstances, so, Massachusetts passed license laws in 1875, which allowed for public drinking places, and led to the growth of saloons. Eventually, Worcester's ethnic working class neighborhoods developed their own saloons, as "male preserves" for leisure activity. Following the Civil War, the temperance movement turned to outright prohibition. In Worcester, there were several more "no-license" periods between 1890 and 1909, which was the last, until the 18th (Prohibition) amendment was passed in 1919.

The secession of the Confederate states was greeted in Worcester and elsewhere in the North with disbelief, outrage, and a burst of righteous patriotism. On April 15, 1861 President Lincoln called for 75,000 volunteers, and loyal states like Massachusetts promptly exceeded their quotas. The 15th Massachusetts Infantry Regiment was organized in Worcester on June 12, 1861 under Colonel Charles P. Devens. The first of two campgrounds for their training was established on the Brooks Farm, named for Deacon Samuel Brooks, one of earliest settlers in South Worcester. A plaque on the wall of the South Worcester Neighborhood Center on Camp Street at Maloney's Field (South Worcester Playground) pays tribute to the soldiers who trained there (fig 6-8).

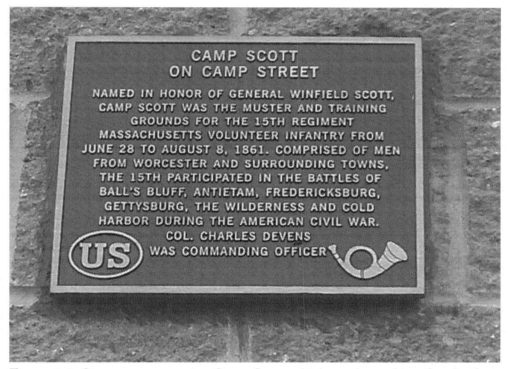

Figure 6-8. Sign commemorating Camp Scott, which was located just South of Cambridge Street and West of the Norwich and Worcester Railroad tracks. (Photo by the authors.)

On the 28th of June, 801 men of the regiment moved into their white canvas tents and went into training. In the weeks that followed, their daily regimen consisted of five hours of drills, morning and evening dress parades, and formations in line. Each company cooked its meals of soup, rice, potatoes, salt beef, and other staples of a dreary diet that was occasionally brightened up with fresh strawberries, contributed by the local citizens. On Sundays, morning drills were replaced by sermons, patriotic addresses, prayers, and band music.

The original plan was to train the men for a month longer, but a disastrous Union defeat at the First Battle of Bull Run (June 21, 1861) forced the government to shorten training. At six a.m. on August 8, the 15th regiment boarded the Norwich railroad train while crowds of onlookers cheered them. They went first to Washington D.C, where they were attached to the Army of the Potomac. They saw their first action on October 21 at Ball's Bluff, Virginia, which was the second major engagement of the Civil War and the second devastating defeat for the Union. Eventually, these unready but willing volunteers would become tempered by fire. Over the course of War, according to historian Charles Nutt, the 15th mustered 1,046 men and lost 398.

While most of the volunteers were motivated by patriotism, others marched off to fight the slavers. Among the latter, was Thomas Wentworth Higginson, the Unitarian minister and radical abolitionist who had organized Worcester's "Disunion" Convention in 1857, and then fought for the Union when the war broke out. In keeping with his convictions, he served as a colonel of the First South Carolina Volunteers, a Union regiment recruited from freed black slaves. In her book "First Fruits of Freedom", Janette Greenwood tells a little known story of other Worcester abolitionist soldiers, who were among the first to invade the North Carolina coast and there formed personal bonds with freed slaves. Out of these bonds, links were established for the migration of many of these former slaves to Worcester and New England. In Worcester, they found a support network made up of sympathetic whites and a welcoming black community, which housed them and helped them find jobs. As a result, they settled readily into the community, purchased homes, and were joined by their families, creating what

Greenwood described as a "northern community with a distinctly southern flavor."[25] In 1870, 524 African Americans lived in Worcester. Over 30% of them owned real estate, 87% could read and write, and more than half of the children attended public schools, which were now fully integrated. Sadly, the "first fruits" of progress didn't last. As Worcester turned its focus from the war to the business of doing business, its industrial leaders chose native white and European immigrant labor for employment, relegating blacks to menial work and the edges of society.

After the civil war, abolition and antislavery reformers remained active until after ratification in 1870 of the Fifteenth amendment, giving male African Americans the right to vote. The struggle for women's rights and suffrage went on with renewed intensity. Women like Abby Kelly, who fought for both causes, were outraged that the Fourteenth Amendment explicitly denied the vote to women. For the rest of their lives, until they were no longer physically able, Abby and her husband campaigned against this injustice. Several times during the 1870s, they refused to pay property taxes in protest. Each time, their farm was seized and auctioned off by the state, and each time, their friends purchased the farm and gave it back. The political struggle for women's suffrage didn't end until the Nineteenth Amendment was passed in 1920.

After his several careers as educator, politician, and antislavery activist, Eli Thayer turned to land investing and development, mostly in the areas of Main South and South Worcester. We will learn more of him in that regard in Chapter 8.

Notes:

1. Worcester Historical Museum, Worcester in the 19th Century: http://www.worcesterhistory.org/19th-transportation.html

2. Rosenzweig, *Eight hours for What We Will,* p. 11-12.

3. London Times, 1878, Triumph of American Machinery. Published By U. S. Commission to the Paris Exposition, 1878, Edward Henry Knight Volume 1.

4. Hovey was an inventive mechanic in his own right, who invented and built improved shearing machines.

5. In 1899, the company he founded was acquired by American Steel and Wire Co., which became a division of US Steel in 1901. It was the largest wire producer in the world.

6. "The result of my building mills is thus far very satisfactory for while I am content with the rent, the tenants deem it very favorable and both mills are filled with good business. The mechanics in these mills work for a certain number of hours and it is therefore important that they should live within a reasonable distance... In the last year I built four houses and refitted another near this mill, which accommodate 7 families and there are at least as many more who wish for houses." Stephen Salisbury II, March 12, 1835, in a letter to Edward Tuckerman of Boston.

7. In addition, Washburn helped build two churches, the Bay State House Hotel, the Memorial Hospital, and the Home for the Female Aged, to name a few. He was also trustee and frequent donor of the Member of Zion's Methodist Society (black) church.

8. Meagher, *To Preserve the Flame,* p. 12.

9. Meagher, *Inventing Irish America,* p.23.

10. Moynihan, *A History of Worcester,* p. 149.

11. Meagher, *Inventing Irish America,* p.137.

12. Hoar, *Celebration of the Two Hundredth Anniversary of the Naming of Worcester,* p. 39.

13. Rice, *Worcester of Eighteen Hundred and Ninety Eight,* p.29.

14. Albert Marble, Worcester Superintendent of Schools Report, February, 1869.

15. The New York Times, New York, NY 16, June, 1854.

16. Nutt, *History of Worcester and its People* , vol. 4 p. 474.

17. Doherty, *Our River,* p. 5-6.

18. All quotes and information regarding trees and parks are taken from *Trees at Risk.* According to Herwitz, Worcester's trees are currently under threat because of neglect, and she warns that they will be lost unless the city takes action. See her website http://treesatrisk.com

19. Rice, *History of Worcester*, p. 123.

20. McCarthy and Doughton, *From Bondage to Belonging*, p. xxviii.

21. Lawes, *Women and Reform*, p. 171.

22. Rosenzweig, *Eight Hours for What We Will*, p. 36.

23. Nutt, *History of Worcester and its People*, vol. 1, p. 505.

24. Rosenzweig, *Eight Hours for What We Will*, p. 38.

25. Greenwood, *First Fruits of Freedom*, p. 8.

— Chapter 7 —
Roots: English Immigrants and the American Textile Industry

From the Worcester Spy, December 23, 1870: "A recent up-tick in English immigration… in the country from England has for a year or two been larger than ever before; and of the whole number of foreigners landing on our shores, the English immigrants have been more numerous than those of any other nation." The article goes on to predict that, "… there will be such an exodus of the bone and sinews of England to our country as will astonish even the most sanguine of us."

The Worcester Spy's prediction, if rhetorically overblown, was grounded in recent trends, and it proved prophetic. At the time it was written, the United States was in the midst of a surge of English immigration that swelled from about 60,000 immigrants annually in 1868 to 75,000 in 1872. This was the second of three "waves" in the ebbs and flows of English immigration during the period between 1820 and 1929, when more than 4 million of them crossed the Atlantic. The first was between the mid 1840s and mid 1850s, and the third wave, the one prophesized by the Spy, averaged 80,000 per year between 1879 and 1893, before tapering off with the depression of the 1930s.[1]

The first and most enduring lure for their immigration was land, and the opportunity to own it. America had it in abundance, it was open to all comers, and it was unbelievably cheap. This was a powerful draw for English tenant farmers and farm workers who labored on rented land and sold their crops at market prices. During the first half of the 19th century, they were being squeezed out by the growth of large-scale farming, and by rising rents and unstable earnings. In America, it was possible to buy land for less than two years rent in England, and so they sold their only assets — their stock and farm implements — and emigrated with their families. Adding fuel to this first wave of immigration was a flood of non-farmers who fell under the spell of the "Agrarian Myth"; a movement that rejected the social "evils" of industrialization and urbanization, and held that farm ownership, and the livelihood gained from it was the only true path to independence, dignity, family cohesiveness, and happiness.

It made no difference that they had never before milked a cow or turned a shovel; they came anyway, bought their farms, and learned on the job. A few of the early ones went first to the northeast where they could still find land in rural areas, or find work in their old trades until they had money enough to move west and buy a farm. But most went straight to the "Old Northwest", which is now the upper mid-west. Surprisingly, they usually succeeded, and it became commonplace to find former English house painters, blacksmiths, storekeepers and even hand-loom weavers, tending farms on the lonely prairies of Wisconsin, Illinois, Iowa, or Indiana. English farmers continued to play a role in the American Westward movement and helped settle the Great Plains and the far western states. In the 2nd half 19th century, English land seekers of a different stripe joined them, hoping to exploit the widely diverse opportunities of a rapidly expanding American nation. They included miners, gold seekers, railroad builders and investors, commercial agents and professionals, and wealthy cattle ranchers.

Immigration author Charlotte Erickson wrote that, as of 1850, only about 1 in 10 of the English immigrants in America were living in the northeastern states.[2] Most of them were farmers; others were in the skilled trades (carpenters, sign painters, tailors, stone masons), or had pre-industrialized skills (hand loom weavers, tool & cutlery makers, iron workers). In smaller proportions, there were some in the professions and commerce (commercial agents, clerks, shopkeepers, schoolteachers, engineers) and a sprinkling of those in domestic service (servants, governesses, gardeners). Some of these immigrants may have been "pushed" from England by the depressed conditions there during the "hungry '40s", but most were "pulled" to the United States by its wide-open job market. But, by the mid 19th century, economic and social conditions in England had radically improved, and moved from the "hungry 40s" to a period "that stretched from 1850 to 1873, during which prices, profits, production and prosperity rose steadily and significantly."[3]

In spite of this "Victorian Boom", emigration from Britain actually increased. This apparent contradiction came about as the transatlantic voyage itself became easier, faster, and more affordable. Until the mid 1850s, transatlantic travel was a daunting experience and a major consideration for anyone contemplating it. Depending on weather conditions, crossing by sail could take anywhere from five to fourteen weeks. The introduction of steamships, which had largely replaced sail by 1865, reduced the time to twelve days. The booming English economy generated higher wages, making emigration affordable for the average worker. And, no longer did tearful goodbyes on the wharfs of departing ships need to mean "forever". As passenger travel became less expensive and continued to improve, emigrants knew they could return home if things didn't work out, or expect to visit with their loved ones again if they stayed. From this point on, the motives for English immigration were almost entirely opportunistic. In increasing numbers, they came to America's northeastern cities and towns, where abundant opportunities and higher wages awaited. By the late 19th century, according to Erickson, their ranks included high proportions of single men and women migrants who were largely "temporary & transient." They could afford to gamble and "tramp" around America to see what it had to offer. Many of them stayed, while others returned home with stories good and bad about their American adventure.

The English immigrants who are central to our book came out of the British textile industry. Their story includes the English inventors who pioneered the industrialization of American textile manufacturers, the entrepreneur-manufacturers who helped build it, and those employed in the industry — the weavers, spinners, loom fixers, foremen, wool sorters, etc., who brought these skills to the United States.

Textile manufacturing had had a long history in England even before the discovery of America. Its rainy climate was perfect for grazing sheep for wool, and flax for linen, and their manufacture into cloth began as a bi-product of farming. Women and children spun the yarn, which then went to a skilled male weaver, who wove the cloth on a handloom. The finished product was either returned to the household or picked up by a merchant for assembly and sale elsewhere. By the late 17th century, cotton became available from India. When spun into thread it made a comfortable, durable and inexpensive textile that was also amenable to machine production. The first improvement was the spinning jenny, followed by the water frame and spinning mule, all of which vastly improved the quality and efficiency of the spinning process; so much so, that attention turned next to the mechanization of the handloom. In 1788, the Reverend Edmund Cartwright of Leicestershire, a man with no weaving experience, invented a power loom that mechanically produced cotton cloth. The mechanization of cotton manufacture vastly increased the demand for cotton, and, after the American Revolution, English cotton manufacturers looked to American cotton plantations to fill that need. But raw cotton had seeds that had to be removed before it could be spun, a prohibitively time consuming process when done by hand. American inventor Eli Whitney solved that problem with his cotton gin, which spurred both the Industrial Revolution in Britain and cotton production in the American south.

Mechanization of cotton textile manufacturing ended the traditional domestic system of textile production. Power looms and spinning machines were concentrated together in mills that were springing up near their power sources along the rivers and in the valleys of northern England. Soon, factory systems developed for the efficient organization of machines and their operators into specific functions and specialized tasks and skills. Farmer-artisans became factory laborers and wage earners, and subject to the authority of the mill's owner. As the first industrialized nation, England was on the way to becoming an economic powerhouse. It had the secrets of the machines, and a factory system that organized them for maximum efficiency and production. It also had a reliable supply of raw material—cotton—from their trading partners across the Atlantic. But, what if America had the machine secrets and controlled the supply of cotton? It was unthinkable. In 1790, the young United States had not one machine for producing thread, and the English government wanted to keep it that way. Laws were passed forbidding the export of machine technology or the emigration of those who were familiar with it.

Looking for a breakthrough, Alexander Hamilton encouraged rewards for those who would bring "improvements and secrets of extraordinary value" to America from elsewhere. Nowadays, we call this "piracy". The answer to Hamilton's call came from one of our most famous English immigrants and the first in our line of textile immigrants. In American histories, he is often referred to as the "father of the American factory system". In Britain he was known as "Slater the Traitor".

Samuel Slater was born of a farming family in Derbyshire, England on June 9, 1768. At the age of ten, he went to work at Jedidiah Strutt's cotton mill, which used the revolutionary spinning frame invented by Richard Arkwright. Also known as the "water frame", it was powered by water and was part of a fully automated process that carded and spun cotton into thread. As a result, cotton spinning moved out of the household and into factory production. About ten years after he began working at Strutt's mill, Slater made plans to emigrate to the United States. Although he had risen to the position of superintendent, he was aware of the rewards offered for "secrets of extraordinary value", and, in late 1789, Slater left England disguised as a farmer, with the secrets of Arkwright's spinning machine in his head. After a brief search for the right situation, Slater offered his expert knowledge of the Arkwright system to the partnership of Almy and Brown, who were attempting to set up an Arkwright-type mill in Pawtucket, Rhode Island. In his reply to the offer, Moses Brown invited Slater to "come and work… and have the credit as well as having the advantage of perfecting the first watermill in America."[4] Slater accepted, and with the aid of local mechanics, he converted the American built machines into a hybrid of Arkwright's. By 1790, the partnership of Almy, Brown, and Slater began operations with the first water-powered and fully mechanized cotton-spinning mill in the United States.

In 1806, Samuel's brother, John Slater, joined the partnership, and together they established the mill village of Slatersville on 122 acres in Smithfield, RI. It was modeled on the factory village system of Derbyshire, with a river-based mill, operating year round and employing entire families, including women and children. These families lived in nearby company owned homes or boarding houses, shopped in company owned stores, and enjoyed company sponsored social activities and a church. Later known as the Rhode Island System, this technological and social model for mills set the standard for those that would dot the entire length of the Blackstone valley, and "define what would become an ionic New England landscape."[5] Slater became a wealthy man, and later built several steam-powered factories in Rhode Island and Massachusetts. The last was the Green Mill, built in 1813 in Webster, Massachusetts, a village just 18 miles south of Worcester. He lived there in a large mansion on the Worcester road until his death in 1835.

Massachusetts-born Francis Cabot Lowell didn't wait for English secrets to come to him. Instead, he went right to the source and got them. In 1811, with the help of family connections, he gained access for a lengthy study of Lancashire's textile mills and their water-powered looms. Two years later, with their secrets memorized, he returned home and hired a skilled mechanic named Paul Moody, who successfully recreated them. By 1814, Lowell and a group of investors formed the Boston Manufacturing Company in Waltham, Massachusetts. They linked their new power looms to previously mechanized processes like spinning, and created the world's first fully integrated mill, where "Cotton entered as a bale and exited as a bolt."[6] The concentration of all operations in one mill led to a more efficient factory/labor organization known as the "Waltham System". Instead of apprentices and family workers, the work force consisted mostly of unmarried females. They worked under contract for wages and were housed in company-provided dormitory style boarding houses. After his death, Lowell's company continued to grow, bringing the Waltham System to larger mills in Lowell and Lawrence Massachusetts, Manchester, New Hampshire, and other industrial centers in New England.

Once English technology was introduced to the United States, further technical improvements were made to it. A West Boylston-born American inventor named Erastus Bigelow invented power looms for weaving ingrain carpets without any stolen British secrets to guide him.[7] Regardless of where these technological advances came from, they were rapidly adopted and used by a growing number of American textile manufacturers. By the 1840s just about every town and city had at least one textile mill of one kind or another, and the industry settled into a period of growth and expansion as textile entrepreneurs built more mills and added niche products of every variety. This brings us to another type of English immigrant—the English manufacturer who came with a deep knowledge of their trade and extraordinary entrepreneurship, and set up mills in America.

One of the first of this type was Henry Whittaker, who began construction of a textile mill on the Tacony Branch of Frankford Creek, in northern Philadelphia. He had once hoped to expand the family textile mill in Rockdale, England, but was discouraged in this by high taxes. The spinning mill he built on 38 acres was typical of English mills of the pre-industrial period; it was powered by water to spin the raw materials that were "put out" to local handloom weavers for finishing. Once established, Whittaker's mill seized on every innovation, and over the years, it grew as sort of microcosm of the industrialization of the American textile industry. By 1824, both spinning and the weaving of cotton were done inside the mill, and three years later, power looms replaced handlooms. The shift to power revolutionized the work force of the entire industry. Operating handlooms had always been a male occupation because of their weight, but power looms could be easily handled by female operatives, and by 1839, 93% of the weavers at the mill were female. In 1831, Henry Whittaker sold the business to his son William, who continued to look for improvements and growth. In 1833 he toured the mills of New England, including the Slater Steam Mill in Providence. When he returned, he purchased a steam engine, and with a combination of steam and waterpower, his mill reached capacity by 1840.

In spite of many ups and downs, the Whittaker mills remained in the family until 1970. There were at least six other textile mills in the Frankford area during that early period, three of which were built by immigrants from the same Manchester area of England. Individually, they were relatively modest, but together, they helped make Philadelphia the leading textile city in America.[8] For the rest of the 19th century, and into the 20th century, more industry builders like these came to the northeast. Two notable examples are Catholina Lambert and William Shuttleworth.

Lambert was born 1834 in Yorkshire, England. After a seven-year apprenticeship in the Boars Head Cotton Mill, he emigrated to America at the age of 17 with little more than a wealth of knowledge in textiles. In Boston, he took a job as a bookkeeper in a silk mill, and four years later, he was made a partner in the firm. He ran the company's New York office for three years, and then bought out his partner and became head of the firm "Dexter, Lambert and Company". In 1858, his company took over a mill in Paterson, New Jersey that produced silk ribbon. His business prospered, and in the late 1870s, he bought more mills there. At their peak, Lambert's Paterson mills alone employed more than 1,000, and the City of Paterson, which was then known as "The Silk City", dominated the production of silk in the United States.[9]

In 1875, William Shuttleworth and his four grown sons came to Glenham New York to establish a new carpet mill for a wealthy merchant named Alexander T. Stewart. The Shuttleworths' came from Halifax, England, and had a long family history and experience in the carpet trade. After William died, his sons moved to nearby Amsterdam and started a carpet company of their own, on the Mohawk River. The Shuttleworth Brothers Company made carpets under that name until 1920, when it merged with a rug company and became the "Mohawk Mills". Shuttleworth descendants continued to manage the company through additional mergers and name changes until the third generation, when Henry Shuttleworth II retired from "Mohasco" in 1980.[10] In 1992, the company went public as Mohawk Industries, which now produces a variety of floor coverings and employs more than 30,000 world-wide.

Charles Nutt, in his History of Worcester and its People, said that up until 1860, "Worcester got few accessions" of English immigrants. "Since 1860, however, there has been a steady contribution to the population from England, but the English become Americans almost as soon as they have made their homes here, and lose their identity and national characteristics."[11] The relatively small number of English immigrants before 1860 was probably due to Worcester's industrial focus on machine and tool making, and it was not yet an important destination for immigrant textile workers, who were going to the large mills elsewhere.

A look at the 1870 census for English immigrants living in the South Worcester part of Ward 6 shows that they were quite typical of those who came to the northeastern United States prior to the mid-1860s, as described above. In a sample of 129 adults, there were 75 males (58%) and 54 (42%) females. Of the males, more than half (42) were single, and 33 were married; 27 of them had English-born spouses, while 6 of these first generation immigrants married native-born (mostly Massachusetts) females. Of the 54 female immigrants, the majority (42) were married; 27 of them were the English wives of immigrant males, while 14 had married native born spouses, and one, an Irish born spouse. These first generation marriages outside their immigrant community help explain why these English immigrants quickly lost their identity and national characteristics.

Occupationally, of the 42 married females, 40 were described in the census as "keeping house" and only 2 of them were employed in the "woolen mill." This suggests that with few exceptions, their spouses earned sufficient wages to support them at home. Of the 12 unmarried females, 6 kept house for boarders, or for unrelated families, or extended families; 2 were domestic servants, 3 were elderly unemployed, and 1 worked in the woolen mill. Of the males, 41 (55%) were employed in two textile mills and in the bleach and dye works. The rest included 9 machinists, and 6 iron and wire workers, who of course, found a ready market for their skills in Worcester; there were 8 in the basic skilled trades (carpenters, painters, tinsmiths); 5 stone cutters, a baker and a watchman; 2 laborers, possibly among those referred to earlier as "on the tramp", looking for their place of opportunity.

There was also one farmer and one retired farmer who, according to the 1870 census, had "no occupation." This was 83 years old John McDollen, whom we met in Chapter 5. He was one of the many early English immigrants who came to America to farm, and one of the few who found that calling in the northeast. He purchased his first piece of farmland from the Patch estate on Pakachoag Hill in 1821, and two years later, he married Mary Stearns, the daughter of his neighbor, Moses Stearns. Was he an ex-tenant farmer fleeing high rents in England? Or did he come from a non-agrarian background, in pursuit of the Agrarian Ideal? The fact that he became a shoe maker in the last days of farming in South Worcester suggests the possibility of the latter. In either case, he found his land on fertile slopes of Pakachoag hill, and never went farther west. As we've seen, he remained a yeoman for most of his life, but the transition from farming to industry in Worcester ultimately caught up his family. In 1833, his son John McDollen Jr. married Lucy Ann Ball, and they got caught between the two worlds of agriculture, and industry. During the 1850s, John Jr. is variously referred to in city directories as a yeoman, a machinist, and an engineer, yet during this time, he and Lucy purchased various tracts of land on Pakachoag Hill from both of their families, suggesting he was unable to find his niche in either world. In 1870, in a deed that conveys frustration as well as land, Lucy's parents sold her a parcel of land on the southeasterly side of Southbridge St. "for the sole use of her and her heirs... free from the interference or control of her husband or his creditors..." In August, 1891, this property went up for sale at auction for failure to pay assessments. The amount assessed was $69.73.[12]

As mentioned above, more than half the male English immigrants and two female immigrants in our Ward 6 sample were employed in two textile mills and the bleach and dye works. The Adriatic Woolen Mills, and the nearby Worcester Bleach and Dye Works, employed some of them. However, most were employed at the Ashworth & Jones Co., where "beaver shoddys" were made. It was located just beyond the western border of South Worcester, in Cherry Valley, and it is a good example those early textile mills that were built by English immigrant entrepreneurs. Its founder, Thomas Ashworth, was born in Lancashire England, in 1822. Like many others of his type, he apprenticed at a young age with a local woolen mill, became well versed in the business, and then decided to look for wider opportunities in the United States. He immigrated in 1848, the year gold was discovered in California, and he went there to try his luck. Some biographies say "his toils were rewarded" and that "he returned with his gold;" in any case, after a couple of years, he left California and went East to work as a weaver in Oxford, Massachusetts. Eventually, he had enough capital to open his own mill. In 1856, he leased a mill in Holden for the manufacture of "shoddy" (yarn from used cloth or rags). He then recruited a "Shoddy Picker" from England, which, in its manual stages, required a skilled fabric sorter.

In 1862, Ashworth moved to Cherry Valley and, in partnership with his brother-in-law Edward Jones, manufactured "Ashworth & Jones Beavers", which used recycled beaver fur in the warp to make a refined and highly desirable cloth. (There was nothing "shoddy" about the finished product.) According to his obituary, Edward Jones "came to this country when a young man, his only capital when he arrived being a thorough knowledge of the woolen business, gained by a long apprenticeship in the factories of England".[13] In 1870 Ashworth and Jones built a large brick mill (fig. 7-1), some homes, a boarding house for their workers and, of course, mansions for themselves (fig. 7-2). Figure 7-3 shows the location and extent of their holdings in 1886.

Prior to 1860, two men of English heritage came to South Worcester and left an indelible mark on that Village. Both were the sons of immigrants from the county of Lancashire, England, but beyond this coincidence, they had little else in common.

James Fitton was the son of Abraham Fitton, a wheelwright, who immigrated to Boston from the "Catholic stronghold" of Lancashire in the 1790s. His mother was also a Catholic, and under their influence, his destiny was set. In his youth he served as an altar boy, and at the age of twenty-two years, Bishop Fenwick of Boston ordained him a priest. Soon after, in 1827,

Figure 7-1. Photo of the Ashworth & Jones factory at 1511 Main St., Worcester, as it appeared in 2015. This was listed on the National Register of Historic Places in 1980. This mill is along the south side of Leicester St. as shown in figure 7-3. (Photo by the authors.)

Father Fitton was sent off to Maine to fortify Catholic Passamaquoddy Indians against the efforts of a Protestant minister named Elijah Kellogg, who was trying to persuade them from their "papist" ways. Fitton lived among them over the winter, and after securing them to the Faith, he returned to Boston. During the 1700s, the number of Catholics in New England was insignificant, consisting mostly of converted Indians of the northern tribes, some French Canadians, and a few Yankee converts, but by the 1820s, bolstered by Irish immigration, their numbers were increasing. In 1821 Bishop Fenwick estimated that there were 3,500 Catholics in his Diocese, which included all of New England, and only about a dozen priests. As a result, they had to cover a lot ground in order to minister to their scattered communicants.

Figure 7-2. The mansion of Thomas Ashworth, which was at 1543 Main St. before being torn down in the 1950s. It became the Tower House Restaurant. From the archives of the Worcester Telegram. (From http://www.telegram.com/article/20140630/THENANDNOW/306309988)

In 1829, Father Fitton ministered to Catholics in Vermont and New Hampshire, and the following year he was sent to Hartford as pastor, responsible for Catholics in Connecticut and Western Massachusetts. As he later wrote, he was "on the road a great deal", preaching, and comforting the sick and dying "wherever a child of the faith was to be found." On one Christmas, for example, he made a 68 mile round trip, by horse-drawn sleigh, from Hartford to New Haven to say Midnight Mass for a group there, then, without food or drink, returned to say Mass in Hartford the next day.[14] Until 1830, a priest could be spared for only two visits each year to Worcester to tend the Irish who had come to the town as canal builders, and settled there as laborers. On Sundays without a priest, they made do with "dry masses"—outdoor prayers and scripture readings led by local lay leaders.

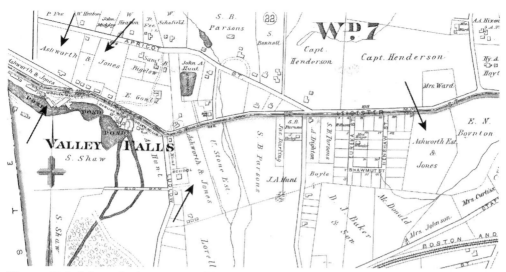

Figure 7-3. Map of what is now Cherry Valley published in 1886 showing the mills and land holdings of Ashworth and Jones (arrows) along Leicester St. (now Main St.). (From Hopkins, G.M., 1886.)

As their numbers grew, Father Fitton began visiting on a monthly basis, and he soon became their chief advocate, as well as their pastor. In 1833, he performed the first Catholic baptism and first Catholic marriage in Worcester, and that year he wrote to Bishop Fenwick proposing a church. In his letter, he estimated there were about 100 Catholics in the vicinity, and he asked, "How are these good people to be attended on Sundays as desired? This [church] will be necessary to preserve the flame at present kindled."[15] Permission was granted, and Fitton, with $500 donated by his Catholics, purchased land on an old cornfield and began construction of the future St. John's Church on Temple Street, south of the present Union Station. Although the building was still unfinished in 1836, 118 adults and children were attending and they had a choir. The same year, Father Fitton organized two Catholic schools; one, a Sunday school, in the basement of the still unfinished church, and the other, an academy for young men, on Pakachoag Hill in South Worcester. The purpose of the academy—to prepare young Catholics for business and commerce—would be a practical fit for Worces-

115

ter's growing immigrant population.

Again, Father Fitton raised funds from sympathetic donors, and on January 22, 1836, he paid $2,000 for 52 acres of land with a house and barn formerly occupied by Henry Patch, on the "northerly side of Bogachoag hill". Then he mortgaged the property to raise money for an academy building, and hired Irish contractor Tobias Boland, one of his most generous donors, to build it. Boland constructed a 70-foot long two-story wooden academy building, and added, at his own expense, a separate cottage for Father Fitton. Fitton then hired his brother Abraham to manage the farm and hired Joseph Brigden, a convert and master of the first Catholic school in Connecticut, as principal of the academy. By August 1836, Mount St. James Academy, named in honor of Fitton's patron saint, already had ten students, with twenty more expected when the building was completed. Students were required to be male, at least eight years old, and to bring with them "a cap and two suits" of clothes, one of which was the school uniform, "a round green cloth jacket, with standing collar, and blue pantaloons." The United States Catholic Almanac for 1837 announced that "the course of instruction comprises all the branches of a sound, correct, and practical English education, such as will qualify youth for usefulness in the various avocations of life." By 1840, the Mount Saint James Academy offered 25 classes in 14 subjects. According to Meagher, "They came from all over the country, and even boasted one scholar from the newly independent Republic of Texas." Students and faculty spent one or two hours outside each day working on the farm, or digging terraces on the slopes of the hill. (This author remembers the terraces as jolting interruptions that ruined his sled rides.)

After the founding of the Academy, Father Fitton, now its President, remained pastor of Christ's (later St. John's) Church and missionary/priest to scattered Catholics throughout south-central New England. As such, he was still "on the road a great deal" while managing his school and his congregation in Worcester. He was still fit enough to handle the physical demands of all these activities, but the mental strains were another matter. The Academy was falling into debt, and Meagher writes that in 1841 he "was sued for a $200 debt by a merchant who had provided 'bread stuff' for the students." His anguish over this, as expressed to the mother of two of his pupils, is palpable: "Judge of my feelings and thoughts this night as I attempt to sleep! Thank Heavens, I have a fund of patience, and am willing to suffer, even in my humble attempt to do good for others, and hope that I may live to meet every debt I justly owe if time is only given me." Fortunately, there was a way out. Bishop Fenwick had a long-held desire to establish a Catholic College, and the site on Pakachoag Hill fit perfectly with his vision. On February 2, 1843, Father Fitton signed the deed for the Academy over to Bishop Fenwick for one dollar and the Bishop gave Fitton $1500 to pay off the mortgage.

Fenwick bought an additional 24 acres from heirs of the late Henry Patch, and in June 1843, he laid the cornerstone of the first building of Holy Cross College. Father Fitton was given the honor of leading the procession at the cornerstone ceremony. Free of his crushing cares and responsibilities, he took his leave from Worcester. He served next as pastor of the Church of Saints Peter and Paul in Providence for twelve years. In 1855, he returned to Boston where he was pastor of the Church of the Most Holy Redeemer for the rest of his life. He died in the church rectory, age 76, and was buried in Malden. In Worcester, in 1905, the new athletic field at the College of the Holy Cross was named in his honor.

The same year Father Fitton's Academy was founded, 1836, William Crompton left his job as superintendent of a cotton mill in Lancashire, England and came directly to the Crocker & Richmond cotton mill in Taunton, Massachusetts.[16] William was a 30-year-old weaver with the kind of mechanical genius thought to be exclusive to Yankees. It is likely that he was invited to the Taunton mill because of this trait, as he was immediately asked by his new employers to develop a loom for a new weaving pattern.

Before the year was out, William invented the Crompton loom, and had it patented the following year.[17] This was the first power loom that could weave cotton into cloth with color patterns in it, and thus it was called a "fancy" loom. In 1838, William returned to England, secured an English patent for his loom, then returned the following year to America with his wife and ten year old son, George. Within a few years he had adapted his loom to weave patterns in wool as well as cotton, and then he contracted with Phelps & Bickford of Worcester to build looms using his patent, on royalty. William continued to make improvements in his looms until 1849, when he became incapacitated just before the patent protection for the Crompton loom was to expire.

His son George, then only 20 years old, was working at the Colt pistol factory in Hartford at the time. He borrowed $50 from the attorney handling his father's financial affairs and went to Washington to argue for an extension of the patent protection. He was successful, and in 1851 he moved to Worcester and formed a partnership with Merrill Furbush to build the looms in the Merrifield Building (fig. 7-4). Three years later, on June 14, 1854, the huge fire at the Merrifield and surrounding blocks of buildings destroyed nearly all of the company's equipment. Instead of filing for bankruptcy as many recommended, Crompton went to all of the people and companies that owed him money and was able to collect enough for the pair to begin again.

They soon leased the old Red Mill on Green Street, which Crompton later bought in 1859. This factory eventually became the Crompton Loom Works (fig. 7-5). By the late 1860s, the Crompton Loom Works was producing a wide range of looms that were being sold in the U.S. and abroad. A crowning achievement was the development of a very large loom later simply called the "1867 loom" (fig. 7-6). One of these was shipped that year to the Paris World Exposition, and it received the only medal awarded for a weaving machine. Crompton later traveled to Paris to accept the medal from

Napoleon III. In 1869, the National Association of Woolen Manufacturers in New York said that this loom was the best worsted loom in the world.

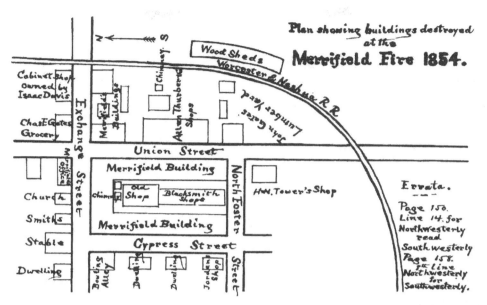

Figure 7-4. Sketch map showing buildings destroyed in the Merrifield fire of 1854. Crompton's shop was in the main building between North Foster and Exchange Streets. Bancroft, James, 1900, p. 155.

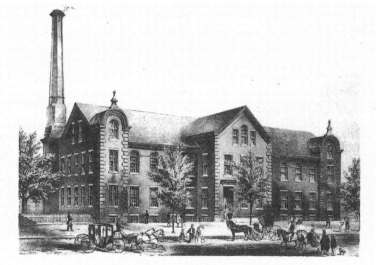

THE CROMPTON LOOM WORKS IN 1867

Figure 7-5. Drawing of the Crompton Loom Works in 1867. The street in the foreground is Green Street. Crompton, W. and Crompton, G., 1949, p. 53.

119

Figure 7-6. Drawing of George Crompton's major invention, the Paris Exposition Loom. Crompton, W. and Crompton, G., 1949, p. 5.

In 1853, Crompton (fig 7-7) married Mary Christina Pratt of Hartford, and they eventually had nine children, all born in Worcester. By 1864, Crompton was wealthy enough to move his growing family into a large home on about twelve acres on the southerly part of Union Hill. Some called it the "Crompton Castle", but he named it "Mariemont" (fig. 7-8). In the census for 1870, George and Mary lived there with seven children, Mary's widowed father Charles Pratt, a "Mrs. O'Neil", six female domestic servants, and one manservant. The stated value of Crompton's real estate was $350,000, an exceptional estate for that time.

In the early part of 1870, Crompton organized the Crompton Carpet Company for the manufacture of Brussels carpets. Previously, this popular carpet was produced almost exclusively in England. Crompton and Horace Wyman invented a loom for weaving Brussels carpets by power and had an American patent to make them.

Figure 7-7.
Portrait of George
Crompton in
about 1885.
Crompton, W.
and Crompton,
G., 1949, p. 58.

Figure 7-8. Mariemont, the home of the George Crompton family after 1864.
Crompton, George, 1952, p. 23.

In July of 1870, the Crompton Carpet Company purchased 52 acres and the water privilege on the Middle River in South Worcester, and immediately started building a mill. In a letter written on April 10, 1871, he described his new carpet company: "After starting with these 16 looms we propose to start some tapestry looms. The building we have these looms in is three stories, the looms on the lower floor sufficiently lighted, heated with steam, lighted with gas, driven by water power the building being 115 x 60'. We propose to build a dye house this coming summer (having our dying now done outside). We also intend to do our own spinning when the tapestry looms are started. We estimate we can produce 500 yards per day on the 16 looms." He added that the estimated water power of the river was 100 horsepower!

The letter quoted above was written to Matthew J. Whittall (in which he mistakenly called him "Michael"), who at the time was a manager of the Severn Valley Carpet Works of Fawcett and Spurway in Stourport, Worcestershire, England. Crompton had never met Whittall, but he had already offered him the position of Superintendent on a recommendation by an employee named Fred Talbot, who had worked for Whittall in Stourport. It was a smart business move. Crompton's expertise was in loom manufacture, not in carpet making, so he imported this expertise from England. The job offered £400 the first year and £450 the second year and included traveling expenses. Crompton finished his letter in this way: "I understand you are a famous bleacher of worsted. Please bring a sample and any other matter which you think will be useful. We are in great need of a superintendent and hope you will use all possible dispatch in serving out your notice and being with us. I expect to see you in two months at the furthest."[18]

Matthew J Whittall arrived in New York City five weeks later, on May 18, 1871. With his arrival in Worcester, Crompton returned his attentions to loom manufacture, where they remained until he died on December 29, 1886. In his obituary, the Worcester Spy said, "He came from a race of mechanics and inventors, and was as ingenious and successful as any of them… He had not much time for public affairs, but his life was that of a private citizen, active and strenuous in business, having not many intimate friends beyond his home circle, but enjoying domestic pleasures with a keen zest and having a cultivated taste for art in all its forms." It is interesting, and unusual for his day, that the obituary didn't tout Crompton's personal or financial support to his city or his church. His true legacy lies in the fact that he revolutionized textile weaving in America and brought carpet weaving to South Worcester.[19]

After his arrival in New York, Whittall probably made his way to Worcester via the Norwich & Worcester Railroad's combined rail-water system, which offered steamboat service from New York City to Norwich, connecting with railroad service to Worcester.[20] The ride through gently rising valley farmlands should have been comfortable, if not particularly exciting. But, as the train passed out of Auburn and into South Worcester, he might have caught a glimpse of his future home. From the Auburn line, the train's route runs parallel to Southbridge Street, and, as it made its way toward the city, Whittall may have seen Stillwater Pond and Pakachoag Hill. He would almost certainly have seen the view of his future workplace with the towers of Fenwick Hall on the campus of Holy Cross College in the background, as shown in figure 7-9.

Past Cambridge Street, the monotony of farmland finally gave way to scenes of growing development, and then, the dense concentration of city commerce. He may has disembarked at the South Worcester station (fig. 7-10). If he stayed in the city while getting established, he could easily commute to South Worcester on the omnibus, a horse-drawn wagon that seated 20-30 people and ran on rails. At that time, the omnibus offered five round trips daily except Sunday, between the Bay State Hotel and the foot of College Hill.

THE CROMPTON CARPET COMPANY

Figure 7-9. Drawing showing the newly constructed Crompton Carpet Company buildings in the early 1870s. The view is from the west and shows Holy Cross College on the hill behind. Crompton, G. and Crompton, W., 1949, p. 60.

Matthew J. Whittall was born of humble origins, but by time he immigrated to Worcester, he had broken out of the working class. He was born March 10, 1843, the first child of Eli and Eliza (Tanner) Whittall, who were married a year earlier in Kidderminster, Worcestershire, England. Eli was a carpet weaver, as was Matthew's grandfather, Eli Sr. and at least two of his uncles. Matthew, his father and his grandfather were all born and raised in the working class neighborhoods of Kidderminster, and lived in rental houses built for weavers and other operatives who worked in the nearby mills. Generally, weavers rented their housing from the manufacturers who employed them, and over time, perhaps because they feared that complaining meant the possible loss of their jobs, these rental houses were neglected by the owners, and the neighborhoods themselves fell into general disrepair.

In August 1843, R. A. Slaney's "commission of enquiry into the State of Large towns" said of Kidderminster, "The Streets where the richer classes live are open and well-drained; but the small streets… inhabited by the working classes are much neglected, are in want of drainage and cleansing;

Figure 7-10. South Worcester Station was located at the junction of the tracks of the Norwich & Worcester and Worcester & Providence Railroads at Southbridge Street. (From the collections of the Worcester Historical Museum, Worcester, Massachusetts.)

the rain water, together with slops thrown from the houses, often lying in stagnant puddles in the ill-made surface gutters." In spite of bouts of disease and deaths from the "Kidderminster fever", "there had been little change by the mid-1860s."[21] Up to this time, the Whittall family had moved several times, possibly in a search for better living conditions. But, Mount Pleasant Street, where Eli Jr. was born (1821), Queen Street, where he lived with his family in 1851, and Broad Street, where he lived with his family in 1861, were all named in the Slaney Commission as among the worst streets in the working class neighborhoods.

In 1861, Matthew, 18, was living with his parents at 66 Broad Street, Kidderminster. The Broad Street address may have been a step up. In the 1840s, "friendly societies" and "land societies" grew up among the working classes to help members gain land ownership. This was a big deal—the Free-hold Land Society, it was said, would place the working man "on the same footing as a capitalist, and enable a man, fresh from the loom or the plough" to buy a plot of land and a house of his own. Some of these houses were built on Broad Street, but we don't know if the Whittalls had yet made the leap to home ownership.[22] According to the census for that year, Mary Jane, Matthew's fifteen year old sister, was employed as a servant, and his brother, George, was thirteen and as yet unemployed. Matthew was employed at the time as a "carpet jobber", a person who buys carpet from manufacturers and sells them to retailers. This suggests he had already refined his skills in the carpet business and may have been earning high wages and helping support his family. By 1871, his last year in Kidderminster, much had changed. Matthew, age 28, was foreman of the Severn Valley Carpet Works in Stourport, Kidderminster and lived there as head of a household that included his wife, Ellen D. (Paget) age 22, her sister, Caroline Paget, and two young children of a second sister-in-law, William and Ellen Hinsley.

Clearly, Matthew J. Whittall has "made it" financially, and he might have remained in Kidderminster and lived a comfortable middle class life. So, why did he decide to emigrate? His stated reasons, if recorded, haven't been found. As we've seen, other men of his type were highly independent, confident, and success oriented. The challenge of running an American mill may have been one consideration. And, England's Victorian class-based society was still based largely on privilege, rather than merit. Access to the great universities, and to political office, for example, were still beyond the reach of the middle class. If the Whittalls were thinking beyond their own futures, to the futures of their children, this may have been another reason. This sentiment is expressed in a letter from an English immigrant, encouraging his brother to come to America: "The laws are excellent, within reach of every man, and every man of 21 years of age has a vote in choosing law givers... The path to science, to wealth, and to honour is open to all... your sons have the privilege of becoming the greatest men in the nation. In fact, this is a free country, and I wish you to think of the advantage it would be to you and your children to come here."[23]

Matthew and Ellen Whittall crossed the Atlantic on the Cuba, an iron-hulled, single screw steamship that was also equipped with three masts and sails. When it was launched in 1864, the New York Times described it as "the finest packet ship ever built on the Clyde." Without doubt, the voyage of the Whittalls was much less traumatic and of shorter duration than the long voyage by sail remembered by earlier immigrants. And, surely, it was much more comfortable. The Cuba catered to first class passengers only, who traveled in accommodations of "such a character as to combine elegance with comfort."[24] The fact that the Whittalls made the voyage together distinguishes them from the working class immigrants who usually left families behind, to be sent for after they got their feet on the ground. And, it suggests this was not a tenuous "toe in the water" visit. They were here to stay, and there would be no looking back.

We have no record as to where the Whittalls lived during their first months in Worcester, but the Worcester City Directory for 1872 gives their address as the "corner of Southbridge and Cambridge" Streets—the site of their future home (fig 7-11). This is the house once owned by Aurin Wood, which we mentioned previously. It was purchased from Wood by Mary Bancroft June 24, 1871, for $28,000, and Whittall purchased the property from her May 29, 1873 for $23,500. The property was financed with two mortgages of $10,000 each and was conveyed to the Whittalls with "rights secured to the Crompton Carpet Co." George Crompton was one of the mortgage lenders and had some sort of interest in the property, which leads us to speculate that the Whittalls moved into it as soon as they arrived and rented it from Bancroft until it was purchased. Once they gained ownership of the property, the grounds around it were extended by the systematic purchase of about 14 adjacent home sites. The lots were originally laid out as a working class neighborhood and were already individually owned. Gradually, during the years 1874 to 1879, Whittall bought them for about $1,550 each. The grounds were planted with trees, lawns and gardens, and the home soon became known as the Whittall Estate.

Figure 7-11. Photo of the Whittall Mansion, formerly at the corner of Southbridge and Cambridge Streets. (From the collections of the Worcester Historical Museum, Worcester, Massachusetts.)

Notes:

1. Hanft, Sheldon, English Americans, Countries and their Cultures website, www.everyculture.com

2. Erickson, *Invisible Immigrants*, p. 13-15.

3. Van Vugt, William E., *Britain to America*, p. 9.

4. Caranci, Paul F., North Providence, *A History and the People Who Shaped It*, p. 57.

5. Worcester Historical Museum, *Landscape of Industry*, p. 5.

6. Yaeger, Francis Cabot Lowell.

7. His Bigelow Carpet Company in Clinton Massachusetts was making some of "the world's best carpets", and Bigelow is now honored as "father of the modern carpet industry." *A Century of Carpet and Rug Making in America, Bigelow–Hartford Carpet Company*, New York, 1925.

8. McConaghy, Mary, *The Whittaker Mill 1813–1843*, p. 3.

9. http://www.lambertcastle.com/lambert_castle_story.htm

10. Cudmore, Bob, *Stories from the Mohawk Valley*, p. 50-52.

11. Nutt, *History of Worcester and its People*, vol. 1, p. 327.

12. Seeley, A.R., ed.,Light, August, 1891, p. 452.

13. Worcester Daily Spy, Monday March 9, 1885.

14. Kelleher, Tom, *Father James Fitton: Missionary Catholic Priest in Early 19th Century New England*, 1997.

15. Meagher, *To Preserve the Flame*, p. 10.

16. Crane, *Historic Homes and Institutions*, vol. 4, p. 308.

17. Tulloch, *Worcester: City of Prosperity*, p. 324.

18. Crompton and Crompton, *The Crompton Loom*, p. 101.

19. George Crompton rests with members of his family in a large stone cottage style mausoleum, in Rural Cemetery. In 1897, Crompton Loom Works merged with L.J. Knowles & Brother Loom Works, to create Crompton & Knowles Loom Works. After World War II, it was one of the largest employers in the area, with more than 3,000 employees. Crompton & Knowles closed operations in Worcester in 1980.

20. Combined Rail- and Water-System Makes Norwich a Key Travel Hub in Mid 1800s. http://connecticuthistory.org

21. Smith, *Carpet Weavers and Carpet Masters*, p. 194-196.

22. Ibid., p 216.

23. Erickson, *Invisible Immigrants*, p. 271.

24. New York Times, "Ocean Steamers" Published December 3, 1864.

— Chapter 8 —
South Worcester: People and Places circa 1870

By 1870, the population of Worcester had grown to 41,115—an increase of 37% between 1865 and 1870, and 70% between 1860 and 1870.[1] It was the second largest city in Massachusetts, after Boston, and its industrial base was expanding rapidly as well. The availability of space in rental or "power factories" continued to foster a staggering diversity of manufactures. Washburn's wire works were the single most important, but eight textile machine manufacturers, including the large Crompton Loom Works on Green Street, produced more than a million dollars worth of machines and employed about 600 workers. The manufacture of arms and cartridges, bolstered by the Civil War, was flourishing, as were machine tools and railroad cars.

Worcester led the country in the manufacture of agricultural tools, boots and shoes, and (locally invented) pre-folded envelopes, and in the southern part of the city, there were eleven woolen mills and two cotton mills.[2] Yet, in spite of its size and industrial importance, some historians have said that Worcester was still a big farm town. Many residences shown on figure 8-1 were likely farms. As late as 1875, one survey reported that the "city embraces the large number of 349 farms", and said that "its hills, vales and plains… are covered with well-cultivated farms, orchards and gardens, interspersed with attractive farmhouses, and often with handsome residences."[3]

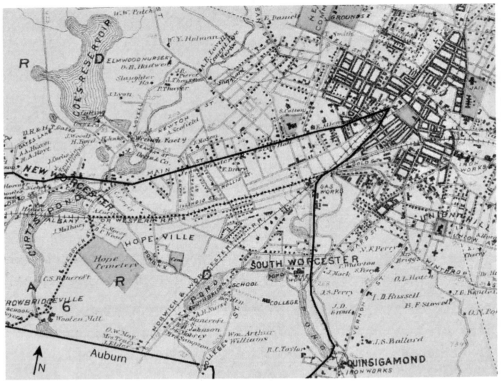

Figure 8-1. Map showing South Worcester and surrounding neighborhoods just before 1870. Dark black line is the boundary of Ward 6. Dotted black line shows the western edge of what we have considered the neighborhood of South Worcester. Large landholders are individually identified, but many individual houses are not shown. See figures 8-2, 8-5, and 8-7 for more detail. Modified from Beers, F. W. and Sanford, G. P., 1870, p. 6. (From the collections of the Worcester Public Library.)

In fact, Worcester was both a center of industry and agriculture; the former in its ascendancy, the latter at its zenith. Another study said that the "Rapid growth of Worcester as an industrial center came with an intensification of the city's agricultural land use—by 1870, Worcester had more farms than any town in the county & more land under tillage."[4] But, for the most part, farming had changed, where it still existed. Subsistence farming, where the primary purpose is putting food on the family table, had been mostly replaced by commercial farming, which benefited in the new economy from the sale of their products to a growing population. There was also a wave of

132

"nostalgia farming" involving the ownership of large farms by wealthy manufacturers who sentimentally kept farms that were worked by hired laborers.
This may explain the "handsome residences" referred to earlier.

If the "hills, vales and plains" of Worcester looked pastoral, the city
center presented a stark contrast to its rural surroundings. In less than 3
decades, the center had spread well beyond its Main Street boundaries. Main
Street, between Lincoln Square on the north and Madison Street in the
South, was almost completely commercial, and was lined with 2-to-6-sto-
ry brick buildings. As commercial blocks took over the center, homes and
streets spread into the surrounding hills — Green Hill, northeast of Lincoln
Square, Chandler, Union, and Oak hills on the east, and up, over, and beyond
the hill west from Main Street. In short, the city, with its distinct commercial
and industrial areas, and its lower, middle, and upper class residential neighborhoods, was far more complex than a simple farm village.

We can only guess at Whittall's first impressions of Worcester, but
in comparison with his ancient birthplace, he was probably struck by the
relative newness of the downtown and all of the construction activity there.
Evidence of change, both recent and ongoing, was everywhere, but most
visible in the construction of new buildings and streets and in the incremen-
tal additions of sewers, sewer lines, gas and water pipes. Shortly after his
arrival, the new City Hospital was established (May 25, 1871) at the Abijah
Bigelow house, which was "hired" for the purpose. New buildings included
the new Water & Sewers Department on Thomas Street, the new Classical
and English High School on Walnut Street, and the Worcester Gas and
Light Company near Kansas Street. Most city streets were still unpaved, but
Main, Mechanics, and the northern part of Southbridge Streets had recently
been completed using the new method of "block paving", and Green and
Lincoln streets were macadamized. Nobility Hill was graded to level Main
Street near Southbridge and Chatham Streets, and Salem Square, which
was once much higher, was graded to its present level. And, the first section

of the proposed "boulevard" around the city was laid out from May Street to the junction of Beaver and Lovell Streets. This would later be called Park Avenue.[5]

The walling of Mill Brook as the main sewer channel was completed from Green Street to Lincoln Square by 1870, and 37 streets now had sewers.[6] Expenses for the main sewer were assessed in the general tax, but street sewers were paid for by a tax on the abutters, "causing much grumbling". Abutters were also assessed for half the cost of street improvements, which caused even "more clamor & dissatisfaction".[7] Many Worcester streets in the city center were illuminated by gas lights, and more were being added. They were lit each evening at dusk by young boys carrying long sticks, with a tip of flame, and smothered by eleven o'clock.[8]

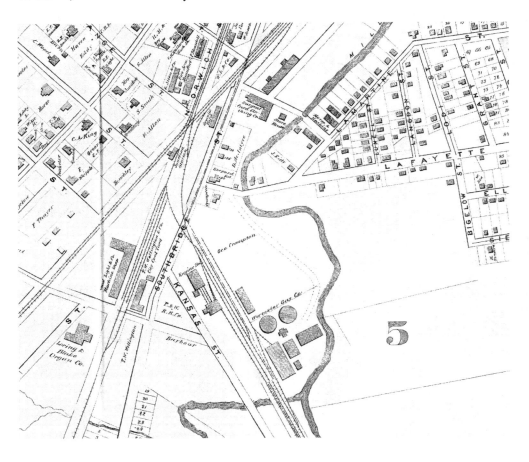

Figure 8-2. (facing page) Map of the northern part of South Worcester and surrounding neighborhoods just before 1870. Modified from Beers, F. W. and Sanford, G. P., 1870, p. 21-22. (From the collections of the Worcester Public Library.)

The gas was provided by the Worcester Gas and Light Company, chartered in 1849. In 1870, the company moved from Lincoln Square to its new location on nine acres just east of Kansas Street (fig. 8-2). (Before electricity made them obsolete, more than 2,000 gas lights lined the city streets. Today, just 27 remain as romantic relics of the past.) Some businesses and residences downtown were getting gas piped in for heating, lights, and cooking, but wood and coal was still the primary source of heat. This gas, often called "town gas" was not the natural gas in use today, but was produced from a distillation of coal and water. Access to running water was gradually being added to downtown businesses and homes. At the beginning of 1870, there were 2477 water users, of which 737 had been added in 1869. That number would continue to grow each year. Food preservation still depended on ice and ice boxes (fig. 8-3).

Figure 8-3. Before electricity was widely available, ice was delivered by horse and wagon. Worcester city Directory, 1873, p. 451. (https://books.google.com/books?id=DgQ-DAAAAYAA-J&q=ice#v=onepage&q=ice&f=false)

This important necessity seems to have had just one supplier, the Walker & Sweetser Company, which harvested 15,000 to 20,000 tons of ice each winter, mostly from Indian Lake, the former "North Pond". Perhaps as a sign of population growth, the December 2, 1870 newspaper reported that there could be no more ice deliveries because the supply cut on lakes the previous winter had been used up.

Schools and school buildings were still trying to keep pace with population growth. Additional schools were being built on the east side and other areas of Worcester, and a new high school on Walnut Street was dedicated in December 1871. During the 1870s, it would offer three separate programs, College, Classical, and English. Not many people went to high school at that time; just 246 students were enrolled at the end of 1869, and attendance was irregular. But all the other public schools were crowded. Almost 9,000 students had some instruction in Worcester schools during 1869, but only 6,454 were in regular attendance at the end of the year. The impact of immigration on school crowding can be seen in the statistics for that year, which showed that the number of students with foreign-born parents significantly exceeded those with native born parents. Of the total students in regular attendance, 6,454, the number with U.S.-born parents was 2,704, Irish-born 2,888, and other foreign born, mostly Canadian, English, German, and Scot, was 888.[9]

In all likelihood, Whittall had some advance knowledge of Worcester before he immigrated. Perhaps, along with correspondence from Crompton, he received copies of the most recent Worcester City Directory and some newspapers. The annually published directories were chock full of information about the city and would have been an indispensable resource for a newcomer. In the 1869 Directory, for example, he would have found about 250 advertisers who sold all the latest means to live, listed alphabetically from "advertising agents" to "yeast". Another section listed the names of every city resident, with address and occupation. The 20-page "Business

Directory" illustrates the relative complexity and sophistication of the city: there were 6 hotels, 45 boarding houses, 11 banks, 8 insurance companies, 63 grocers, 41 attorneys, and 50 physicians, including 5 Homoeopathists, 3 Clairvoyants, 1 Thompsonian, and 1 "Vegetable". Also, there were 8 photographers, 3 weekly and 2 daily newspapers, 3 publishers, 3 periodicals, 12 booksellers, 17 music teachers, 8 stationers, 17 eating houses, 3 telegraph offices, and 5 libraries. (Earlier, the Free Public Library announced that its reading room would be open to the public on Sunday mornings, having concluded that the public's "right to know" trumped religious Sabbath law!)

The remainder of the directory provided useful information about the city — its institutions, services, and government, including the names of every city, state, and federal representative. An "Associations and Organizations" section listed the Grand Army of the Republic, the YMCA, Worcester Agricultural Society, the Antiquarian Society, the Public Library, the Lyceum and Natural History Association, the Worcester Horticultural Society, the Mozart and Beethoven Choral Union, eight lodges of the Free Masons, and five Temperance organizations. Twenty-four churches were listed, including the original First Congregational Church (Old South), and a range of other denominations including Catholic, Baptist, Methodist, and Episcopal. Several pages were devoted to the public and private schools, with details about curriculum, grading, schedules, school committee members, and more. It said that there were 105 schools in the city, with 110 female teachers and 9 male teachers.

Another section listed railroad, stage, and omnibus schedules. These three modes of transportation made it possible and relatively convenient to get anywhere from Worcester and back. Four railroads connected the city to the outside world. The Norwich & Worcester ran twice daily from Worcester to Long Island Sound and its steamboat connection to New York. One could head west via the Boston & Albany (then called the Western Railroad) and connect there with the Erie Canal. This was an extension of the original

Boston & Worcester line; its Eastern Division now offered seven departures to Boston "every week day", and its Western Division ran five trains daily to Albany. The train that finally doomed the canal, the Providence & Worcester, provided daily service to Providence and places between. In addition to these links to the east, west, and south, the Worcester & Nashua opened service to the north in 1848, and these trains by 1869 departed Worcester three times daily.

Stages provided service to Holden, Shrewsbury, Paxton, and most of the other towns in the county, and omnibuses provided service within Worcester itself. This was a recent innovation, but the South Worcester omnibus was already popular. The newspaper of January 29, 1869 reported that "The ladies of South Worcester made Mr. Goodwin, their popular and obliging omnibus driver, the recipient of a surprise gift in the shape of a set of furs and muffler". In November 1870, the Worcester Street Railway purchased land in New Worcester near Coes Reservoir (fig. 8-1) for stables and accommodation of railcars. That year also saw the completion of track through Webster Square to New Worcester, the village west of Webster Square. By late December 1870, they had 40 horses at work. In ensuing years, this company would combine with others to become the Worcester Consolidated Street Railway. These lines would eventually be electrified and run along Cambridge, Southbridge, College and Clay Streets in South Worcester.

Worcester's major newspaper at the time was the weekly Massachusetts Spy, which came out every Friday and also in a daily edition. Newspapers were different in those days. There were no phones or radio or television, so they were the main source of information. Much of the news was international and national, and, thanks to the telegraph, coverage was thorough and timely. (After a decade of experimentation, dependable transatlantic service had been in existence since the mid-1860s.) Columns with headings like "News from London" or "News from Paris" kept readers informed of events around the world, and national coverage included lengthy descriptions of the active committees of Congress and presidential and other political speeches, often in full length. One column railed against "Ku Klux Klanism", and "its efforts to restore the old order of things in the South." County and city news rounded out the paper, and this is where a newcomer could get information about the opportunities and amenities, as well as the growing pains and problems, of the city of Worcester.

One issue, for example, reported that in 1869 there were 2,304 arrests, and the diversity of those arrested reflected the diversity of the population as a whole. Of the total, 644 of those arrested were born in America, 13 of which were "African". The rest were foreign: 1,080 were born in Ireland, 90 in England, 73 in Canada, 24 in Scotland, 20 in Nova Scotia, 15 in France, 11 in Germany, 3 each from Italy, Wales, and Denmark, and 1 each from Greenland, Egypt, and Poland.[10] The "melting pot" had truly arrived in Worcester! Drunkenness was by far the most common cause for arrest, even though it was illegal at the time to sell liquor in Worcester. Effective July 1, 1869, state law limited the sale of alcohol in Massachusetts to wine or liquor packed and sealed in foreign countries and to patent medicines that contained alcohol. In the years that followed, many raids on eating and drinking establishments produced arrests and destruction of illegal liquor. In addition to serious crimes, there were arrests for playing cards on Sunday, being a suspicious person, insanity, and burning grass.

Each January, the newspaper reported the number of deaths for the previous year. Infant mortality was high. Of the 831 deaths recorded in 1869, 239 were of infants under one year old, and 114 were children 1 to 5 years old. The leading causes were consumption (tuberculosis) followed closely by cholera infantum, premature birth, lung fever, typhoid fever, and scarlet fever. The first case of smallpox in Worcester was reported in November 1869, and by June of 1870 there were 80 known cases. School children were required to be inoculated, and an office was set up in City Hall to inoculate the general public.

There were 27 deaths from accident and a few from criminal acts. Accidental deaths and injuries were often reported in grisly detail, as with these examples from September 16, 1870: "As Rev. Thomas O'Sullivan, Catholic priest of Springfield, was about to step upon the 3:30 train for Boston Monday afternoon, from the platform at Washington Square, while the train was in motion, he lost his footing and fell cutting a deep gash in his head through the flesh to the bone from his forehead nearly to his left ear causing him to bleed profusely. Officer Colby took him to Dr. Sargent's office where his wounds were dressed and the patient was taken to the residence of Rev. P.T. O'Reilly, where he died Wednesday night at about eight o'clock… Charles Brown, son of Mr. D.W Brown, engineer at Court Mills, and one of the carriers of the Spy, cut off all the fingers of his left hand Wednesday while playing with the machine for trimming slate. While Drs. Kelly and Simpson were busy dressing the hand, a laborer name Patrick Markham was brought to their office with one foot so badly crushed that it was afterwards found necessary to amputate it just above the ankle. He met his accident while at work on the Nashua railroad."[11]

Not all the city news was disease, death, and mayhem. The paper also reported court cases, divorce decrees, school graduations, temperance and other association meetings, guardians appointed, local entertainment, and sporting events. For example, there was a less than favorable review of dramatic readings performed by Mrs. Scott-Siddons, whose "beautiful face and floral decorations would have found favor, if her dramatic faculty were less admirable." And, a rowing challenge was issued by a Worcester man for a "scull race of three or five miles against any sculler in the United States for the sum of $500 a side." A $50 deposit was enclosed. Another article took note of a missed opportunity to preserve a downtown lot for a park. The lot on Main and Wellington had just been purchased for a large double house, "So the opportunity has gone by, and that green spot in our midst will soon be 'like a tale that is told' with bricks and mortar."

The 1869 paper also announced a new mode of transportation that had just been introduced. The velocipede, an early form of the bicycle, was demonstrated downtown at the opening of a velocipede riding school and exhibition in February, 1869. "So great was the interest in the affair that for two hours before the hall was open crowds of men and boys gathered in the entrance waiting to get a glimpse of the 'steed' and its riders... All voted the velocipede and its prospects in Worcester a success." In the following year, velocipede rides to surrounding towns were organized with great emphasis placed on how quickly one could get to places like Millbury!

An accident that shocked the entire population of Worcester happened in mid-December 1870. James Blake, who had just been elected to a 6th year as mayor of Worcester, was killed a week later in a huge explosion at the new gas works. The gas service for the city was interrupted for nearly a week. On December 23, the paper reported, "the improvised methods for lighting up the stores and the offices on Main Street... gave a strange contrast to its usually brilliant and lively appearance of a Saturday evening... The stores where lamps could be bought were the only ones in which a lively trade was carried on; and in these the rush was astonishing, and the stock of lamps and candles, lanterns — in fact everything, from which the feeblest ray of light could by any manner of means be extorted — was soon sold out, and many orders were taken for goods which the traders ordered from Boston by telegraph, and delivered yesterday."

If Worcester *was* an overgrown farm town in 1870, its center was truly a city, with all the opportunities, vitality, cultural amenities, and social ills that city life entailed. After decades of lawyer-politicians, businessmen now dominated public office; commerce was their passion, progress and growth were their goals, and the pace of change was rapid. But Worcester seemed to have had a split personality. Outside the city, the pace of change varied by region. As we have seen, farming was still important and much of the land was still pastoral. A growing city created a growing commercial market for farm products, and savvy farmers made a living from it. Elsewhere, the pace of change followed the growth of industry, and in those areas, red-brick factories and mills spawned new working class neighborhoods. With the exception of Washburn's North wire works, most of these were in the south half of the city. In the southwest, textile factories spurred residential development in the small villages of Cherry Valley, Jamesville, New Worcester, and Tatnuck, and in the southeast, at Quinsigamond. Between them, two key industrial sites prompted significant residential development in South Worcester, which already had extended from the city center to the northern border of Cambridge Street.

In 1870, the Village of South Worcester lay entirely within Ward 6, which, according to the census, had a population of 6,244, with 799 dwellings and 1,303 families. But it was only a portion of Ward 6. It does not include that part of Ward 6 west of Webster Street, Webster Square, or Main Street—all of which have residential development around the mills there (fig. 8-1). So the population of South Worcester was less than the Ward 6 totals, perhaps about 5,000. About a quarter of them were foreign born; the majority (63%) were Irish, followed by French Canadians (20%) and English (11.7%). The remaining (4%) were Scots and Germans. The two waves of English immigrants anticipated by the Worcester Spy, were yet to come. The City Directory put the location of South Worcester "At the intersection of Southbridge with Cambridge Streets." This is considered to be the heart of the Village, even to this day. The Atlas of Worcester County, published in 1870 by F. W. Beers, allows us a precise view of South Worcester at that time, and it will be our guide for the rest of this chapter (fig. 8-2, 8-4, and 8-7).

Figure 8-4. (facing page) Map of the southern part of South Worcester and surrounding neighborhoods just before 1870. Beers, F. W. and Sanford, G. P., 1870, p. 27-28. (From the collections of the Worcester Public Library.)

142

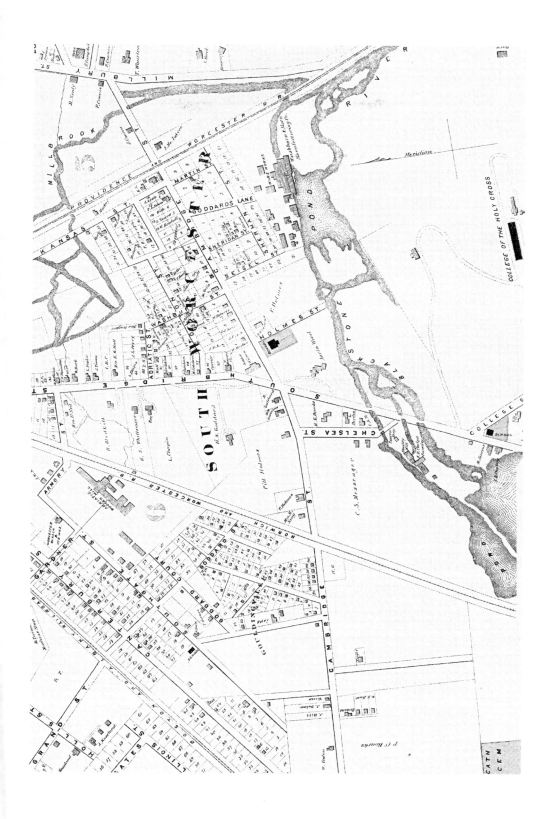

143

By 1870, Southbridge and Cambridge Streets were fully laid out, and had their modern names. North of Cambridge Street, between Canterbury Street and the Norwich & Worcester railroad tracks, new neighborhoods occupied the area once known as Raccoon Plain. These were clearly planned as working class residential neighborhoods, with access to nearby centers of employment. The woolen industry was just beginning to grow in South Worcester. The Adriatic Woolen Mills near Armory St. (fig. 8-5) was the earliest textile mill in South Worcester. Eli Thayer, of Kansas anti-slavery fame, originally built it in 1854. It was 400 feet long, forty feet wide, and two stories high, and may have been originally designed as a rental factory. It was sold in 1859 to Benjamin F. Joslyn, the arms manufacturer who developed the first breech-loading rifle. The Jordan Marsh Company purchased the property in 1863 and expanded it for the manufacture of textiles. The finishing and weaving operations on the 1st floor used looms made by George Crompton, and the 2nd floor was used for carding & spinning. By May 1869, the complex employed 220 people.[12] The Adriatic Mills were later owned by the Worcester Woolen Company and were used for textile production into the 1920s. They were added to the National Register of Historic Places in 1980. The nearby Worcester Bleach and Dye Works (fig. 8-5), founded in 1865, dyed and bleached wool yarn and cotton threads and may have provided these services to the woolen mill. Across the street was Chandler and Carr's dry goods store (fig. 8-4). Other nearby manufacturers included Wood, Light & Co. and the Loring & Blake Organ Company (fig. 8-2), incorporated in 1868, which later claimed that its Palace organs were "The Best in the World" after winning highest honors at the 1889 World Exhibition in Melbourne, Australia.

Canterbury and Southgate are the oldest streets in this area. They were laid out by John P. Southgate and Thomas M. Rogers, who began as partners in the "leather and shoe findings business" in 1842.[13] Rogers later became wealthy as a real estate developer and was president of the Worcester Elec-

tric Light Company when he died in 1901. Canterbury, Southgate, and Goddard Court streets run parallel to the Boston & Albany tracks, and were intersected by Gardner, Goddard, and several other streets not yet named. All were lined with about 200 small house lots that had been platted, and were partly inhabited. As expected, many of the inhabitants had textile-related jobs, such as wool sorters, weavers, and dyers, but there was also a good mix of laborers and trades people such as machinists, boot-makers, stone masons, and painters and store owners. A testimony to that area's growth is the school that was built for its children on Southgate Street (fig 8-4). It was called the Adriatic School, and it was built in 1866 to relieve the pressures of a growing population. According to the school report for that year, "this new house has somewhat relieved the pressure at South Worcester" which then had two schoolhouses. The other, as we will see, was on Cambridge Street.

The eastern borders of Cambridge Street, between Southbridge and Kansas Streets, were intensely developed by this time. Washburn & Moen's central wire works, on the Middle River (fig. 8-4), was the employment magnet there. Washburn bought the property and the water rights in 1840, and put the mill in the charge of his first partner, Benjamin Goddard, who lived in the area. Goddard was Superintendent of the mill until his death in 1867. All three of his sons, Delano, Henry, and Dorrance apprenticed there, or at the nearby Quinsigamond works. Two of them followed their father's footsteps in the wire business. By 1870, neighborhood blocks surrounded the wire works from the south side of Cambridge Street to Adriatic Street on the north side. These were fully laid out with the platted lots and the small wooden homes of the working classes; three-deckers were not yet in vogue. Some of the lots were yet uninhabited, but among those that were, there was a strong showing of Irish names—Kelleys, O'Niels, Callihans. By this time, the Irish were a significant part of Washburn's workforce, about a third. Another string of lots line Southbridge Street from Adriatic Street to the junction (fig. 8-2, 8-4). These would have easy access to the junction shops and the Adriatic Mills. A branch of Mill Brook meanders through a low area east of these lots before it rejoins its other half a bit north of Cambridge Street. This was swampland and was yet unwanted for development.

Between the two developed areas north of Cambridge Street (between Southbridge St. and the railroad), the map (fig 8-4) shows a wedge of lots that were owned by just eight individuals. Some were large enough to hold blocks of working class houses and appear to be awaiting development. Pitt Holmes, the carpenter/developer we met in Chapter 5, owned one of them. His large lot and residence sat on the north side of Cambridge Street, across from its junction with Chelsea Street. East of Holmes' lot, there are two small lots at the corner of Cambridge and Southbridge Streets. One is owned by Caroline Stebbins, the 46-year-old widow of George Stebbins, who was a wire drawer. Her son, a teamster, and three boarders helped make ends meet. The modest lot bordering the corner contains the residence of Henry Goddard, who became superintendent of the nearby central wire works after his father died. North of these lots is the huge lot and residence of his brother, Dorrance S. Goddard. The lot is about ten or more acres, part of which might have been orchard or otherwise cultivated. According to Nutt, after attending public schools and Worcester Academy, Dorrance "rapidly advanced step by step" until he became superintendent of the Quinsigamond works. It seems he lived life much larger than his brother and neighbor, Henry. His large lot might hold about 20 lots the size of Henry's, and his home was grand as well. Nutt writes, "His chief recreation in life was reading and travel. In his beautiful home in South Worcester he had a well selected library of the books he loved."

North of this "beautiful home" was another large lot and the residence of Lewis Chapin (fig. 8-4). The city directory called him a "Farmer" but he was now 77 years old, and retired. Lewis was the son of Thaddeus Chapin, who, as we've seen, was one of the earliest settlers of South Worcester. His farm extended into Auburn, and Lewis retained a farm there until about 1863, when he moved to this present location. It was probably an investment, rather than a farm, and he also owned several small lots on the east side of Southbridge Street. North of the Chapin lot, Henry S. Whittemore has a slim but long lot that extends from the Norwich and Worcester tracks to Southbridge Street. The 1871 city directory says Henry S. Whittemore has an "eating house on 48 Front Street" and he lives at 163 Southbridge. Another large lot north of Whittemore's is owned by Hamor Gledkill, the Superintendent at Adriatic Mills. He and his wife Elizabeth were from Scotland. Her obituary reports that she often told of her trip to America in a sailing vessel, a trip that took 46 days. In 1850, the day after their wedding, "she and her husband left Berry Brow for Liverpool, traveling most of the distance by stage coach and on foot."

The south side of Cambridge Street, except for the residential development around the wire mill, was still sparsely settled and lightly developed. Bordering this development, Pitt Holmes had another large lot between Seigel Street and Holmes Street, his namesake. Its Seigel Street border was already lined with lots. Aurin Wood owned the large lot between Holmes and Southbridge Streets. This is the future site of the home of Matthew Whittall.

According to Nutt, Aurin Wood "was one of Worcester's pioneer mechanics and inventors." About 1850, he organized the firm that later became Wood, Light, & Company on Hammond Street, which won a national reputation as machine builders and tool manufacturers.[14] A curved driveway on Wood's lot provided access from Southbridge Street at Cambridge Street, and another point farther south, and his residence was a large one, reflecting his wealth and success. The opposite corner of his lot belonged to the city. This was the site of the then new Cambridge Street schoolhouse (fig. 8-4).

In 1852, the School Committee reported that "The school house at South Worcester is in a condition utterly unfit for use and should be replaced by a new one without delay, preferably in a location which will allow the great majority of small children to approach it without crossing so many bridges as are now in the way." The specifics are unclear, but the school was replaced sometime before 1857 with a new one on Cambridge Street, and that year, 51 pupils were in attendance. An 1866 summary of real estate belonging to the school department reported that the South Worcester school building was a two-story brick structure, with two schoolrooms. This was still not enough for a growing population. The addition of the Adriatic School in 1867 helped relieve the pressure, but just two years later, in 1869, Superintendent Marble reported that, "The house at South Worcester was enlarged to six rooms and a commodious hall." These modifications were designed by local architect Eldridge Boyden and built by Larned and Clough at the cost of $18,828. Five women were teaching at the school during this transition, and they had the task of Americanizing a majority of their students. That year, the children of Irish born parents exceeded those with native-born parents by more than two to one.

The southwest corner of Cambridge and Southbridge Streets is bordered by Chelsea Street, which has access to both. There were three properties within its borders in 1870. Horace E. Brooks lived with his mother at 1 Chelsea Street. Horace was the son of Nathaniel Brooks, and a descendant of Deacon Samuel Brooks, one of the earliest families in South Worcester. He was wounded in the Civil War, and was a surveyor in 1869. His lot would become the present home of St. Matthew's Church and parish office. Lewis Boyden lived south of it, at 9 Chelsea. Lewis was a retired blacksmith and blind. He was a brother of Joseph Boyden, who lived nearby, and a descendant of pioneer settler Lieutenent John Boyden of Auburn. In his late 60s at the time, he lived with his wife Betsey, and daughter, Ellen Maria, age 25. Ellen was single, and was one of the five teachers at Cambridge Street School. The third Chelsea Street lot was owned by Charles S. Messenger, a land investor who was living in Brooklyn, New York. Messenger had purchased this lot, and another 40 acres of land just west of it (fig 8-4), in 1865 from Joseph Boyden. The property included the site and water privilege of the old White & Boyden machine shop, which burned down in 1863, and had remained idle ever since. A bit southwest of the site, near where the Blackstone River crosses Southbridge Street, a shoddy mill recycled cloth from used rags, collected by "rag men". As late as the early 1950s, one still clattered through our neighborhood on a horse-drawn wagon, shouting "Rag, rags, bring your rags!" He was generally unkempt, bearded, and un-smiling—"scary" to children, but most women gladly gave him what rags they had. Next to the shoddy mill was the F.F. Phelps Iron Foundry where, among other things, they produced the Worcester Clipper stove. Phelps and partner Henry Cooley had a store on Front Street (fig. 8-6), for the sale of stoves.[15]

The area south of the foundry to the Auburn line and west of it to Webster Street, was mostly the reserve of two cemeteries (fig 8-7). St. John's Cemetery (Catholic Cemetery on fig. 8-7) was opened 1847 for Catholic burials. The original 16 acre tract was purchased from Eli Thayer, for $100 per acre. An earlier attempt to purchase land from Deacon Samuel Brooks failed when he learned it would be used for a Catholic cemetery.

Figure 8-6. An ad for Phelps & Cooley, stove manufacturers in South Worcester in the early 1870s. From the 1873 Worcester City Directory, p. 491. (https://books.google.com/books?id=DgQ-DAAAAYAA-J&printsec=front-cover&source=gbs_ge_summary_r&-cad=0#v=snip-pet&q=1&f=false)

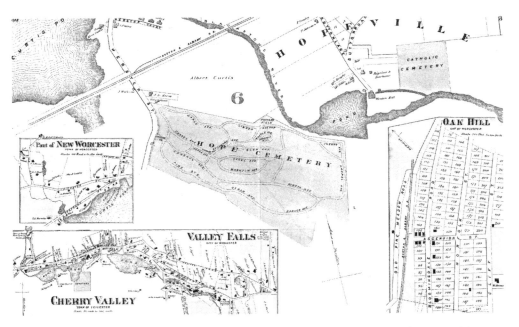

Figure 8-7. Map the western part of South Worcester and surrounding neighborhoods just before 1870. Beers, F. W. and Sanford, G. P., 1870, p. 30-31. (From the collections of the Worcester Public Library.)

150

Over the years, St. John's cemetery has spread from its borders on the Middle River to its current entrance on Cambridge Street. In 1851, the city purchased 50 acres for a public cemetary, at a cost of $1,855. It has since expanded to about 168 acres. According to the Friends of Hope Cemetery web page, this was "Worcester's second garden cemetery, born of the rural cemetery movement inspired by romantic perceptions of nature, art and the themes of death, as well as by the realities of civic development and identity. The first was Rural Cemetery in North Worcester [fig. 6-4]. Hope Cemetery replaced as many as six earlier burial grounds that were overwhelmed by the growing city. By the end of the century, remains from Mechanic Street, Tatman and Pine Meadow cemeteries were reinterred at Hope, and in the 1960s, graves were moved here from Worcester Common." Other than the cemeteries, there were two textile mills in this area. Bigelow and Barbour's satinet factory, on the southwest edge of St. John's Cemetery, is on the Middle River at the old Sutton Mill site (fig. 8-7). This factory later became the Hopeville Manufacturing Company. On Kettle Brook, near the southern end of Webster Street, there is a woolen mill owned by Albert Curtis. According to Rice, Curtis grew up on his father's farm in Auburn and, at the age of seventeen, apprenticed at the White & Boyden machine shop until he gained his majority.[16]

The corner of College and Southbridge streets was at that time called Auburn Square. Just west of it, across Southbridge Street, were the homes of Moses P. Stearns, who once had a large farm there and was in 1870 a machinist, and Isaac Chesley, a granular fuel dealer who had a shop on Foster Street. South of these properties, the old White & Boyden dam had ballooned the Middle River into a large pond (fig. 8-4). It sits on the western border of Southbridge Street and extends nearly to Malvern Road, and fills the low area between Southbridge Street and the Norwich & Worcester Railroad. The pond, which covered the early Trowbridge, Nathan White and

Thaddeus Chapin farms, was called Stillwater Pond. There were two other man-made ponds nearby, at Washburn's Central Wire Works and his South Works at Quinsigamond. By 1870, water power was no longer necessary for many industries because steam provided more power and was more dependable. But, access to running water was still necessary for the steel industry, and textile mills for washing wool and dying textiles. Unfortunately, these waters also carried off their waste!

A mixed group of people lived on Southbridge Street between its junction with (yet unnamed) Malvern Road and the Auburn line (fig. 8-8).

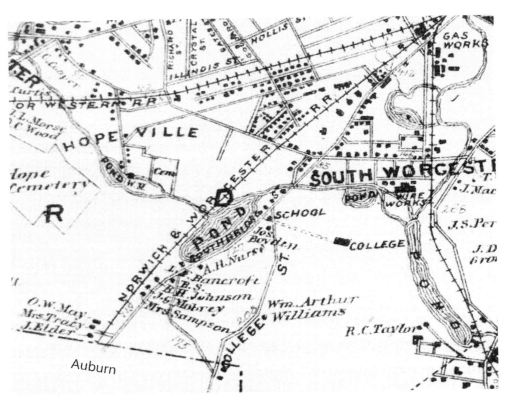

Figure 8-8. Map showing South Worcester just before 1870. Note names of property owners discussed in text. Modified from Beers, F. W. and Sanford, G. P., 1870, p. 6. (From the collections of the Worcester Public Library.)

Among the most interesting are the families of two pre-Civil War former slaves. Clark University professor Janette Thomas Greenwood recounts that, "Robert H. Johnson was one of the few members of Worcester's black community born in the South." He and his wife Mary were born into slavery in Maryland, and somehow migrated to Worcester. Arriving here in 1856, Johnson established himself as a self-employed truckman. During the Civil War, some local Union soldiers from the 25th Massachusetts Volunteer Infantry, became the first leg of a network that helped escaped slaves, called "contraband", migrate to Worcester. Johnson, by this time a respected resident of Worcester, worked with other activist members of the last link in the network, which helped find them find jobs and homes. In 1870, Johnson lived on Southbridge Street with his wife Mary and 6 children. Johnson's neighbor, and also former slave, J.G. Mowbray and his wife Elizabeth also fled Maryland and found their way to Worcester in the 1850s. Mowbray found work as a paperhanger, and he and Elizabeth became prominent members of the black community and were activists in the contraband network. They hosted seven southern migrants in 1865.[17]

Nearby, Mrs. Caroline Sampson, a 60-year-old widow, kept house for several boarders. A.H. Nourse had a sand and stone supply business, and Loring Bancroft, a former farmer and Civil War veteran was in the "Submarine Business". This entry in the City Directory makes no sense until we realize that the nearby Washburn Wire Company was making transatlantic cable at the time. Close to the Auburn line on Southbridge Street, James Elder, the grandson of Loyalist William Elder, was retired, and lived on a remnant of the family farm on the Auburn/Worcester border. The Tracy homestead was still occupied by the family. Mercy Tracy, the 65-year-old widow of shoemaker William Tracy, kept house for four adult children. Her neighbor, Oliver May was a 76-year-old carpenter who kept a small farm near the Tracy's and rented his home to six boarders. This farm was the smallest of four remaining farms in South Worcester. In 1870, it was 13 acres, had 2 "milch cows", and it produced rye, hay, and 40 pounds of honey. The other three farms were on Pakachoag Hill.

The northwestern section of Pakachoag Hill begins near the junction of Southbridge and College Streets. Our map shows that the first South Worcester public school house was still standing there, within the notch formed by the junction (fig. 8-4, 8-8). Nearly two decades had passed since it was deemed "utterly unfit for use" and later replaced at Cambridge Street, and it was probably a neglected eyesore. Next to the school, and extending up the southern side of College Hill, was the farm of Joseph Boyden. (Caro Street would later cross this farm.) Boyden's is another of the four farms that remained in South Worcester and one of three on Pakachoag Hill. All four had long since transitioned to supplemental commercial farming. Although Boyden retained his farm, he had become a successful jeweler years ago, and, like his brother Lewis on Chelsea Street, he was blind and had retired in 1870.

The agricultural census for that year records that his farm consisted of 66 total acres, 20 of which were improved, and 6 of which were wood lot; its stock was 1 cow, and 1 horse, and the farm produced for sale, 45 bushels of barley, 60 bushels of potatoes, 20 dollars worth of orchard products, and 18 tons of hay, for a total value of $496.

Jubal Boyden, of the defunct White & Boyden shop, lived on the farm with Joseph and his family, but he, too, was aged and no longer an active farmer. Clearly, farm production here was the work of hired farm labor. Higher up the hill, on its north side, was the farm of William A. Williams. We are unsure as to where Williams came from or how he came by this farm. It occupies the general area of the farm once owned by John McDollen, who quit farming and became a shoemaker (see Chapter 5). Williams later shows up in census reports as a farmer in Paxton. In 1870, his College Hill farm was 66 acres, of which 60 were improved and 6 were a wood lot. For stock, it had 2 horses, and 1 milk cow, and it produced for sale, barley, orchard products, hay, and 200 bushels of Irish potatoes. The fourth farm was owned and operated by Holy Cross College. From its very beginning, a farm was kept there as a source of food and exercise for its students, who often worked along with farm laborers and enjoyed its abundance.

It should come as no surprise that Pakachoag Hill was the last bastion for farming in South Worcestor. Nearly two centuries earlier, in 1674, Daniel Gookin first described it. "Pakachoog", he wrote, "is seated upon a fertile hill and is denominated from a delicate spring of water called 'pleasant water'." It has been described that way ever since, as if the very essence of Pakachoag Hill is its fertility and abundant clear water. In an article for the Spring, 2010 issue of Holy Cross College Magazine, Jack Dempsey writes: "A farm diary from 1869 gives one an idea of how busy a place it was. The 'Account of Stock' includes 'one fullblooded Jersey bull 2 years old, 4 heifers, 1 steer, 2 oxen, 2 calves... 2 sows — one suckling the young ones... 2 workhorses both old too light for hill work, 2 family horses used for the missions.'... The farm was still providing food for the Jesuit and student kitchens in the late 1950s. Former superintendent of grounds Jim Long recalls there being five or six farmhands at the time. The present site of Hogan [Hogan Campus Center] 'was all vegetable gardens and nurseries,' he says, and the College still had a huge domed oven for baking, and even a cider press. Long and his co-workers would occasionally ride the farm's horses for recreation. The old hill is still full of water. Even the new soccer field, located on the top of the hill, needs judicious drainage. 'Touch a spot with a backhoe and all the water pours out,' says George Query, greenhouse manager and landscape foreman. 'The land is all ledge, and if you disturb it the water will find its way out.'"[18]

In 1862, Holy Cross expanded its campus by an additional 48 acres, purchased from Moses Stearns, John McDollen, and other nearby farm owners. A year later, the college was empowered by the legislature to confer degrees, and post-war prosperity brought further expansion and a growing enrollment. In 1867, Fenwick Hall was expanded and redesigned by Eldredge Boyden, who added its iconic spires. Between the years 1861 and 1870, enrollment rose from about 80 to nearly 150 students. During those early days of the college, students and locals alike enjoyed swimming in the Middle River, which was yet unsullied by upriver mills and their poisonous discharges. Newspaperman William Larkin wrote, "The Middle River, after it left what was then called Stillwater Pond, formed a pond at the foot of College Hill that was called College Pond. Here the boys and men of South Worcester used to go swimming… and they went in the altogether because there were so few houses within eyesight of the swimmers."[19] This idyllic scene was about to change.

During the 1870s, the Irish would continue to move south into new neighborhoods along Cambridge Street, while Quinsigamond's Swedish immigrants would spread north and up the eastern slopes of Pakachoag Hill. These two divergent immigrant groups would soon be in hot and sometimes hostile competition for jobs and living space. Matthew J. Whittall was in the vanguard of a third immigrant group that would settle among them.

Notes:

1. Massachusetts Spy, January 7, 1870.

2. Massachusetts Historical Reconnaissance Survey Town Report: Worcester, 1984, p. 15.

3. Nason, *A Gazetteer of the State of Massachusetts, 1890*, p. 712-720.

4. Massachusetts Historical Reconnaissance Survey Town Report: Worcester, 1984, p. 16.

5. Rice, *Worcester of Eighteen Hundred and Ninety-Eight*, p. 46.

6. Massachusetts Spy, January 7, 1870.

7. Rice, *Worcester of Eighteen Hundred and Ninety-Eight*, p. 49.

8. The Flame that Keeps on Burning, The New Worcester Spy, February 17, 2012

9. Worcester City Document No. 31, 1876, p. 346.

10. Massachusetts Spy, January, 1870.

11. Massachusetts Spy, September16, 1870.

12. Massachusetts Spy, May 21, 1869.

13. Nutt, *History of Worcester and its People*, vol. 4, p. 567.

14. Nutt, *History of Worcester and its People*, vol. 3, p. 369.

15. Massachusetts Spy, May 21, 1869.

16. Rice, *Worcester of Eighteen Hundred and Ninety-Eight*, p. 592.

17. Greenwood, *First Fruits of Freedom*, p. 50-53.

18. Dempsey, Holy Cross College Magazine, 2010, vol. 44, number 2, Flashback – Cool, Clear Water.

19. Larkin, William J., *Looking Back on a Half Century, A retrospective newspaper series published by the Worcester Evening Post*, p. 21.

— Chapter 9 —
The South Worcester English Enclave 1872–1901

Our ancestor, George Jones, was among the earliest of the Kidderminster carpet weavers who settled in South Worcester. The U.S. census reports for 1900 and 1910 inform us that he immigrated in 1871 at the age of 21. He was born in Kidderminster on New Years Day 1850, the fourth of ten children born to John and Emmeline (Baker) Jones, who lived in an area of rental houses for carpet workers called Pantile Row. This was in the same vicinity that young Matthew Whittall lived and had similar working class characteristics, such as back-to-back houses with rear courtyards where residents shared privies, washhouses, and water pumped from wells.

By the mid-19th century, power looms were making inroads on hand looms, causing a general lowering of wages and unemployment among the hand weavers. John Jones was a former hand loom weaver who saw the future and adapted; the 1861 census describes him as "Power loom weaver". By that time John and Emmeline had eight children and had moved to nearby Clensmore Yard, likely for want of more space. George Jones, then 11 years old, was already at work in the local carpet company as were his two older brothers, William, 13, and Henry, 15. Another brother, John Albert, was 9 years old and still in school, but he would soon join his brothers in the mill. An education wasn't necessary for a future in carpet weaving, and their income was needed at home. One family memory has it that George

Jones never did learn to read or write very well; later in life, his wife read the newspaper for him.

George married Eliza Carr in August 1869, and when the 1871 census was taken, they were living on Lark Lane, Kidderminster, with their 9-month old son, Albert. In this census, his occupation is simply "carpet weaver" but we know from later records that he was also a "loom fixer", meaning that he had acquired the skills needed to maintain and repair power looms. This would have made him a valuable employee in any carpet mill of that period. What or who initially lured this young family to South Worcester is not known. We had always assumed that Matthew Whittall was the pied piper, the one who went there first and induced George Jones to follow. But ships' passenger records tell it otherwise.

In the early summer of 1870, George, Eliza, and her father, John Carr, made an advance trip to Worcester and then returned to England. (She gave birth to son Albert on the ship). Their purpose must have been to scout things out before deciding to immigrate, and they must have liked their prospects, because they returned to Worcester as immigrants later, in the year 1872. We wonder if his scouting results were passed on to Matthew Whittall, who at the time was weighing those prospects himself. He and George Jones must have known each other as they were neighbors in Kidderminster, were only 7 years apart in age, and born into the same trade. By this time, however, their careers had clearly diverged, with Whittall a superintendent at a mill and George a weaver. In any event, Whittall immigrated in 1871 without an advance scouting trip, and within a year, he and George both became employees of the Crompton Carpet Company in South Worcester. They were neighbors once more, but in spite of their common experience and common origins, their lives would take separate paths. By 1873, George and Eliza were living on the first floor of a two-story tenement near the mill on 7 Cheever Street, and his younger brother John Albert, who immigrated in 1872, lived on the second floor with his wife Isabella Starr. Matthew and

Ellen Whittall were settled in their mansion on Southbridge Street.

They had barely enough time to adjust to their new jobs or their new country when the unexpected happened. The "Panic of 1873" was a financial crisis that brought on the first global depression in industrialized Europe and the United States. When the year began, the Crompton Carpet Company had 36 looms and two spinning mills and showed great promise, but the onset of the panic broke its momentum, and it struggled during the lengthy depression years that followed. In July 1879, the company closed its doors and sold its looms to W.J. Hogg, who leased its buildings and began to manufacture carpets as the Worcester Carpet Company.

One might suppose that Matthew Whittall was the logical successor to the Crompton Company, because George Crompton had invited him to come and run the company in the first place. But, it wasn't Crompton's decision alone, as he was just one of nine shareholders in the company and owned just 200 of 650 total shares. Did Whittall make an offer to buy? That would have been a more direct approach to ownership than the one he took, but if he did, Mr. Hogg made the better offer. In any event, when the doors closed on the Crompton Carpet Company, Matthew Whittall and George Jones joined the ranks of the unemployed.

By all accounts, Whittall saw this as an opportunity rather than a calamity, and the speed with which he seized it suggests advance planning. Before the year was out he had made a round trip voyage to England, purchased eight Crossley power looms and returned to Worcester with some weavers and his nephew, Albert Thomas. By 1880, the looms were set up in a one-story building he leased from George Wicks at the site of the old White & Boyden machine shop. Ironically, this building sat just a stone's throw away from the mill of his former employer, Crompton, which was now occupied by his competition, W.J. Hogg's Worcester Carpet Company.[1] A prominent advertisement in the 1880 Worcester City Directory announced the new carpet company: "Matthew J. Whittall, Manufacturer Of Wilton &

Brussels Carpets." In the logo, the company is called the Stillwater Carpet Mill, named for the pond that helped power it (fig. 9-1, 9-2).

Figure 9-1. Advertisement that announced Whittall's new Stillwater Carpet Mill from the 1880 Worcester City Directory, p. 554. We can only wonder what thoughts his former employer, George Crompton and his competitor, W.J. Hogg had when they saw it. (https://books.google.com/books?id=uwMDAAAAYAA-J&q=carpet#v=snippet&q=carpet&f=false)

Whittall's carpet company was immediately successful, so much so, that in hindsight it seems predestined. It helped, of course, that the depression was over, and America's economy was booming again. Within a year, Whittall had built a mill on Brussels Street, on land he had purchased from George Crompton. It was still new when additions to it were already necessary to meet growing demands from consumers. They were completed by Thanksgiving Day, 1883, and Whittall celebrated the occasion by hosting a supper for his employees. One more component for a self-sustaining carpet mill remained, and here, fate did play a role in Whittall's favor. Thus far, he had relied on the Pakachoag Spinning Mill for his yarn, which was still owned by George Crompton, who had held on to it when his carpet company closed. It was a profitable business, and he apparently had every intention of retaining it.

This is where fate stepped in—on May 15, 1884 the Pakachoag Spinning Mill burned to the ground in a tragic and spectacular fire, during which a young boy and two firemen were killed, and many of the mill's operatives were severely injured. The Worcester Daily Spy's report of the Pakachoag

Figure 9-2. Map of part of South Worcester published in 1878 showing the Crompton Carpet Company and Wicks Manufacturing in the southern part of the map, and the location of the original St. Matthew's Chapel shown by arrow. From Triscott, S.T.R., 1878. (From the Boston Public Library, Leventhal Map Center Digital Maps.)(http://maps.bpl.org/id/12943)

Mill fire reveals an all too common danger in those days before public fire safety laws. The report states that there were 75 to 100 female employees at work in this three-story building when the fire broke out. Since the building had no fire escapes, most were forced to jump to the ground from windows that were twenty to thirty feet above the ground. Many of them sustained burns, cuts, broken bones, and other severe injuries. It is interesting to note that none of the injured were taken to hospitals; instead, they were initially treated at the scene by physicians, then taken to nearby homes for further care and recovery. Firefighters were able to save nearby buildings owned by the Wicks Manufacturing Company and Whittall's carpet works, but the Pakachoag Mill (fig. 9-3) burned "until there was nothing left to burn." Although the building was fully insured, George Crompton never rebuilt it.

Terrible as it was, it proved the old adage that "one man's loss is another man's gain." In 1885, Whittall purchased the land and ruins of the Pakachoag Mill from Crompton and built the Edgeworth Spinning Mill (fig. 9-4), which he named after his daughter; then he put the mill under the management of his nephew Alfred Thomas and made him a partner.

The following years brought uninterrupted growth and further additions. By 1891, he had two more mills, which together with several additions would ultimately cover nearly 200,000 square feet of land. In 1892, he bought the Palmer Carpet Company in that nearby town, with its 24 looms and 100 employees. A second depression swept the country in 1893, this one much worse than the one that brought down the Crompton Carpet Company. Nevertheless, Whittall kept his company running on a reduced 3-4 day work week while many other companies failed or had to suspend operations. On June 14, 1901, W.J. Hogg sold his Worcester Carpet Company to Whittall for one dollar and other valuable considerations. This sale has the ring of surrender about it. In its wake, Whittall emerged as the only carpet manufacturer in South Worcester, and the largest individual maker of Wilton and Brussels carpets in the world.[2]

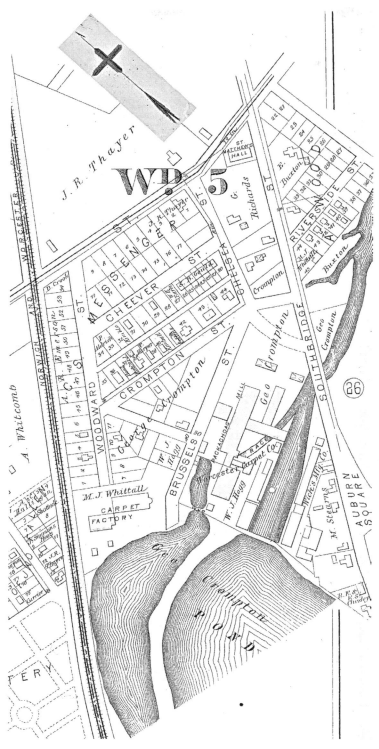

Figure 9-3. Map of part of South Worcester published in 1886 showing the Worcester Carpet Company owned by W.J. Hogg, the Pakachoag Mill, a spinning mill owned by George Crompton, and the new M.J. Whittall Carpet Factory (the Edgeworth Mill). (Hopkins, G.M., 1886) (From the State Library Digital Collection.)

165

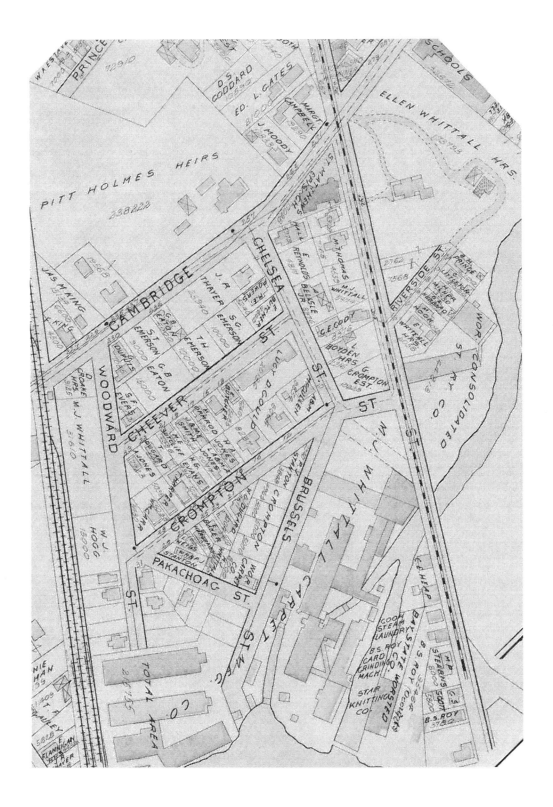

166

Figure 9-4. (facing page) Map of part of South Worcester published in 1896 showing the extent of M.J. Whittall Carpet Manufacturing. Compare with figure 9-3, dated 10 years earlier, which is in the same orientation. Note that what was Wicks Manufacturing Company on the 1886 map is now B.S. Roy Card Clothing. The mill complex including Pakachoag Mill, which burned in 1884, are owned by M.J. Whittall on the 1896 map, and his new mill is called the Edgeworth Mill. Note that there are significantly more houses in the residential neighborhood north of the mills as well. (Richards, L.J., 1896) (From the collections of the Worcester Public Library.)

The founding of Whittall's carpet company in 1880 signaled the beginning of the English enclave that grew around his mills in South Worcester. By this time the earliest members of the enclave, Matthew Whittall and George Jones, had been living there for almost a decade. It was becoming a community (fig. 9-5).

The U. S. Census gives us a good look at Whittall's household as it was then:

Worcester Massachusetts Ward 6, U.S. Census 1880

Whittall, M. J. age 35, b. England "Proprietor, Carpet Mill"

Helen, wife, age 29, b. England "Keeps House" (should be Ellen)

Matthew P. son, age 5, b. Mass.

Daisy E. daughter, age 3, b. Mass.

Caroline Bagget, sister-in-law, age 55, b. England (should be Caroline Paget)

Charlotte Insley, sister-in-law, age 48, b. England (should be Hinsley)

Ellen Insley, niece, age 13, b. England (should be Hinsley)

Alfred Thomas, Nephew, age 22, b. England

Annie Dagnin, age 21, b. Ireland

After we get past the hilarious mangling of names by the census taker (who phonetically recorded what he heard from his English informant, complete with dropped "Hs"), we can see that Whittall's household had grown significantly. He now had two American-born children, and an extended family that included two sisters-in-law, a niece, and his young nephew, Alfred Thomas. He also had an Irish maid. More than anything, the census gives us insights into his mindset. Clearly, he wouldn't have beefed up his household like this if he had the faintest thought of failure.

The Jones family handled their unemployed status with the same air of aplomb and confidence in the future, a future they connected to Whittall and his leadership. Had it been otherwise they might simply have gone to work at Hogg's Worcester Carpet Company. Instead, they made a round trip of their own to England. It was a chance to visit home and family, and perhaps a chance to gain familiarity with the Crossley machines they'd be working with in Worcester. During this interlude, Rose, the fifth child of George and Eliza, was born and baptized in Kidderminster in May 1880. The exact date of their return to Worcester is unknown, but according to the city directory of 1881, George Jones was there as a weaver at Whittall's. Working beside him were his brother-in-law, William Carr, his brother Albert J., and their brother Thomas Jones, who brought their widowed sister with him. On October 28, 1886, George, Albert J., and William Carr went to the courthouse together, where they renounced their allegiance to England and became American citizens. They settled with their families on Crompton and Cheever Streets (fig. 9-4) where they formed a nucleus of the English community that would grow and spread well beyond those confines over the next three decades. That growth would include one more brother, Henry A. Jones, who arrived with his family in 1891.

As we've seen, the development of English enclaves wasn't a new phenomenon. They had popped up elsewhere in the United States wherever skilled English workers were needed or preferred. Instead of being recruited by employers, most evolved through a process historians call "chain immigration", where earlier

Figure 9-5. (facing page) Bird's eye view of Worcester in the late 1870s. North is to the left. The mills being discussed are the complex west of Southbridge Street. Holy Cross College and College Square are along the lower edge of the painting. Cambridge Street is the main East-West street. The large complex of buildings near the center of the painting is the gas works. (Bailey, O.H. and Hazen, J.C., 1878) (From the collections of the Worcester Public Library.)

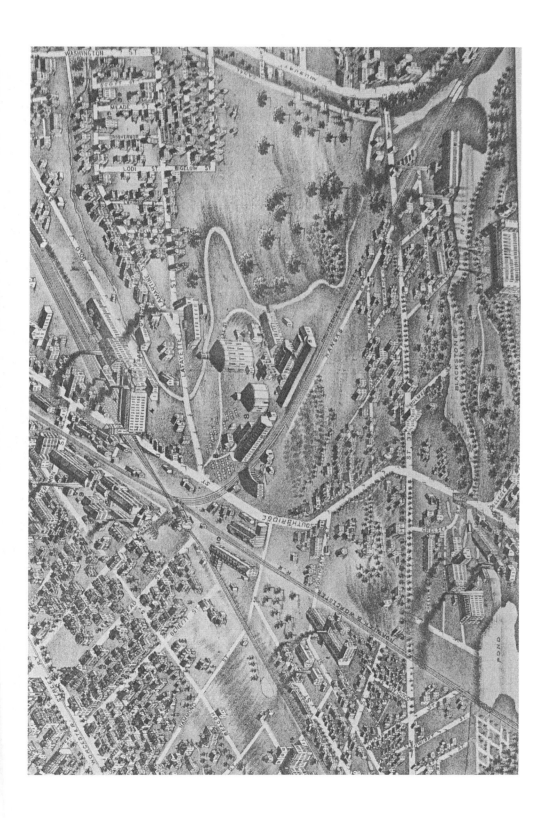

169

immigrants encourage their relatives, friends, and co-workers, to join them. An article in the *Worcester Sunday Telegram*, October 13, 1963, "How the Rug Weavers Came to Worcester", describes the origins and growth of the Whittall enclave. "Between 1800 and 1915 hundreds of rug weavers and machinists came… Some came from Scotland, and a few came from Yorkshire. The majority, however, followed Matthew John Whittall from the center of English carpet weaving, Kidderminster, and knew that jobs and homes awaited them upon arrival."

How and why they knew this is indicated in a letter from Tom Gardener, an early immigrant, who urged John Reece to "come immediately", and to 'bring a pair of iron shuttles by all means from Brinton's, it is partly through the iron shuttles that I got the loom for you." He also suggested that Reece should "bring some music, and some weavers tools", and warned him "Do not bring any cord trousers with you because they do not wear them here, & do not bring any White fronts because they laugh at them."

John Reece immigrated alone in 1885 and "married an English lass he met in South Worcester, but many brought their families with them…often interrelated by blood or marriage so that newcomers were warmly greeted." The earliest of them lived on Cheever, and Crompton Streets; later, as the mills expanded, the growing neighborhood expanded to Camp, Cambridge, Riverside and "other streets within walking distance." Their homes were "plain but comfortable" "with big kitchens that became family rooms with comfortable chairs"—in all likelihood, much improved over the ones they had left behind in Kidderminster. John Giles, who immigrated in 1895, said, "those first weavers worked by the light of oil lamps." He described the "hours as long, and the work as hard" but added "It was a good place to work. We had a good life." Work at Whittall's was often a family affair. Benjamin Barber, who immigrated in 1892, said that "he and his two oldest sons went to work in the rug mills the day after they reached Worcester, and his younger children, except Ben, followed as soon as they became 14." Typically, these youngsters started in the mills as "creelers" (helping the weavers

170

with bobbins) and then worked their way up. This is how Alfred H. ("Cap") Underwood learned the weaving trade and became a master weaver. One of the rugs he wove at Whittall's was exhibited at the Metropolitan Museum of Art in New York.

The children of the enclave attended Cambridge Street School, an easy walk from their homes. As late as 1883, city school reports still called it the "South Worcester School" and at that time, Principal Carrie A. George and eight other teachers, all female, taught grades I-VII. This was typical at a time when over 90% of teachers were unmarried females. Teaching was practically the only middle class occupation open to them, and it was considered improper for married women to have a career outside the home. "Miss George" taught there until her death in 1892. In an article for the Worcester Magazine, she recounts how she asked Matthew Whittall, whose mansion was right next door, to allow tours of his gardens as an "enjoyable and inspirational activity for her pupils." Permission was granted, and this became an annual event, "providing the students with an image of what hard work brings." [3] Like every other public school in Worcester, Cambridge Street School was a place where the children of different ethnic backgrounds first got to know each other. In its classrooms and playground, the children of English, French Canadian, and Irish immigrants learned and played together, and became Americans. Another institution of importance to every neighborhood—its place of worship—is where they celebrated their religion and maintained their ethnic identities.

When George Jones and Matthew Whittall and their families first settled in Worcester, they likely attended services in a small wooden chapel at the corner of Southbridge and Adriatic (now Washburn) Streets. It was built by the congregation of All Saints Church as the first of four proposed "mission" chapels, and it was dedicated on St. Matthew's Day, September 21, 1871. This humble structure served the spiritual needs of the local English immigrants for the next two decades (fig. 9-6). When the mission became a parish (May 5, 1874), Matthew Whittall was one of its charter members, and a Church Warden. For the rest of his life, Whittall was intimately involved with and influenced every aspect of the church. In fact, it can be said that he devoted almost as much attention to the growth and success of St. Matthew's Church as he did his carpet business. When St. Matthew's Parish Hall opened, December 1882, it was no accident that it was built on a lot at the corner of Southbridge and Cambridge Streets—right across the street

Figure 9-6. The original St. Matthew's Chapel, which opened on September 21, 1871. It was located at the corner of Southbridge and Washburn Streets. (From the collections of St. Matthew's Episcopal Church, photo provided by Rev. Nancy Strong.)

from his home, and in the heart of the mill neighborhood, where it could serve as gathering place and social center (fig. 9-7). St. Matthew's historian Paula Rowse Buonomo says that the hall "became the meeting place for parish organizations such the St. Margaret's Guild, Ladies Parish Aid Society, Men's Guild, Dramatic Society, Debating Society, Young Ladies Guild, and was the site for Strawberry Festivals, Tissue Parties, English Tea Parties, Harvest Festivals, and entertainments by the Minstrel Troupe." "The bowling alleys and billiard tables, as well as the reading room, became gathering

172

places for members of the neighborhood."[4]

In 1890, plans were underway to build a new church. The wood structure that was the "Old St. Matthew's Church" burned to the ground January 6, 1893, but by then, it had already been decided to move the parish hall to Chelsea Street and build the new church on the corner lot it occupied. The new St. Matthew's Church was built in the "English Gothic Revival" style that writer Katherine Murphy described as a medieval form that emerged in England in the 1830s and was adopted by high church Episcopalians in America "to distinguish themselves from other American Protestants" (fig. 9-8). It was built by local architect Stephen C. Earle and was constructed by Norcross Brothers of Worcester (fig. 9-9), and after it was consecrated, Matthew Whittall assumed the $30,000 debt owed to the builder. As Ms. Murphy pointed out, this could be seen as one of Whittall's "contributions to urban beautification and the advancement of taste", thus "fulfilling the Gilded Age's Gospel of Wealth." And, she adds, "perhaps St. Matthew's could even be viewed as Whittall's declaration of his successful material and social advancement, by owning and expressing England's upper-class ideals."[5]

Figure 9-7. The first St. Matthew's parish house as it looked in 1893. It was dedicated in 1882 and was located at the corner of Southbridge and Cambridge Streets. (From Buonomo, Paula, 1995, p. 11.)

173

Figure 9-8. The "new" St. Matthew's Church (right) and the Rectory (left). (From the collection of Paula Buomono.)

High School House, Built by Norcross Brothers.

NORCROSS BROTHERS,
Contractors and Builders.

Estimates made and Contracts taken for Building

Churches, School-Houses, and other Public Buildings,

STORES, DWELLINGS, &c., &c.,

OF STONE, BRICK, OR WOOD.

124 Southbridge Street,

WORCESTER.

Figure 9-9. Advertising for Norcross Brothers, Contractors and Builders. They built the new St. Matthew's Church shown in figure 9-8, several of Whittall's mill buildings, and many other public buildings in the city. Worcester City Directory, 1874, p. 535. https://books.google.com/books?id=DgQDAAAAYAAJ&printsec=-frontcover&source=gbs_ge_summary_r&-cad=0#v=snippet&q=1&f=false

174

St. Matthew's Church was the last link in a triangle of institutions that bound the English enclave together as a complete community. The Church was its spiritual center, the Mill its workplace, and the parish hall, its social center. They were all very much intertwined. The first service at the church opened with the newly organized Men's and Boy's Choir, under the direction of Whittall's nephew and partner, Alfred Thomas. The St. Matthew's cricket club was formed and played on a field of four acres with a clubhouse and a grandstand, all donated by the Worcester Cricket Club in 1899. This later became the home field of the Whittall Company's soccer team, known as Whittall F.C., which became nationally and internationally competitive during the early 1920s.

Many members of the enclave participated in several national English-American organizations that were active at the time. The Prince Consort Lodge Number 20, organized in 1877, was a Worcester chapter of the Order of Sons of St. George, a fraternal benevolent society for Englishmen, their sons and grandsons. Princess Alice Lodge No. 1, Daughters of St. George, was founded in 1882 and had the same purpose. Both organizations offered sick and death benefits to its members, and held dances, picnics, and other social activities. [6] The British American Society started in 1887 in Boston, as a response to the rise of Irish Catholic power in that city.[7] When that year began, first and second generation Irish made up more than 57% of Boston's population, and they controlled the city's government. "The mayor, president of the Board of Aldermen, president of the Common Council, and the City Clerk were all Irish Catholics." [8] Although they thought of themselves as loyal Americans, their success in America was a source of ethnic pride, which they had been celebrating publicly and ever more frequently with St. Patrick's Day parades and other demonstrations since the early 1880s. At the same time, they were emotionally tied to what was going on in Britain, where a heated debate over Irish home rule was raging. This spilled over into Boston politics when its Irish leaders and Irish organizations began hosting home rule advocates from Britain and presided over a series of "monster meetings" in Faneuil Hall on behalf of their cause. Meanwhile, the population of protestant immigrants coming to Boston from Britain or Canada had risen to 40,000 by 1887. They, too, kept their eyes on the home rule debate and took the opposing side.

Stirred by their own ethnic pride and feeling their strength, British and American Protestant groups decided to hold a celebration of Queen Victoria's Golden Jubilee June 1887 at Faneuil Hall. When the city approved the use of the Hall for this purpose, Irish politicians reacted with outrage that the "cradle of liberty" would be used to celebrate "British tyranny". The day before the planned celebration, the city withdrew approval, which sent the British groups into an uproar. With the Hall closed to them, they met elsewhere and formed the British American Society. Branches of the British American Society spread quickly, and soon nearly every town in the state had one. Worcester Branch Number 36 was organized in Worcester in January 1888.[9]

At the time, Worcester echoed on a smaller scale the same population makeup and pressures as Boston, having its own large Irish population and a growing number of English and Canadian Protestant immigrants. The Faneuil Hall incident happened at a time when elements of the Yankee Protestant populations in both cities were feeling increasingly overwhelmed by Irish Catholic immigrants, and it rekindled a smoldering undercurrent of anti-Catholic nativist sentiment. Sympathetic Protestant preachers and Republican legislators joined forces with the British American Society to combat the rise of Irish power in city offices and schools.

Irish historian Timothy J. Meagher makes it clear that Worcester's Irish population had no friends or allies among the other immigrant groups of significant size. By the late 1880s, there were over 5,000 French Canadians with three neighborhoods in the city, and although they were staunch Catholics, they were committed to their own culture and considered the

Irish their "worst enemies". An equal number of Swedes lived in the city, attracted first by Washburn & Moen Company, which sought skilled iron workers, and later by the Norton Company, seeking experienced potters. Among them were "fervent evangelical Methodists, Baptists, or Congregationalists" whose sentiments fit perfectly with those of the British American society and its anti-Catholic Yankee allies. According to Meagher, by the late 1880s French Canadians and Swedes were edging the Irish out of neighborhoods and jobs, and the English "woolen workers" who came to work at Whittalls' became another group hemming them in. "Staunchly Protestant and steeped in loyalty to the crown the new British immigrants appeared to have arrived in Worcester eager and ready to battle their hereditary Celtic enemies." "Throughout the 1890s", Meagher says, the British Americans were "noticeably active in the various nativist anti-Catholic associations that rose and fell during that decade."[10]

For the most part, their "battles" took the form of bombast and petty insults. In 1892, the York Commandery No. 4, Uniformed Sir Knights Order, Sons of St. George, was instituted "To promote the interests and welfare of the Sons of St. George through the attractive medium of public parades and military displays…" etc., and perhaps, incidentally, to taunt Irish onlookers. Among its members was a musician named Charles Mapp, who in his day job was a weaver at Whittall's.

Ten years after the Faneuil Hall incident in Boston, Worcester's British-Americans concocted a proposal to donate a drinking fountain to their city in honor of Queen Victoria's Diamond Jubilee. As they must have anticipated, "Worcester's Irish community exploded with frantic demonstrations and heated rhetoric."[11] A hearing was scheduled by the city council for November 8, 1898 and both sides were invited to debate the matter. According to the Worcester Telegram, it was one of the "hottest" city council hearings "in a long time." Neither side listened to the other, and both sides traded insults and ridicule. In the aftermath of the hearing, the city aldermen tabled the proposal and the fountain was never built. The English Natural-ization Club was organized October 1, 1895 with a more practical objective. Calmer heads realized that if Worcester's English immigrants wanted to gain relevance and power, they needed to get naturalized and become voters. To promote that effort, they set up an office at the corner of Cambridge and Camp Streets. Albert J., the brother of George Jones was president of this organization in 1917. Later, after ethnic tensions cooled, the Naturalization Club was re-purposed as the English Social Club, and it continued under that name and at the same address until quite recently.

As we've seen in a previous chapter, the efforts of the combined forces of Yankee and immigrant Protestants to keep Irish Catholics out of power at City Hall came too late. By the end of the 19th century, Worcester's Irish population exceeded 40,000, and they had a powerful political organization of their own—The Ancient Order of Hibernians. In 1901, they helped elect Worcester's first Irish Catholic Mayor, Philip J. O'Connell.

Every ethnic group had its own political and social organizations in those days. They provided comfort, security, and a sense of pride and be-longing to immigrants as they were getting their bearings in a new country. And, it's a very rare thing when a dominant culture quietly surrenders its status to outsiders. But, the fact is, the Anglo/Protestant and Irish/Catholic "battles" that took place in Worcester in the 1880s and 1890s were basically a side-show presented by the hot-heads among them. They did not repre-sent public life in Worcester, where many of its Protestant Yankee leaders spoke out against nativism, extolled immigrant contributions, and still got elected to public offices and school committees. Meanwhile, Irish, English, French and Swedish children attended public schools together, and some of their men and women intermarried. John Albert Jones, of the Kidderminster immigrants, was among the first of that group to do so: in 1884 he married Mary A. Neill, who was born in Ireland. If Matthew Whittall or George Jones took part in any of these ethnic demonstrations, we are unaware of it. In Whittall's case, it is unlikely, because he was then a rising member of Worcester's business community which was above the fray and socially progressive. George Jones may have followed his lead and stayed out these squabbles, which were mostly working class and conservative. According to the city directories for 1887 and 1888, his title at Whittall's is "foreman" and he had become a member of the middle class.

Evidence of his status is suggested by an extravagant and very unusual journey George made with his entire family in the closing months of 1888. On the 10th of October, he and Eliza arrived at Sydney, Australia with their six children, who ranged in age from eighteen years to "infant." At the time, one of the only ways to get there was by sea, across the Atlantic from New York to London, and from there, by sea to Australia. Steamship travel was no longer daunting, and the Atlantic crossing had become comfortable and affordable enough for routine family visits and other round trip travel. The opening of the Suez Canal (1869) and improved steamship technology and design made the eastern route from Britain to Australia increasingly more comfortable and efficient, if not brief.

The voyage lasted about 45 to 50 days, but it passed through exotic countries and cultures rarely seen by the average Englishman. The Jones family made their journey on the S.S. Austral (fig. 9-10), the pride of the Orient Line of steam vessels that boasted electric lighting and hot running water in each cabin, music, smoking and dining rooms, and organized games like cricket on the main deck.

This would have been a memorable adventure for any class of traveler then; and even today, as modern cruise lines have re-opened the route for pleasure trips. Unfortunately, we can only surmise what prompted the trip and led the Jones family to make it. We believe it was a trip that mixed business with pleasure and that Matthew Whittall subsidized it. In an advertising brochure, Whittall explained that "Domestic wools are too fine and soft to be durable in carpet fabrics, and so the wools which are woven into even the most inexpensive of the Whittall fabrics are imported."[12] Sydney was one of the world's major exporters of wool, so George Jones was probably sent there to arrange for the purchase and delivery of that product. (Only a trusted and experienced member of the company would be given this responsibility. Alfred Thomas, Whittall's nephew and partner, made at least one wool purchasing trip to Scotland in the early 1900s.) The Jones family remained in Australia for about 3 months. Daughter Emily (Emeline) Jones was given a parting gift of a bible from her classmates and teacher at St. Barnabas Sunday School, Sydney, inscribed January 1889. Soon after, they began the long journey home.

Figure 9-10. Painting of the S.S. Austral, a "compound steamer", meaning it used sail for backup and to preserve fuel (wood) when the winds were up. Its route as of 1883 was London-Gibraltar-Port Said (Egypt)-Port Aden (Yemen)-Suez-Columbo (Sri Lanka) then across the Indian Ocean to Australia. A brochure promised travelers that, "instead of 90 days just a month on a floating hotel takes you through some of the most beautiful and interesting scenery in the world." (From the National Maritime Museum, Greenwich, London, Cairo Collection.)

They were back in Worcester by March 24, 1890. We know that, because that is where and when Eliza Jones died of heart failure at the age of 38. Four days earlier, she had delivered an unnamed baby that didn't survive. "Baby Jones" would have been the tenth child born to George and Eliza Jones in the span of just twenty years; four others, born in the 1880s, had already preceded Eliza in death. This left George a widower, with five living children who ranged in age from four to twenty years, but this was only a temporary status. Just six months later, September 27, 1890, he married Mary Jane Gardner. He was 40, she was 20, and Eliza's niece; beyond that, we know very little about his second wife. However, there is nothing heartless or unusual about this hasty marriage arrangement, which it clearly was. In those days, before social security, day care, and other public services, it was common for a widowed spouse to re-marry for practical reasons; she, for security and companionship; he, for companionship, housekeeper, and stepmother. George and Mary Jane had one child, Herbert, who died in his first year, in 1892. Mary Jane died two years later, July 16, 1894, of consumption, an early name for tuberculosis. We need to pause here, in this as yet unfinished record of one family's mortality, so we can offer some context for it. Because it is not only the tale of one unlucky family, it's also a representative story of the health hazards of that time.

In the late 19th century, conditions in urbanized American cities were ripe for a shocking increase in mortality caused by contagious diseases that killed indiscriminately, but were most deadly to young children, infants, and women in childbirth. In 1890, 2 of 10 children died before they reached their 5th birthday. Gastrointestinal diseases, (enteritis, diarrhea, cholera infantum) and respiratory diseases, (pneumonia and bronchitis) were the most deadly, but other infectious diseases, such as measles, scarlet fever, diphtheria, whooping cough, and smallpox took a large toll. Tuberculosis, (also commonly referred to as consumption and phthisis) was significant in adult deaths, killing 15% of those over the age of 15. Although Eliza's cause of death was recorded as "heart failure", it may have been brought on by puerperal fever, or "childbed fever", a disease that in the 18th and 19th centuries was the single most common cause of maternal mortality, second only to tuberculosis as a killer of women of childbearing age. Of course, it didn't help that she gave birth to 10 children in the span of 20 years. Statistically, if a woman gave birth to eight or ten children, her chances of eventually dying in childbirth were pretty high.

These diseases had two things in common; they were bacterial infections and they were highly contagious. But they weren't new; they had killed for centuries, and were accepted for the most part as God's will, or punishment. By the mid-19th century in England and late 19th century in America, mortality intensified in the industrialized urban centers where people were crowded into smaller spaces where poor sanitary conditions existed. Disease and death struck the countryside as well, but by mid-century in England it was apparent that people were dying more rapidly in the cities, and that is where demands for inquiry and solutions first arose. Medical science, such as it was at the time, offered theories, but no science. For most of the 19th century, the primary theory held that sickness came from "miasmas" in the environment. A miasma was the term for foul air, the kind that arises in baking hot summers around cess-pools, privies, and contaminated swamps.

Rapid industrialization and urbanization had created a host of filthy and foul-smelling city neighborhoods that tended to be the focal points of disease and epidemics. Ironically, proponents of the miasma theory positively influenced public health reforms. As mentioned in a previous chapter, the Raney commission in England undertook a town-by-town cleanup of these neighborhoods during the mid-1860s, under the incorrect belief that conditions there hosted disease-causing miasma; nevertheless, by improving the sanitation and general cleanliness of these areas, the levels of disease began to abate. Unfortunately, the miasma theory locked medical practice in the use of treatments that didn't work. That theory held that miasmic air caused an excess of bodily fluids that upset the natural balances of the body, so medical practitioners sought the release of excess fluids with purgatives like calomel, or with camphor, which induced perspiration, or through bloodletting. Patients expected and often demanded aggressive use of these methods from their physicians, and saw the release of copious amounts of blood, sweat, and other bodily fluids as proof that proper medical care had been rendered. Aggressive practices such as these were given the name "heroic medicine".

We shouldn't be surprised that it took so many years and so much convincing to develop a science of disease where none had previously existed. The germ theory—that infection was caused by a living organism—first appeared in 1840, when a German pathologist named Friedrich Henle wrote, "The material of contagions is not only an organism, but a living one and is indeed endowed with a life of its own, which is, in relation to the diseased body, a parasitic organism."[13] This theory was supported by later studies of English physicians John Snow and William Budd, but miasma theorists were unmoved. Some minds began to change in the 1860s when French chemist Louis Pasteur demonstrated that bacterial organisms were responsible for souring wine, beer, and milk, and showed that boiling could kill them. German physician Robert Koch, who isolated the cholera bacteria in 1884, finally and conclusively established the germ theory. His findings were circulated worldwide, but it wasn't until the end of the century that scientific advances began to catch up with the medical needs of the public in the United States. By 1900, much more was known about infectious diseases, but care still centered on prevention, such as personal cleanliness, food preparation, and isolation of patients, rather than treatment.

During the last quarter of the 19th century, public Boards of Health sprung up in cities throughout the United States. As with the Raney Commission in England, their responsibilities focused on the regulation of sanitary conditions, such as waste disposal, water purity, and later included inspections of milk and food. According to Charles Nutt, "Intelligent supervision of Public Health did not begin {in Worcester} until April 3, 1878, when the Board of Health was organized." In addition, an isolation ward for tuberculosis patients was set up in Belmont Hospital. Nutt wrote this in 1919, and he goes on to say that "the death rate was reduced almost one-half since the board was established and kept records."[14]

For those who lived before medical advancements and public solutions, there could only be acceptance and reorder. Twice married and twice widowed, George Jones once again wasted no time rebuilding his family. Just two months after Mary Jane died, he traveled to England to meet his soon-to-be third wife, Annie (Dudley) Farndon, taking his young son Frank, with him. They arrived at Southampton on September 18, 1894, just two days after Annie baptized her two children, one month old Ethel, and 19-month old Frederick, in Birmingham, Warwickshire. Less than two months earlier, Annie's husband Frederick William Farndon had died, leaving his widow with two young children to care for and support. Since she had no family of her own to fall back on, she was left with only a couple of options. The local workhouse was one option she must have dreaded, having lived there herself from the age of six years until she was old enough to "work on her own", as she later wrote. Or, if fortunate enough to find a willing, proven, and available provider, she might remarry. Her meeting with George Jones was clearly arranged beforehand with this purpose in mind, and it proved mutually acceptable.[15] George was back in Worcester by mid-November 1894, and Annie followed shortly after. They were married in Worcester on January 12, 1895; he was 45 years old, she was 24. They suffered their first loss as a married couple about two weeks later, when Annie's son Frederick died on January 30, 1895.

The ravages of death and disease made no distinctions of class or wealth. Matthew Whittall shared the same air and space as his employee-neighbors, and he had his full measure of loss and grief. His sister-in-law Caroline Paget died in 1894, and his wife Ellen died November 25, 1895, both, of tuberculosis. During their marriage, Matthew and Ellen had five children, of whom only two survived into adulthood — their son Matthew Percival, and daughter, Edgeworth Paget, who was more commonly known as "Daisy". His remarriage would also be arranged, but a man of his position would require time to find a suitable partner.

As the 20th century began, George and Annie Jones were already well underway toward building their new family and a new life together. When the 1900 census was gathered, they were living in one apartment of a "three decker" at 20 Crompton Street with his son Frank, her daughter Ethel, and their two children, Ada and Roy (fig.9-11). George's brother, Albert J., and his oldest son Albert and their families occupied the other two floors. His brothers Henry and Thomas and brother-in-law William Carr also lived on Crompton Street with their families. All together, they formed a large and tight-knit family group that provided mutual support during their times of personal loss.

Figure 9-11. George Jones (left) and his wife Annie Farndon Jones (right) in 1898 with their children Frank (between them), and (L to R) Ada, Ethel, and Roy. (From the Jones Family collection.)

185

Matthew Whittall, on the other hand, was much more alone. The 1900 census finds him living as the head of a diminished household that consisted of his daughter Edgeworth, his sister-in-law Charlotte Hinsley, and two domestic servants. Mysteriously, they were living on Mill Street, which is west of south Main Street, and outside our South Worcester boundary. We can only speculate as to why he was not in his Southbridge Street mansion; perhaps it was a form of self-quarantine from the home where tuberculosis struck twice, or maybe he found its empty halls too depressing.[16]

It's not surprising that as the 19th century came to a close, the Jones families were searching for someplace new, away from past ghosts. The mill neighborhood was getting old and packed, and brand new suburbs were opening to the south. On May 21, 1900, George and Annie Jones purchased a parcel of land on southerly side of Boyden Street, and their extended family soon followed.

In 1880, the mill neighborhood consisted of 25 households and 141 residents. By 1900, there were 125 households, and 537 residents. The streets that served them—Brussels, Cheever, Crompton, Chelsea, Riverside, Woodward—were pretty much built out, as was Cambridge Street on their northern border. Hemmed in on the west by cemeteries, and on the east by the homes of wire-workers, the logical place for growth was south, on Pakachoag Hill. Already, there were three new suburbs planned there:

—The Boyden Estates, with house lots along Southbridge Street from College Street to Boyden Street and along Caro and Clay Streets; (fig. 9-12)

—the plans of real estate developer George H. Dutton that laid out several tracts on the north side of College Street above Holy Cross College and included City View, Dutton, Epworth, Kendig, and Davenport Streets (fig. 9-13)

—the "Malvern Heights" plan developed by Eli Thayer, of Kansas emigrant fame, that climbed east up Pakachoag Hill along the recently named Malvern Road from Southbridge Street (fig. 9-13).

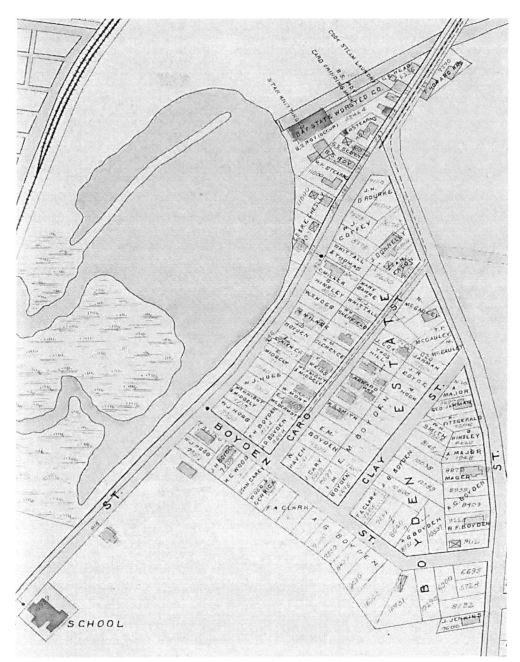

Figure 9-12. Map of part of South Worcester showing the plan for the Boyden Estate published in 1896. North is toward the top of the map. Note Malvern Road School, on Southbridge Street is in lower left of this map. This area is north of that shown in figure 9-13. Richards, L.J., 1896. (From the collections of the Worcester Public Library.)

In May 1896, Eli Thayer sold a tract of land at the corner of South-bridge Street and Malvern Road to the city of Worcester for a school. Malvern Road School (fig. 9-12, 9-13) opened the following year for Grades I-VI with two teachers: A. Theresa Timon and Jennie H. Quinn. Both were young unmarried Irish women, and representatives of a changing social order. School teaching offered them an alternative to domestic work and an entry into Worcester's growing middle class. According to Meagher "By 1910, over half the teachers in the Worcester Public Schools were second generation Irish women."[17] In the years to come, a second generation of English children from the new suburbs on Pakachoag Hill would learn their ABCs from second generation Irish women.

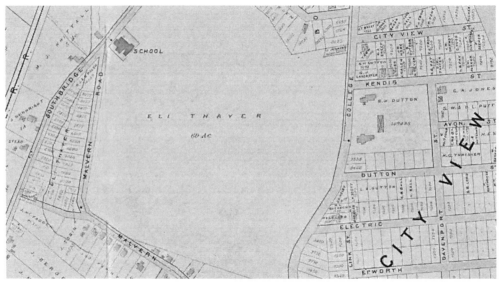

Figure 9-13. Map published in 1896 showing the planned City View neighborhood at the top of College Hill and the future Malvern Heights planned neighborhood. North is toward the top of the map. This map shows the area South of Boyden Estates shown in figure 9-12. Note that Malvern Road School is near the top of this map. A large, unplatted tract was still owned by Eli Thayer. Richards, L.J., 1896. (From the collections of the Worcester Public Library.)

188

Notes:

1. William James Hogg was born in Philadelphia. He and his parents came to Worcester in July 1879 to buy the Crompton Carpet Company. Hogg made several improvements to the mill, where he made high-grade Wilton & Brussels carpets. He was also active in the development of building lots in the southwestern section of Worcester, where he owned several large tracts of land. (Morris, *Famous Men and Great Events of the Nineteenth Century*, p. 311.)

2. *America's Textile Reporter*, vol. 16, p.1052, 1902.

3. *Worcester Magazine*, vol. III, January–June 1902, p.102-106.

4. Buonomo, Paula, *Forward Through the Ages*, p.10.

5. Murphy, K., *An English Gothic for 19th-century Worcester*, p. 1-2.

6. Nutt, *History of Worcester and its People*, vol. 1, p. 330.

7. Connolly, *The Triumph of Ethnic Progressivism*, p. 18-19.

8. O'Toole, and Quigley, *Boston's Histories*, p. 126.

9. Rice, *Dictionary of Worcester*, p. 18.

10. Meagher, *Inventing Irish America*, p. 214-222.

11. Ibid, p. 221.

12. M. J. Whittall Associates, Ltd., *The Making of Whittall Rugs and Carpets*.

13. The Editors of the *Encyclopedia Britannica*.

14. Nutt, *History of Worcester and its People,* vol. 1, p. 425.

15. This marriage was likely put together by William Jones, the oldest brother of George Jones, and the only brother who didn't follow the family carpet weaving tradition. Instead he went into the brass industry in Birmingham, Warwickshire, which was also the home of the Farndons who were also employed in that trade.

16. This census record is garbled and barely legible; for example Matthew J. Whittall is recorded as "Whitte" Matthew J., Edgeworth Paget is "Elizabeth Pears", and Charlotte Hinsley is "Charlotte Komalay".

17. Meagher, *Inventing Irish America*, p. 112.

— Chapter 10 —
Worcester and its South Worcester Suburb 1900–1925

"With the year 1898, Worcester passed the Fiftieth Anniversary of its incorporation as a City. The period of fifty years just closed has been one of continual accretion, rich experience and worthy achievement. Few municipalities have within any single half century been more favored in everything which could contribute to material prosperity, local expansion, and real advancement in the line of human progress."

Franklin Pierce Rice, 1899.

The above quote is from the book, *Worcester of Eighteen Hundred and Ninety-eight: Fifty Years a City,* and as the title suggests, it is a celebration of Worcester, so some hyperbole can be excused.[1] All the more so, because the essence of what Rice said is true. Two years earlier, in 1896, Worcester's population exceeded 100,000. It was the second largest city in population in the state, third in New England, and third largest inland city in the United States. Worcester was also one of the economic powers in the country. According to Rice, "It produced a greater variety of manufactured products than any other city in the United States."[2] Worcester's industries had not only grown, but were changing to compete nationally and internationally. Although most were still local and owned by the individualistic entrepreneurs who built them, some, like Reed & Prince, Crompton & Knowles, and Wyman & Gordon had merged into larger corporations to compete in a broader market. This trend accelerated in the early 1900s, and when completed, "Worcester, the town of farm-boy mechanics and small producers, would be gone forever."[3]

In another celebratory book, *Picturesque Worcester*, published 1895, its author claimed that, "There is no city in America, possibly excepting New York, that has such a cosmopolitan population as Worcester." "Main Street on a pleasant Saturday night is worth an hour of loitering, simply to watch and study the immense crowd which parades up and down the sidewalks." Here, "the Armenian jostles the Kurd, Russian Poles and Finns walk side by side, Arabians and Chinamen, Turks and Yankees, Negroes and Swedes, Danes and Norwegians, Japs and Hungarians—these and many other people, talking in their native tongues, help in that Rabble of tongues, which the listener may puzzle himself to comprehend."[4]

Exaggeration? Perhaps, yet according to the U.S. Census of 1900, of the total population of Worcester, 118,421, just 38,337 were of native parentage while more than twice as many—80,084, were of foreign parentage. Although the major foreign groups at the time were Irish and French Canadians, the city added 20,000 new immigrants between 1895 and 1900 alone: Italians, Russian Jews, Poles, Syrians, Greeks, Armenians, and even a smattering of Asians. Along with their "rabble" of tongues, they brought new religious denominations and added their churches and synagogues to Worcester's increasingly diverse neighborhoods.

Hyperbole notwithstanding, Worcester boosters had much to celebrate as their city entered the 20th century. By every measure, it was in the top ranks of American cities in population and economic importance. And if there were still rural features in its outskirts, downtown Worcester was unmistakably and utterly modern. The old mansions of the wealthy were gone from Main Street and replaced by a solid mix of department stores, retail shops, corporate headquarters, banks, and other commercial buildings (fig. 10-1). Worcester's first "skyscraper", the second State Mutual Life Insurance Company, was built in 1896, and at 10 stories, it towered over a wall of buildings on both sides of Main Street that extended north to Lincoln Square. The nine-story, 800-room Bancroft Hotel, completed in 1912, dominated the sky line on Franklin Street, on the south side of Worcester Common and claimed itself "a model of luxury for its patrons and a center of social life in Worcester". Along the opposite side of the common, another solid wall of commercial buildings lined the north side of Front Street.

Figure 10-1. View down Main St. at Harrington Corner at about the turn of the century. (From the collections of the Worcester Historical Museum, Worcester, Massachusetts.)

A number of still-new public buildings stood at the northern end of Main Street near Lincoln Square—the Armory, the Worcester Historical Society, and a new courthouse. And on May 1, 1898, a proud city government occupied their new City Hall on the Common: a sixty-room granite structure built in the Italian renaissance style with a Florentine tower.

Although many of its streets were still unpaved, those in the central district were edged with concrete sidewalks, and on July 17, 1914, they were illuminated electrically. "That evening, 100,000 citizens packed the city's center to cheer as Mayor Wright pressed a small electric button and then, silently, instantly, luminously, the lights shone forth."[5] Where hogs and other livestock roamed less than a century earlier, electric "trolly" cars ruled the center of wide streets and shared space on both sides with a mix of horse-drawn carriages and automobiles. The Locomobile, a small inexpensive steam powered automobile first made its appearance on Worcester streets in 1901. A few years later, it was replaced by internal combustion-powered automobiles, and by 1909, "reckless Automobilists" had become a menace. "On the new street called Park Avenue, motorists were breaking the speed limit of eight miles per hour on a daily basis. Some automobiles were clocked at 40 miles per hour and better. The lives of citizens were being put at risk and the 'tarviated' roadbed was being ruined."[6] On the positive side, on March 1, 1909, a new public automobile taxi service called the Worcester Taxi Rail "took two gentlemen from Pearl Street to Norton Company in Greendale in 10 minutes with careful running."[7] The gasoline motor truck was replacing the horse team for hauling, and telephones were losing their initial awe as a "wonder" and becoming more common.

Outside the city center, working class neighborhoods near the factories had grown in size and shifted in ethnic composition as waves of new immigrants moved in. Since the early 1880s, the small single-family homes once built for their use had been replaced by a burgeoning number of three-deckers. These large wood-frame structures allowed interior space for three identical apartments stacked one on top of each other. Each was designed to provide accommodations for a single family, and generally included a parlor, kitchen, dining room, pantry, laundry, three bedrooms, and a bathroom (fig 10-2, 3). Figure 10-4 shows a view along Southbridge Street showing three 3-deckers on the east side of the street.

The exterior offered abundant windows for light and visual communication, a small yard space for a garden and relaxation, and most included a "piazza"—a covered porch deck for hanging out laundry, or a play area, or a place to relax. There is at least one claim that the three-decker originated in

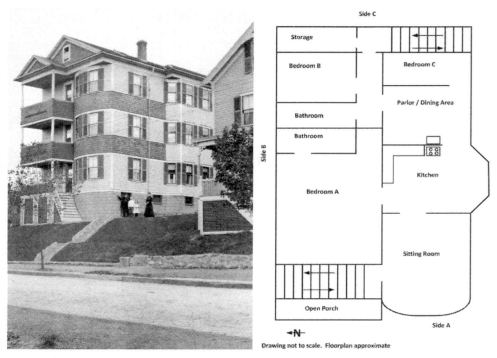

Figure 10-2. Photo of typical South Worcester three-decker taken relatively soon after construction. (From the Jones family collection.)

Figure 10-3. Note that each floor could comfortably house a family with 2 or 3 children. (From Center for Disease Control and Prevention, NIOSH, Fire Fighter Fatality Investigation and Prevention Program, June 25, 2012. http://www.cdc.gov/niosh/fire/reports/face201130.html)

Worcester, while others claim that they evolved from the wooden row houses in Boston, or from elsewhere.[8] Regardless, they became so prevalent that they have ever since been closely identified with Worcester as the quintessential working class home and neighborhood. They were an ideal solution for the housing needs of an exploding immigrant population for several practical reasons. By building upwards, three homes could be built on small narrow lots, while requiring only one hook-up for sewers and utilities. This made them less expensive to build, to own, or rent. Owners could offset their costs by renting out their second and third apartments, and three workers, rather than one, could live within walking distance to their work. But they were not popular with Worcester's elite citizens. In 1912, the Worcester Board of Trade referred to them as a "blight" that "presents an unattractive and unhealthy appearance".[9] They obviously preferred the Queen Anne, Colonial Revival, and English Revival (Tudor) single-family houses that were being built in the more affluent subdivisions on the West Side.

Figure 10-4. View north on Southbridge Street in about 1890. The former Hope Church is the building on the left. (From the collections of the Worcester Historical Museum, Worcester, Massachusetts.)

The Board of Trade was formed in 1874 in order to "concentrate the influence of business men in forwarding movements that tend toward prosperity of the city." In January 1901, they inaugurated the first issue of "The Worcester Magazine", which would be their voice.[10] As prominent members of the business class, they shared the same outlook as those of their type who served in city government, the difference being, that they advocated for what they felt the city should strive for and the mayor and his government decided what could be done within the constraints of a parsimonious budget. In the first issue of the magazine, the Board named one of the city's most pressing needs. "We will never outgrow the appearance of an overgrown country town until we have a modern hotel and modern pavement to it".

In 1914, two years after the Bancroft Hotel was completed, the Board took credit for promoting it, and announced that it fulfilled its promise, having hosted four State conventions and up to 1,000 delegates and guests. Modern street pavements would have to wait until the increased use of automobiles and "auto" trucks made hard and durable streets an absolute necessity. Finally, with financial support from the State, and with improved materials like concrete, tar and asphalt, Worcester historian Charles Nutt could write that by 1919, the paving of Worcester's streets was showing "great progress."[11]

In the May 1902 issue of the magazine, the Board of Trade said that sewage purification was needed because the "discharge of crude sewage into the local water courses is the constant cause of offense to riparian owners and people traveling in the vicinity." In 1890, the city had completed a costly disposal plant below Quinsigamond Village that removed pollutants from raw sewage by chemical precipitation before it was emptied into the Blackstone River. This helped, but not enough. An additional, but separate, system completed in 1903 was still inadequate, and frustrated over multiple costly disposal plans, one city councilman proposed that the sewage should simply be carried out to sea. (Another councilman asked which sea he intended to favor with Worcester sewage). Eventually, further improvements were made, but they were costly. By end of the year 1917, Worcester had a state of the art system with 243 miles of sewers and a large and efficient purification plant. It had cost the city more than seven million dollars. Another "paramount necessity", according to the Board, was "to promote instruction in mechanical pursuits… in order to maintain Worcester's place as "the ideal home of the ideal mechanic". The age of the apprentice was gone, so their goal was to bring an apprentice setting into a new type of public school. The driving force behind this concept was Milton P. Higgins, who had founded the Norton Emery Wheel Company in 1885. His vision of an Apprentice Trade School came to fruition in 1910, when Boys Trade School opened to 52 students. A year later, in 1911, a Girls Trade School opened to 75 students.

Generally, the Board of Trade focused on issues they believed to be practical and necessary, like paved streets, fire and police protection, and schools. Yet, they also sought "wise provision for city parks and playgrounds", and an "accumulating fund for the commemorative adornment of public squares and buildings". However, even these "pleasing" city enhancements were seen as serving practical objectives. In their view, public parks were places of "popular refinement" where "common citizens would be exposed to aesthetic ideals." [12] And, well-designed thoroughfares and public buildings would enhance the "nobility" of the city and attract other manufacturers to it.

In 1908, Worcester voters endorsed the Massachusetts Playground Act, which mandated at least one playground for every 20,000 city residents. At last, the east side could have its playgrounds, while the west side retained its scenic parks. But even these, city leaders decided, must have a practical purpose. On May 15, 1911, the city organized a Playground Commission to develop and maintain east side playgrounds staffed by paid supervisors and focused on organized activities like storytelling, basketry, physical education, sewing, and folk dancing. In short, they were intended as outdoor educational centers, where working class children would be "refined" and made into Americans. Not surprisingly, the children found them tedious, and in 1912, the Worcester Telegram ran a series of articles about the needless extravagance of "taking the fun out of play".

Out of these practical sentiments (everything pleasing must serve a purpose), the Board strenuously urged that Lake Quinsigamond be made a State Park and linked to the city and the rest of the county by a suspension bridge and a boulevard. They viewed the lake as the "greatest asset" to the business interests of Worcester, and argued that a water park in this section of New England would bring "thousands of pleasure seekers" to the city each summer. That vision was not accomplished. Meanwhile, the old causeway that crossed the lake on Shrewsbury Street was crumbling under the weight of an increasing number of automobiles and trucks. It was finally replaced with a modern span in 1919, but only after an agreement that shared its costs between Worcester, the town of Shrewsbury, the state, Worcester County, and the Consolidated Street Railroad. It was hard then, as it is today, for government leaders to increase taxes for pressing necessities like infrastructure. But there were a few who called for more vision, and more courage. One of them wrote an article for The Worcester Magazine (1911) titled "Where There is No Vision the People Perish." In it, he wrote that, "our community lacks imagination" and has "little comprehension that where we now have 150,000 people, we will soon have 200,000 people, acting as if we live in 1811, not 1911. Nothing is being done to provide to them; afraid it costs money, and money means tax increases. We have arrived at that period in life when we must plan for the future. He is not a great citizen of Worcester who argues that the tax rate must be kept low regardless of what suffers, he alone is a good citizen who says the city shall have what it needs for responsible development no matter what the tax rate."[13]

During its brief existence (1901–1916) the Worcester Magazine ran numerous articles about the successive waves of foreigners that turned

Worcester into a city of immigrants. Overwhelmingly, they revealed a generous and welcoming attitude toward Worcester's foreign population. After noting that the 1900 census showed that ⅔ of the population is of "alien birth", one article said, "Some in Worcester are concerned, but shouldn't be; they soon become 'Worcesterites' no matter what country of origin." Another article titled "Pilgrims of Today" called for patience and understanding: "The process of assimilation can only be slow at first. It cannot be brought about at all without our aid. It requires on our part intelligent recognition of their difficulties, the cultivation of a mutual understanding, patient and persistent effort on either hand." For some, this generosity was at least partly due to the recognition that the foreigners brought much needed unskilled and skilled labor to the city — and it helped that this labor was relatively docile. A promotional article that listed the "Advantages of Worcester as a Manufacturing Center" boasted that the city "attracts large numbers of skilled mechanics from other countries and foreign laboring classes who do not "affiliate" with each other, and therefore, do not "organize".[14] What they are winking at here, of course, is that Swedes, Irish, and French Canadians were too divided by their ethnic differences to join together in disruptive labor organizations. Whether for reasons practical or sympathetic, this welcoming of foreign workers prevailed among Worcester's ruling class, but it wasn't universal. At least one article in the magazine railed against that "great influx of Continental and Eastern immigrants, who… look to government as the "Good God" from whom all bounties should be received and expected." It concluded that, "We must teach these foreigners, who come to us from a weaker civilization, to rely on their own strong arms as did the builders of this nation."[15] This and other articles in Worcester Magazine suggest that the real distaste for foreigners, where it existed among the upper classes, was not their ethnicity, but their poverty.

In the first issue of the Worcester Magazine (January 1901), the President of the Board of Trade, R. B. Fowler, wrote that one of Worcester's most pressing needs was a "distribution of public alimony which discourages pauperism and inspires and encourages manhood". This was another way of saying what many felt; that poverty was a character deficiency that shouldn't be encouraged through financial aid. In a later issue, his successor wrote, "The Worcester of to-day, like the Worcester of early days, is made up of a conservative, industrious, persevering and hard-working people".[16] Here we see the echoes of Puritan values that were still ingrained in the mind-set of Worcester's Yankee elites. Although most of these latter day Puritans now tolerated ethnic and religious differences, they still viewed poverty as a failure of character, if not caused by infirmity or the death of a breadwinner. But times had changed. With the industrial age, loss of employment became the new poverty creator, and there were as yet no private or public safety nets for it, other than the poor-house, where conditions were purposely made unpleasant in order to discourage dependency.

During the Panic of 1873, Worcester's diverse economy enabled most laid off workers to find work with another employer. In addition, Mayor Davis put the rest to work on public works programs, such as the extension of Park Avenue, which furnished the "means of an honorable existence". Twenty years later, the deeper depression of 1893 temporarily shut down even the strongest industries, including the Washburn & Moen Wire Company. This time, a public works program was insufficient. New charitable organizations sprung up in Worcester that offered some relief, and the City reluctantly decided that temporary payments for the "deserving poor" would be less of a burden on city coffers than the almshouse. The "dole" ultimately expended for the "outdoor poor" as they were called, was mere $4,300.27.

Care of the poor was a civic responsibility administered under direction of the Overseers of the Poor, a group appointed by the city council. Since 1885, the Overseers had under their direction the Alms-house, formerly called the Poor Farm, the Truant School, and all resident and non-resident paupers of the city, and the State Lunatic Hospitals. Built on the old Jennison homestead off Lincoln Street, the Alms-house had grown to 376 acres, and was considered a model (and self-sustaining) institution for the poor. The farm provided work for the inhabitants, and produced meat, poultry, eggs and milk for their use and for other institutions that had indigent residents. It also cleaned up and disposed of the city's waste, using an early form of recycling. Twenty double horse teams made daily service runs to various sections of the city to collect "offal" which would then be fed to the hogs on the farm's "piggery." In their report for the year 1884, the Overseers said, "The experience of upwards of 20 years confirms us in the belief that three quarters of the poverty existing here is the direct result of intemperance, improvidence, and shiftlessness." The conflict over who among the poor were worthy of "charitable consideration" and who were not raged on, and still lingers to this day. In the early twentieth century, the Alms-house was given a softer, more welcoming name — "Home Farm". But the taint of residing there endured even after it closed its doors forever in December 1956.

In the last year of its existence, 1916, the Worcester Magazine expressed a steady optimism over Worcester's growing material prosperity and a growing anxiety over the war in Europe. Shortly after the Great War broke out, the December 1914 issue had argued against involvement in that "... gigantic wrestling match now going on on the floor of France and amid the Austrian plains..." Instead, the writer cynically suggested that "Uncle Sam" should stand by and take advantage of Europe's problem. "The baud of Fate plucked Uncle Sam out of the wings of time and threw him into the middle of the world's stage. Nothing on earth will have such a sobering effect on the European nations as to discover that in the midst of their reversal to type, we are with characteristic Yankee audacity walking out with their foreign trade."[17] By March of 1916, the articles were more serious, and more ominous. "America is unprepared for defense", they said, and military preparedness became the new cry. At the same time, business was booming. The April 1916 issue boasted that, after a few "lean years", Worcester had its full share of prosperity. There was more than full employment and the demand for labor exceeded the supply in a variety of professions for men, (toolmakers, machinists, cotton and woolen mill workers, rubber shoe workers, and clerical work) and for women (stenographers, typists, office workers, corset and envelope factories, power machine stitchers, and woolen machine help.) Another piece in the May 1916 issue described the impact of prosperity on housing trends. "Without prosperity in the mills and the fat pay envelopes in all the shops, building would be slow. Only a busy, growing city builds new houses and homes." "Until recently," it continued, tenements once sufficed for families, but now "the trend is to single or double houses. The hope and desire for a home is now being realized earlier than ever before." As a result, "The city is stretching out along every highway toward the country, and from the main thoroughfares, side streets are building up rapidly." [18]

The old cliché *a rising tide lifts all boats* aptly describes Worcester's economy in the first quarter of the twentieth century. It was the tide that lifted its citizens into prosperity, or, at least, hopes for its eventuality. With a little night school and a lot of hard work, even the most "foreign" foreigners could become "Worcesterites". They gave city manufacturers a constant supply of unskilled labor while earlier assimilated immigrants and native-born citizens occupied skilled jobs or moved into white-collar positions. In these circumstances wages were going up, work hours were going down, and there was more time for leisure and more discretionary income for leisure spending. Although numbers varied by State and among industries, a U.S. Census Bureau study reported that the standard work-day for most establishments in 1830 was eleven hours or more. Under pressure from labor reform movements the work-day declined, and an 1883 Bureau of Statistics of Labor report concluded that the ten hour work day was "normal" in Massachusetts. [19]

During the next several decades, the numbers continued to decline, and by 1919 the average number of weekly hours worked was about fifty hours. [20] At same time, an increasing number of employers required only half a day's work on Saturdays, and the number of legal holidays increased from five in 1870 to nine in 1920. Summer vacations were becoming common in management and upper class circles, but were not yet a fixture for the lower classes, although occasional days off came from paternalistic owners like Matthew Whittall, who in 1895 treated his workers to a spectacular picnic at Lake Quinsigamond to celebrate his son's 21st birthday and to an extravagant company "Anniversary Fete" at Fitton Field on September 23, 1922. Another social event recorded on film was the appearance of Whittall's Unique Wooden Band (fig. 10-5).

Figure 10-5. A group called "Whittall's Unique Wooden Band". Presumably most were Whittall employees and their families. (From the collections of the Worcester Historical Museum, Worcester, Massachusetts.)

As work hours decreased, there was a corresponding increase in the growth of saloons, and by the turn of century, spending time in the saloon was the primary leisure activity for working class men. They were social places, where lower class males could enjoy companionship and conversation with their peers. According to Rosenzweig, Worcester's larger ethnic communities developed their own saloons, and even the "smaller community of English carpet workers in South Worcester appeared to have supported three or four saloons."[21] The upper classes and owners were against them for reasons both practical and moral, and they conducted an ongoing campaign to keep them closed that lasted until national prohibition made the issue moot in 1920. Beyond the saloons, working class males participated in organized sports, went bowling, played billiards, and joined fraternal organizations, while women socialized with relatives and neighbors and took part in church activities. The upper classes enjoyed a separate sphere of leisure activities, like balls, social events, concert halls, theater, rowing, social clubs and golfing. In 1888, the Worcester Club opened to an extremely select group limited to 150 men, and the Hancock Club opened soon after, for the relaxation and diversion of the "prominent men" of the city. In 1900, the Worcester Country Club was founded, and in 1913 it built an 18-hole private member golf course that was dedicated a year later by ex-President William H. Taft.

During the first 20 years of the 20th century, the combination of increased leisure time and fat pay envelopes gave rise to "new kinds of commercialized amusements that radically reshaped the nature of American leisure activities" which had previously been segregated on the basis of gender, and class.[22] By the late 1890s, vaudeville circuits played in houses small and large in almost every sizeable city including Worcester. "In the following decade, those with only ten cents to spend could sit in the gallery of Lothrop's Opera House and watch melodramas and minstrel shows or visit the nearby Front Street Musee for burlesque or vaudeville. And such outlets for cheap amusement multiplied further in the first decade of the twentieth century."[23] Another entertainment outlet opened with the development of commercial amusement parks. In 1905, a wealthy retired boot and shoe manufacturer named Horace Bigelow opened an amusement park he named White City, on the Shrewsbury side of Lake Quinsigamond. In this venture, he turned his considerable skills as a producer and promoter of shoes for the masses into a career as a promoter of commercial entertainment for the public. Although he initially offered separate and more sedate leisure activities for the middle and upper classes, like summer homes and boating clubs, he was the first to design and offer inexpensive entertainment aimed at the larger and as yet untapped working class market. White City opened with a wide variety of exciting side-shows, merry-go-rounds, food courts, a dance hall, and a challenging roller coaster called the "Zip." "On its first July Fourth in business, 30,000 people paid the 10-cent admission charge."[24]

Although most of these new commercial entertainments enjoyed mixed gender participation, they remained working class oriented. Then movie theaters came along; or as Roy Rosenzweig called them, "the class equalizers". He tells us that movies first came to Worcester late 1890s, and by 1904 they were a regular feature at two of the city's vaudeville theaters. The Nickel Theater, Worcester's "first full time movie theater" opened in the fall of 1906 "with a program of motion pictures and illustrated songs… and claimed 10,000 customers in its first week of business." Over the next several years, the showing of movies spread to several smaller theaters that "had an ethnic or working class management, an immigrant, working class clientele, and the lowest prices in the city… By 1910 nickel theaters in Worcester had about 4,250 seats devoted exclusively to showing movies." They attracted low wage immigrants with cheap prices, and the silent pictures presented no language barriers. They were democratic and informal, and the audience could loudly cheer their heroes and sing along with "filler" reels of illustrated songs.

At first, the upper classes were offended and suspicious as they so often were with uncontrolled amusements of all kinds. Self censorship and outside censorship of movies quieted their initial concerns about immoral content, but this only shifted complaints to the theaters themselves, as dark places where immoral activities might take place, or as places of filth and foul odors. These accusations gradually led to the building of new, more majestic, palace-like theaters with plush interiors monitored by uniformed ushers who maintained proper order. The Plymouth Theater on Main Street was characteristic of this period. Built in "the ornate Egyptian-style", its interior included velvet curtains, columns, a large central chandelier and other elegant architectural details. When it premiered on November 25, 1928, "its 3000 seats were filled with an audience that included "bankers in evening dress. By the 1920s, movies had cut through all segments of American society and touched the lives of people who had little else in common."[25]

Another theater was built in 1904 near the intersection of Main and South-bridge Streets (fig. 10-6). It later became the Grand, then Poli, and in 2008 the Hanover Theatre for the Performing Arts. The following is a quote from their website: "in 1925, Sylvester Poli of New Haven, Connecticut hired Thomas W. Lamb, one of the world's leading theatre architects to make major additions and alterations to the building. Lamb designed a 3,000-seat theatre, decorated with ornately painted plasterwork, marbleized columns and many elaborate furnishings. It offered its early patrons mirrored walls, a grand staircase, a large chandelier and a two-story lobby.

Figure 10-6. Photo of the Grand Theater at 2 South-bridge Street taken in about 1924. (From the collections of the Worcester Historical Museum, Worcester, Massachusetts.)

On June 26, 1902, Matthew J. Whittall wrote to the Worcester Board of Health about a matter "that is of great importance to my business and to the people in the section near my mills in South Worcester. When the mills were established" he said, "we had a fair water privilege and good clean water for dyeing and manufacturing purposes. This has gradually been deteriorating through the effects of other works up the stream emptying their refuse and sewage in it." He went on to say that, "Aside from the effects on our business, in my opinion it is dangerous to the public health. The smell along the stream is almost unbearable. It is having a bad effect upon our help, for we are constantly having malarial sickness among the work people, and they are beginning to object to live in the vicinity of the mills." After an investigation, the Board of Health confirmed that the stream above Whittall's mills was indeed polluted by a number of up-stream concerns, such as the Curtis Manufacturing Company and the Worcester Bleachery and Dye Works. However, it noted that, "sewers have become available for the removal of sewage and manufacturing wastes" from all but one of these upstream factories. Then, in what seems like a slap at Whittall, the Board concluded that, "The most serious pollution of the stream, however… was caused by the sewage and manufacturing waste discharged by your factory. Under the circumstances, it does not appear to the Board that further action on its part is necessary at this time."[26]

Whittall wasn't the only one complaining. Soon after this exchange of correspondence, the Worcester Magazine ran a couple of articles about the widespread existence of malaria in South Worcester and Quinsigamond. The January 1903 issue reported that it received a letter "a year ago from the manager of the steel works at Quinsigamond saying that one of the mills was practically closed on account of the prevalence and severity of the disease among the workmen. It has also seriously interfered with the attendance of the children at school."[27] In a follow-up article, the magazine published a detailed report by William McKibben, M.D., who identified the source of the disease: "In the center of St. John's Cemetery is a marsh which, with the help of Stillwater Pond and a small grassy stream emptying into it near Malvern Road, in a large measure are responsible for the scourge brought on to South Worcester. Here it is an interesting fact that east rather than west of Southbridge Street by far the largest number of cases exist, due apparently to a gentle and continuous west wind blowing the female Anopheles from Stillwater Pond to that section." One of the two South Worcester physicians consulted for the article reported 500 cases of malaria during the past summer, while the other had 125. "They report some streets on which every house has its shaking-individual, and especially on those streets running back to the river, they say it is the rule that almost everybody on the street has had chills and fever."[28]

When George Jones and other members of the mill community moved to the Boyden Street neighborhood, they may have had hopes of escaping the malarial outbreak. If so, they would have been disappointed, because their new homes were right in the bulls-eye of the "west wind blowing the female Anopheles from Stillwater Pond to that section". Fortunately, later articles in the Worcester Magazine reveal an awakening, that mosquitoes were indeed the carriers of malaria and, that their extermination could eliminate the disease. A successful program was later undertaken to fill stagnant pools and "petrolize" (with a film of oil) known breeding places. If the Jones family were among those that suffered from the disease, they all survived it. According to the census for the year 1910, George and Annie Jones owned a home on 6 Boyden Street where they lived with their blended family. Shortly after they moved there, members of their extended family, and several close friends and fellow Kidderminster immigrants like Frederick and Phoebe Jarman, followed them to the neighborhood (fig. 10-7). But just beyond Boyden Street, on Southbridge, Caro, and College Streets and on Malvern Road, there was more diversity, with neighbors of Scotch, Irish, Canadian, and American heritage.

Figure 10-7. Boyden Street neighbors, from left to right: Frederic and Phoebe Jarman, Mabel and Thomas Jones, in about 1910. Behind them is Boyden Street, just downhill from the corner of Caro Street. They appear to be standing at the site of their new homes, across the street from the lot owned by George and Annie Jones. (From the Jones Family Collections.)

In microcosm, this new neighborhood signaled the beginning of the breakdown of the English enclave in South Worcester. Not only had these English immigrants moved from their core "settlement" near the carpet mill, many of them owned their homes, a circumstance unimaginable in their youth and one that made them more American. And, the Whittall Carpet Company was no longer the primary source of employment for their children. Again in microcosm, we see this reflected in the children of George Jones. His first son, Albert, (born 1870) is the only one of his children who became a weaver and made that occupation his life's work. William, (born 1875) went to college and obtained a Ph.D. from Brown University, Frank (born 1886) became a bookkeeper with a building contractor, Roy (born 1897) became a purchasing agent with Gratton & Knight, and Milton (born 1907) became a clerk in the order department at Norton Company. George's daughters—Rose, Emeline, Eliza, Ada, and stepdaughter Ethel

Farndon did follow tradition and worked briefly at the carpet mill before they married, but that was likely related to the female employment options of the times, rather than preference.

The majority of George's surviving children (seven of nine) found spouses within the community who, like them, were first generation descendants of English born parents. Of his five daughters, three — Eliza, Rose, and step-daughter Ethel — married English born weavers and remained within the community, but two of them, Emeline and Ada, married American-born machinists and moved away from it. His four sons, Albert, Frank, Roy, and Milton, all married daughters of English parentage. Frank married Beatrice, the daughter of close neighbors Frederick and Phoebe Jarman. The other spouses lived outside the immediate neighborhood, but no matter; they were all members of St. Matthew's Church, and they sent their children there.

Between the years 1906 and 1910, George Jones purchased additional parcels of land from the Boyden Estates plan. There were two lots on Boyden Street, and one lot at 10 Clay Street, which is where they were living when he died on April 6, 1915. As a skilled weaver/mechanic he is representative of all those early immigrants from Kidderminster who crossed the Atlantic when it was still an adventure, and helped Matthew J. Whittall build a world-famous carpet company from the ground up. Like them, he wasn't pushed to America by poverty or persecution, but was pulled by the promise of a better future for himself and his family. He had lived a full life marked chiefly by hard work and marred by far too much grief; over the course of it, he outlived two of his three wives and nine of his fifteen children. But he also knew the joys of a close family and of friends bound by common ways and hopes, experience, and accomplishment.

In later years, Annie Jones wrote that her husband had left her "well taken care of", and the 1918 Worcester City Directory seems to bear that out. Her real estate holdings are listed there as follows: On Clay Street, a building worth $5,000 on a 6,600 foot lot worth $300. On 1 City View

Street, a building worth $3,050 on a 5,558 foot lot worth $400. On 33 Caro Street, a building worth $4,500 on a 7,200 foot lot worth $400. On Clay Street, a 6,600-foot lot worth $300. And, Annie was an enterprising and independent person in her own right; the city directories for 1919 to 1923 record that she lived at 87 College Street and owned a grocery store on the basement floor. But when the 1920 census was taken, Annie, and her sons Roy (22) and Milton (13) lived on one floor of her three-decker at 1 City View Street. Renting another floor of the building is her daughter Ethel, and her husband Harry Rainsford, a Kidderminster weaver who immigrated to Worcester 1907. (They were married in 1915, but Ethel liked to joke that she "got him right off the boat.") Annie's other daughter, Ada, had married and moved away, which left Milton as her only remaining responsibility. Presumably, her rental income and Roy's was more than sufficient.

By 1920, the word "enclave", if applied to South Worcester's English community, is misleading, if not inaccurate. Their homes are too scattered and their neighborhoods are too diverse to fit its definition as a "distinct area or group enclosed within a larger one." Most of its dispersed members lived in the new neighborhoods opening up on College Street, Malvern Road, and the streets between them—Southbridge, Caro, Clay, City View, Boyden, Glade, and Kendig Streets (fig. 9-12, 10-8, 10-9). Note that on the 1896 maps (fig. 9-12, 9-13) the area south of Boyden Street was undeveloped. By the time the 1922 maps (fig. 10-9, 10-10) were made, all present day streets had been laid out and were being built along.

In the 1920 census, English-born heads of households were the largest single ethnic group (43%), but not the majority, in these neighborhoods. American-born households (32%) were found on every street, and a good showing of Irish (7%) and Canadian (7%) households were scattered among them. In these circumstances intermarriage was inevitable, and nearly one-third of the English-born heads of households were married to American or foreign born wives.

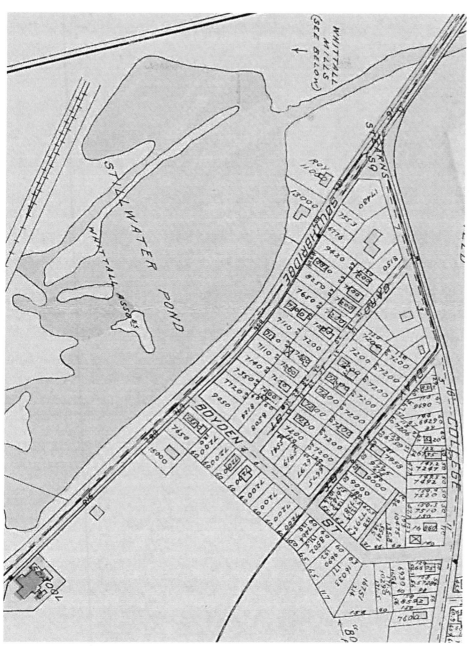

Figure 10-8. Published in 1911, this probably represents the neighborhood about a year earlier than that. Compare to the same area shown in figures 9-12 (1896) and 10-9 (1922). Richards, L.J., 1911, Plate 14. (From the State Library of Massachusetts.)

Figure 10-9. Published in 1922, the map of Boyden Estates probably represents the neighborhood about a year earlier than that. Compare to the same area shown in figures 9-12 (1896) and 10-8 (1911). Richards, L.J., 1922, Plate 14. (From the collections of Clark University.)

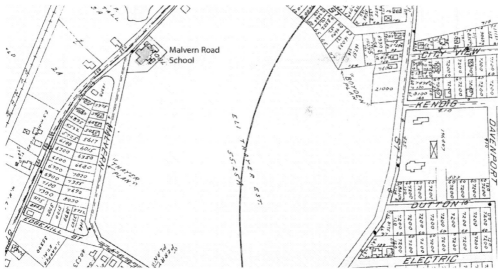

Figure 10-10. Published in 1911, the map of the Malvern Heights Subdivision shows the Thayer property not yet platted into house lots. Stillwater Pond is just north of Malvern Road School. Compare to the same area shown in figures 9-13 (1896) and 10-11 (1922). Richards, L.J., 1911, Plate 14. (From the collections of Clark University.)

Occupational diversity was even more pronounced. Although 66% of the English born heads of household worked at Whittalls', about one-third (34%) worked elsewhere. Of equal interest is that 13% of non-English heads of households were employed at Whittall's, and most of these were American-born, suggesting the increased availability and hiring of American workers. Outside the carpet mill, machinists and wire-workers were the two most common occupations, but white-collar occupations like stenographers, teachers, bookkeepers, and clerks were also found there. Other occupations included plumbers, laborers, salesmen, printers, janitors, dressmakers, engineers, firemen, and even a tailor, a butcher, and a lawyer. Overall, whether white collar or blue, this neighborhood could best be described as a working class one. The working class character of the area is reflected in the homes that were built there. Three- and two-decker tenements dominated its earlier streets, but some later lots on upper Boyden and Glade Streets, and most of Kendig Street favored single-family homes. This may have reflected both the growing prosperity of these later homeowners, as well as the declining popularity of multi-story tenements. By the time these lots were being opened, banks were expanding mortgage opportunities to qualified working class buyers through a program that the Worcester Magazine referred to as the "Cure for the Three Decker."[29] Regardless of home styles, the lots in these "new suburbs" were generally ample, with large back yards and generous space between them. Unlike the more crowded working class neighborhoods to the north, they were pleasant places to live and raise children, who had plenty of room for play. Although early plans called for more intense development of this area of Pakachoag Hill, they were later modified, and about thirty acres of the upper portion of the hill were saved from development and eventually became Cookson Park (see chapter 11). This may have in part been due to the fact the Consolidated Electric Railway once ran along Clay Street on its way from Washington Square in the city to the Auburn line, and may have owned the land there. In any event, much of the area along Clay Street from College Street to Malvern road remained open woods and fields — a free playground for summer and winter activities, controlled only by their own imaginations (fig. 10-11). Downhill (west) of it, Stillwater Pond lined the length of Southbridge Street from Malvern Road to College Street. It was unsuitable for swimming, but children could skate there in the winter, or dare their friends to walk the thin ice without crashing through. And in the early days, when automobiles were still rare, they could ride their sleds down the length of College Street while police officers watched at its top and bottom to ensure their safety. By 1920, 236 children from this area attended Malvern Road School where eight teachers taught kindergarten to eighth grade under principal Carrie A. Hildreth. Six of the teachers were first generation Irish-Americans females who lived outside the neighborhood. The others were Agnes W. Hines, who was born of American parents and also lived elsewhere, and Annie F. Cox, a first generation English-American who lived on Caro Street.

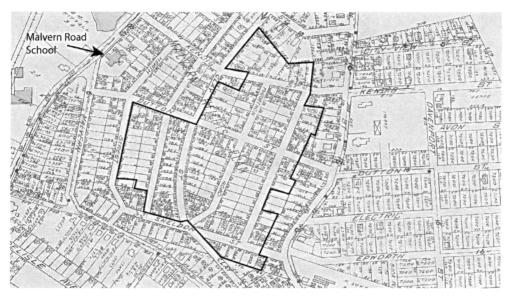

Figure 10-11. Published in 1922, the map of the Malvern Heights Subdivision shows nearly all of the area platted into house lots. The dark outline shows present day Cookson Park, which was never developed. Stillwater Pond is just north of the words" Malvern Rd." Compare to the same area shown in figures 9-13 (1896) and 10-10 (1911). Richards, L.J., 1922, Plate 14. (From the collections of Clark University.)

For the English homeowners who lived in this area and worked at Whittalls, work, church and parish hall were a bit more distant, but still within walking distance, perhaps 10 to 20 minutes. Although separated by this distance, they remained close to their old neighbors and countrymen through their common work and worship centers. According to Paula Buonomo, "Thirty-five percent of the City's English and Scottish residents were [still] concentrated in Ward 5, near the church and mill."[30] While that neighborhood was undergoing dispersal, it retained its "Englishness" through the ongoing arrival of later English immigrants. Their children, like those before them, still attended Cambridge Street School. Not blessed with the "wide open spaces" of their Malvern Road School cousins, the parents of these children had been pushing for a playground for years. A recommendation to infill Stillwater Pond was considered and declined before the City

217

Playground Commissioners chose a 4.5-acre tract off Cambridge Street, just west of St. Matthew's Church called "Maloney's Field"[31] (fig 10-12).

Farther west, off Cambridge Street, South High School opened on Richards Street in 1901 with four hundred students. This helped fill a great need in the City, and signaled a surge in the growth of secondary schools

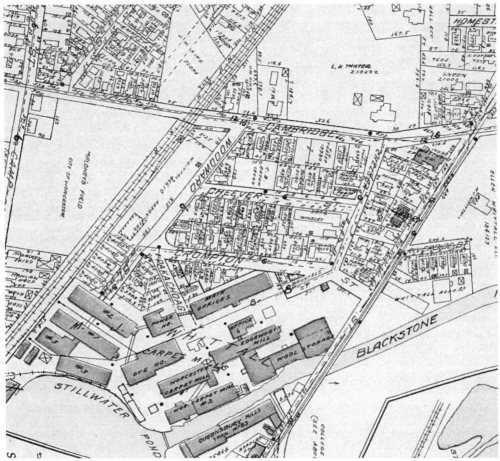

Figure 10-12. Map from 1922 of the nucleus of the South Worcester neighborhood. Maloney's Field is just west (left) of the railroad tracks, at the corner of Camp and Cambridge Streets. The dark gray buildings along Stillwater Pond were by this time all part of the Whittall Carpet Mill. The Whittall mansion is on the far right of the map, south of the intersection of Cambridge and Southbridge Streets. Across Southbridge Street from the mansion are St. Matthew's Episcopal Church and South Worcester Branch of the Public Library, both shown in dark gray. Richards, L.J., 1922, Plate 14. (From the collections of Clark University.)

in Worcester. North High opened its doors in 1911, Commerce High in 1914, and Classical High reorganized and relocated that same year. Over the years, several generations of South Worcester's children attended South High School, which was "seen as an exemplary educational model with over 80 percent of its graduates going on to college and university studies."[32] Many of them would go on to their studies just a short walk away at Clark University, which opened its doors on October 2, 1889. Jonas Gilman Clark built the University that bears his name on undeveloped pasture-land he purchased on South Main Street from the famed "Free Kansas" leader, Eli Thayer.

It is interesting to note that Jonas Clark was not a Worcester native, and had never even resided there until after he made his fortune and decided to use his wealth to build a university which "would incorporate the best features of universities in continental Europe and America." Donations made by Clark during his lifetime (about $1,000,000) and a bequest after his death ($2,915,000) set his namesake university on its way to its current renown as one of the forty "colleges that change lives".[33]

By 1911, Clark's neighbor, Holy Cross College, was the largest Catholic undergraduate college in the nation, and had an "academic program that was gaining broad acceptance." Holy Cross historian Anthony J. Kuzniewski calls the years that followed the "Halcyon Years" of unprecedented growth and expansion that included new dormitories for a growing student body, a chapel and a library, and a broadened athletic program that included track, baseball, football, and basketball teams.[34] Even before the turn of the century, Holy Cross baseball had become a favorite source of entertainment for Worcester residents. The Holy Cross Purple Magazine reported that after Holy Cross defeated Harvard at Cambridge on June 10, 1891, "not only the college but the people in the city began celebrating in a fitting manner. The route to the college was ablaze in fireworks, and Mr. M.J. Whittall paid the team a nice complement by illuminating his house and decorating his grounds with Japanese lanterns in honor of the victory."[35] Later that year, the magazine wrote that, a happy multitude of 10,000 "good people of Worcester" attended a baseball game at the home campus where "thirty electric cars awaited patiently the ending of the game."[36]

Without doubt, many of those "good people" who cheered the local Catholic college were members of St. Matthew's Episcopal Church, which was coming into its own halcyon years as a beautiful place of worship and as a stronghold for its English congregation. This is where their remaining "Englishness" would be reinforced and celebrated in its liturgy, its choir, and its consciously styled English architecture. During the first two decades of the twentieth century, the installation of Tiffany windows that began in 1896 was completed with the "Life of Christ" series on the side walls, donated by the managers of Whittalls. In 1926, with the help of a generous donation by Mr. and Mrs. Matthew P. Whittall, the interior of the church was refurbished in the style of an "old English church"[37] and the Parish Hall retained its importance as a community bond and social center. The Men's Club gathered to play cards and enjoy candlepin bowling, the Girl's Friendly Society and several other clubs held meetings and parties, the Men's and Boy's Choir went off on yearly outings, and the St. Matthew's basketball team played in the Interchurch Basketball League. St. Matthew's wasn't unique in this regard. Every neighborhood and every denomination had its own place of worship that functioned as ethnic "bastions" in much the same way. It took more than two pages of double columns in the 1920 City Directory to list them all. Most were Roman Catholic, Baptist, and Congregational, and many were Methodist, Lutheran, Episcopalian and Jewish, but Armenian, Church of Christ, African, Unitarian, Friends, Christian Science, and several other denominations were also listed.

In South Worcester, close by St. Matthew's, Sacred Heart Church served the nearby Irish community. In 1867, Bishop O'Reilly, then pastor of St. John's Catholic Church, purchased a lot on Cambridge Street for the

future he foresaw. The building of the mills at Stillwater and the Quinsigamond mills made him realize that the "city was to grow in that direction."[38]
Ground was broken in 1879, and the new Church of the Sacred Heart was
named on January 24, 1880. Rev. Thomas J. Conaty rented a house on the
corner of Sheridan and Cambridge Streets and said his first mass in the
completed church building on Easter Sunday 1881. Within the decade, another place of worship, Hope Congregational Church, was founded (1889)
just a few blocks away, at 595 Southbridge Street (fig. 10-4).

At Whittall's carpet company, prosperity proceeded apace with the
general prosperity of greater Worcester. In 1906, the company was re-organized as the Whittall Associates, with Matthew J. Whittall as President
and Treasurer, and his son, Matthew Percy Whittall as Assistant Treasurer.
After a brief economic slow down, Worcester's industries enjoyed a period of
substantial growth during the years 1909–1914, and this was especially true
for Whittall Associates. Even with his great financial success, it appears that
Matthew J. Whittall was a hands-on manager and was always advancing his
craft. Figure 10-13 shows copies of a patent application signed by Whittall
as inventor.

In the fall of 1909, Norcross Brothers was awarded a contract for
$100,000 to erect a new mill for the company that added 80,000 square feet
of floor space. In January of the following year, Whittall opened extensive
new showrooms on Fifth Avenue in New York City, taking up the entire
thirteenth floor with over 16,000 feet of floor space for display. This growth
and prosperity meant "fat pay checks" and the rights to more leisure time
for the company's skilled weavers (fig 10-14). The February 1910 issue of
the Worcester Magazine reported that, "the weavers in the M. J. Whittall
carpet mills will receive an advance of five per cent in wages as well as the
benefit of the fifty-six hour law". Later that year, Matthew Whittall attended the formal opening of his "magnificent" new showrooms in New York,
and according to one account, after checking the order books, "he went away

for his summer vacation with a smile on his countenance, and knowledge that his mills would be kept busy during his absence." He was right, and the benefits of the fifty-six hour law would have to wait; while he was off touring England and the Continent, his workers were working fifty-eight hours per week and getting paid for sixty. [39] Figure 10-12 shows the extent of the Whittall mill complex some time just before 1922. When the Great War in Europe broke out, Whittall Associates was at its peak with 500,000 feet of floor space, 350 looms, and 1500 employees.[40]

The pre-war years between 1909 and 1916 were probably the best of times for Whittall and his employees. But during the World War, inflation ate away at the purchasing power of consumers, and a sharp post-war downturn in the economy made things worse. About this time, the close bond

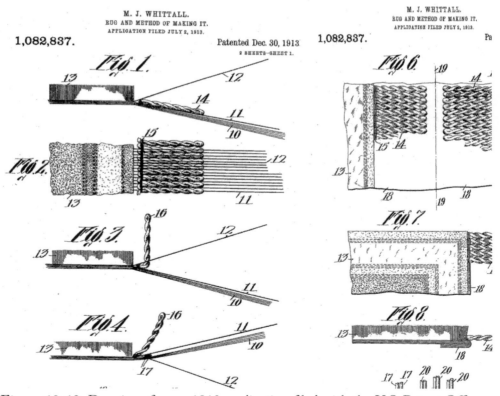

Figure 10-13. Drawings from a 1913 application filed with the U.S. Patent Office that show Matthew J. Whittall as the inventor of a new carpet weave.

Figure 10-14. Carpet weavers at work in the Whittall mill. (From the collections of the Worcester Historical Museum, Worcester, Massachusetts.)

between Matthew Whittall and his employees began to erode, as sheer size and organizational layers put more distance between them, and the first immigrants who helped build the company had retired or passed on. As a result, Whittall employees were no longer beyond the lure of labor movements that were on the rise and fighting management for improved working conditions, and they had become accustomed to a certain standard of living. Faced with a declining post-war economy, Whittall called for a reduction in wages, and his weavers promptly went on strike. It was a bitter experience for all concerned. The carpet mills were practically shut down in January 1921, and in July, after months of frustration, Whittall Associates announced it was starting classes for inexperienced weavers to replace its striking weavers.[41]

223

They finally went back to work on August 12, 1921, after accepting a 20% reduction of wages for weavers and a 10% reduction for loom fixers, under an agreement worked out with Federal arbitrators.[42] By the following spring, all seems to have been forgiven. On March 4, 1922, Whittall Associates began distributing monthly bonuses to their employees for increased efficiency and production, in accordance with a plan worked out in the settlement.[43]

For Matthew J. Whittall and his family, these were years of momentous personal change. His son, Matthew Percival Whittall, married Betsey Whitin in 1900, and five years later, on June 6, 1905, his daughter Edgeworth "Daisy" Whittall, married James E. Whitin. Betsey and James Whitin were siblings and descendants of Col. Paul Whitin (1767–1831), the American industrialist who, in 1831, established the Whitin Machine Works, which became the largest maker of specialty textile machinery in the world. In 1835, the town of Whitinsville (Massachusetts) was named for the factory, which remained in the hands of the family until 1946.

The joining of these two prominent and wealthy families in marriage was typical. Rarely did the children of these wealthy scions marry outside their class. They grew up in a privileged lifestyle that held no prospects of a future of long dreary hours among noisy machines for wages. They lived in mansions, were attended by maids, and dressed in the latest fashions. In their teen years, they enjoyed parties and gatherings with others of their class, and this is how they met each other. Daughters were expected to marry well, and sons were groomed to enter the business careers laid out by their fathers. A report of Daisy's marriage said that, "Miss Whittall is a great social favorite, as is also Mr. Whitin, who is a member of several leading clubs in Massachusetts." The wedding was typical in its extravagance. On the evening of the wedding, a reception was given by Matthew Whittall for his employees, and about "1,200 to 1,300 employees and their wives accepted." "Committees were detailed to attend the doors, at the stairs, in the billiard room, where the gifts were displayed, in the library, reception, and other rooms."[44]

(George Jones, and presumably, his wife Annie were there, and we can only wonder at their thoughts about this extravagant and dazzling evening.)

In his youth, "Percy" Whittall had a taste for powerful boats and fast automobiles. In 1905, the Worcester Automobile Club sponsored the first one-mile race up Dead Horse Hill on Stafford Street. The Worcester Gazette reported that "more than 7,000 people attended, jostling to see Pierce-Arrows, Stanleys, Stevens-Duryeas, Franklins Pope-Toledos and Mercedes tear up the steep grade, which was then unpaved." "The winner in Category One was… Percy Whittall, the carpet king. His Pierce Arrow whizzed up the steep slope in two minutes and 15 seconds."[45] On April 10, 1908, Prial, the Motorboat Magazine, reported that Percy purchased a boat "26 feet 6 inches long, with a 5 feet 2 inches beam" for use on Lake Quinsigamond where he was a member of an exclusive boat club. Before his marriage, Percy attended Worcester Polytechnic Institute for a couple of years, and then went off to Harvard. After his graduation he began the career he was destined for. The November 1917 issue of the Journal of Worcester Technology reported that, "Percival is one of M.J. Whittall Associates" and is a "live wire in the business." There, he settled into life as a "prominent man" and like his father, he joined exclusive clubs, board memberships, engaged in philanthropy, and became a church warden at St. Matthew's.

Almost a year to the day after Daisy's wedding—June 4, 1906—Matthew J. Whittall was married in a ceremony that was in stark contrast to hers in style and extravagance. His bride was Gertrude Littlefield Clarke, the only daughter of Henry T. and Martha Fielding Clarke of Omaha, Nebraska.

Henry Taft Clarke was a wealthy and prominent railroad builder and merchant who owned a successful wholesale drug business in Omaha and a branch in Lincoln. Gertrude was born on October 7, 1867, and like her future step children, she grew up in a privileged life of wealth. A biographical sketch tells us that, "She was educated chiefly under private tutors" and "she cultivated her special interests in music, literature, art, French and Spanish early in life. Her cultural background was enriched by independent study at the Sorbonne, and by wide travel in Europe and South America."[46] When not on these sojourns, she lived with her father. Her marriage to Whittall was announced in the spring of 1906, and until then, there is no evidence of a previous courtship or even any personal contact between them. This, and the 24 years that separated the couple in age, suggest their marriage was a practical arrangement, but how it was arranged and by whom, is a mystery. In any event, Matthew and Gertrude seemed to have enjoyed a comfortable companionship during his last years.

Figure 10-15. Matthew J. Whittall (portrait from him at the John Matthew Whittall Masonic Lodge memorial.) and his second wife, Gertrude Clarke Whittall. (From the Library of Congress website: http://lcweb2.loc.gov/diglib/ihas/loc.natlib. ihas.200152689/default.html)

At home, they enjoyed their flower gardens, music concerts, golf, and social gatherings. They also enjoyed travel, and made several trips to England and the European continent together. In 1910, they lived in the South Worcester mansion with Matthew's elderly sister-in-law Charlotte Hinsley, three servants, and two gardeners. In 1912, the couple moved to a new and even more grandiose Georgian estate on 100 acres of land in Shrewsbury that overlooked Lake Quinsigamond. They named their new home "Juniper Hall". From the sun porch of their magnificent home they could look out on formal gardens that they opened to the public for visits during the summer and during "Lilac Week".[47]

Figure 10-16. Juniper Hall in Shrewsbury, Massachusetts. In 1927, Gertrude Whittall deeded the estate to the Grand Lodge of the Masons Massachusetts in memory of her husband, Matthew. The building was razed in 1979. A portion of the estate now remains as Prospect Park. (From the collections of the Worcester Historical Museum, Worcester, Massachusetts.)

In these lovely new surroundings, Whittall enjoyed a life of gentile tranquility, far away from the crowded masses and the smelly river near his former home at the corner of Cambridge and Southbridge Streets. But he also no longer lived among his English compatriots and co-workers, or across the street from his beloved St. Matthew's Church. This physical distance may have been a reflection of a growing emotional distance between him and his employees that was exposed during the strike of 1921. In the summer of 1922, Vice-President Calvin Coolidge visited his friend Matthew Whittall at Juniper Hall. Surely, this was a highlight in what would be the last year of his life.

Matthew J. Whittall died on October 31, 1922. In a statement that followed his death, Massachusetts Governor Channing H. Cox praised Whittall's honesty, industry, public service and "his beautiful character". Mayor Peter F. Sullivan of Worcester ordered all city flags lowered to half-mast, and called Whittall the "highest type of citizen" who was "broad-minded and liberal toward his fellow man."[48] He also referred to Whittall as a "big man", which was clearly a reference to his character, and not his physical size. In those days, when eulogies of prominent men praised their industriousness and moral character, the unusual descriptions of Whittall as a "big man" with a "beautiful character" ring more true and heartfelt. In his public philanthropy, Whittall was no match for men like Stephen Salsibury II, or Ichabod Washburn. His charitable contributions were directed mostly to St. Matthew's Church, and St. Mary's Church in Kidderminster where he donated $40,000 for a chapel that bears his name. His most significant contribution to his adopted city was a donation of land in 1913 for a branch library that was built next to St. Matthew's in South Worcester. His employees remembered him as a "down-to-earth man… who took care of his workers."[49] True, it was a paternalistic kind of care. Paternalism of this kind was common among the manufacturers of that era who mastered a trade, built a business from it, and tended it like a man might tend a growing family. In the early years of his carpet company, Whittall surrounded himself with skilled workers who shared a mutual pride in their product. That relationship, if not friendship, was similar to the bond formed between a respected coach and a talented team. Whittall frequently sponsored picnics, outings, and other events for his employees to promote a "team spirit" in the same way Norton Company promoted the "Norton Spirit" in their employee magazine. This is seen by some critics as a sop to distract workers from their long work-days and low wages. More likely, it reflects the bond of fondness that develops between people who are different, but who build or achieve something important together. That relationship is difficult to understand in our era of giant corporations. As early as 1903, the Worcester Board of Trade saw the coming breakdown of this relationship. They agreed that the eventual consolidation of Worcester's independent home-grown industries was necessary, yet they lamented the rise of "soul-less" corporations and the loss of those days when owner and workers worked side by side.

While Matthew and Gertrude Whittall were enjoying their last years together, the United States went to war in Europe. Whittall Associates wove cotton webbing for the War Department, and, "One hundred and forty-three young men from St. Matthew's joined the ranks in the fight for freedom."[50] Roy Jones, the 19-year old son of George and Annie Jones, enlisted in the United States Marine Corps and went off to the fields of France with them.

Notes:

1. Rice, *Worcester of Eighteen Hundred and Ninety Eight*, p. 5.

2. Ibid, p. 361.

3. Meagher, *Inventing Irish America*, p. 210.

4. Kingsley and Knab, *Picturesque Worcester*, vol. 1, p. 63.

5. John Hammond, *Worcester Evening Gazette*, July 18, 1914.

6. Albert B. Southwick, *Park Avenue Speed Demons*, Worcester Telegram, February 8, 1915, www.telegram.com.

7. The Worcester Magazine, *Taxicabs in Worcester*, March 1909.

8. Breisch and Hoagland, *Building Environments, Perspectives in Vernacular Architecture*, p. 57.

9. The Worcester Magazine, Vol. 15, July 1912, pp. 194-195.

10. Ibid, Vol. 1, January 1901, p. 305.

11. Nutt, *History of Worcester and its People*, vol. 1, p. 471.

12. Herwitz, *Trees at Risk*, p. 71.

13. The Worcester Magazine, October 1911, p. 647.

14. Ibid, July 1902, p. 204.

15. Ibid, January 1903, p. 27. (From an article by Robert W. DeForest)

16. Ibid, April 1901, p. 87.

17. Ibid, Vol. 17, December 1914, p. 376

18. Ibid, May 1916, p. 103-109.

19. Rosenzweig, *Eight Hours for What We Will*, p. 38-39.

20. Whaples, *Hours of Work in U.S. History*.

21. Rosenzwieg, *Eight Hours for What We Will*, p. 50.

22. "Comercialized Leisure" online: http://www.digitalhistory.uh.edu/disp_textbook.cfm?smtID=2&psid=3316

23. Rosenzweig, *Eight Hours for What We Will*, p. 194.

24. Ibid, p. 180.

25. Ibid, p. 192-215.

26. Annual Report by the State Board of Health, Massachusetts. Volume 35, 1902–1903.

27. The Worcester Magazine, January 1903, p. 10.

28. Ibid, February 1903, p. 47-52.

29. Ibid, Vol. 15, July 1912, pp.194-195.

30. Buonomo, Paula, *Forward Through, the Ages* p. 25.

31. Worcester, Mass. City Document No. 66, 1912, p.1206.

32. Fisher, *Educating the Human Race: The Evolution of an American High School.*

33. Jonas Clark Biography, Clark University, Worcester, Mass, 2015. http://www.clarku.edu/research/archives/archives/JC_bio.cfm

34. Kuzniewski, *Thy Honored Name*, p. 227-269.

35. Holy Cross Purple, June 1899, vol. 8, p. 320.

36. Ibid, p. 372.

37. Buonomo, Paula, *Forward Through the Ages*, p. 31.

38. Sacred Heart Review, Volume 16, No. 13 September 26, 1896, online at Boston College, 2015. http://newspapers.bc.edu/cgi-bin/bostonsh?a=d&d=BOSTONSH18960926-01.2.69&e=-------en-20--1--txt-txIN-------

39. The American Carpet Journal, Volume 28, June 1910.

40. Zuckerman, Amy, "Mathew Whittall – the Ultimate Paternalist". The Evening Gazette, Worcester, July 2, 1982.

41. Textiles: A Monthly Technical Journal, July 1921. "Here and There in the Mills", p. 46.

42. Textile World Magazine August 20, 1921, p. 1123.

43. Ibid, March 4, 1922, p. 1431.

44. American Carpet and Upholstery Journal, vol. 23, June 1905, p. 90.

45. Southwick, Albert B., *Park Avenue Speed Demons*, Worcester Telegram, February 8, 1915, www.telegram.com. Southwick writes that this dramatic hill climb would grow over the years to include some of the most famous drivers in this country and some of the best-known cars of both American and foreign make. It was the most exciting thing to hit Worcester until the 1950s.

46. Biographical Sketch: "Gertrude Clarke Whittall." Library of Congress, Washington D.C. 2005.

47. Website "Friends of Prospect Park, Inc." Shrewsbury, Mass. 2015

48. "State and City Join in Tribute to M. J. Whittall" Worcester Telegram, Worcester Mass. November 1, 1922

49. Zuckerman, Amy "Matthew Whittall – the Ultimate Paternalist". The Evening Gazette, Worcester, July 2, 1982.

50. Buonomo, Paula, *Forward Through the Ages*, p. 23.

— Chapter 11 —
The English Community: Depression, War, and Decline

"On Oct. 22, 1929, the Worcester Telegram ran a headline on its financial page:

STOCK MARKET COLLAPSE

But the story didn't make it to the front page. The next day, after a brief rally on Wall Street, the newspaper tried to be cheery. "Brisk Recovery Develops" "Government Undisturbed by Stock Market" and "Financiers Swing Stocks Into Rally" were typical headlines.

But then came Black Thursday, Black Friday and Black Monday—Oct. 24 to 29—during which the market lost half its listed value and financial people were beginning to grapple with the fact that the nation was skidding into the worst financial panic in a century and more. The Telegram reported that some local brokerage firms were "steeped in gloom" and that "hundreds of thousands of shares were dumped overboard by Worcester traders," but to most people the collapse of the stock market was not an immediate concern. It was something far removed from daily life — at least that was the general impression in those early days.

I have only vague memories of the great Wall Street crash — I was only nine — but I clearly remember the grinding Great Depression that set in during 1931-32. That was when my father started losing many of his properties through tax foreclosures and after my older brother, just out of college, got a job with one of FDR's alphabet agencies. He joined a crew that was mowing grass by hand scythe around Worcester's reservoirs. It paid $15 a week and was the only steady income my family had for months."[1]

The stock market crash and the ensuing Great Depression surprised and stunned Americans, who had enjoyed unprecedented prosperity and were brimming with confidence and optimism. From 1920 to 1929 stocks had quadrupled in value while investors borrowed money to invest in a market they believed was a sure bet. But in October 1929, the bubble burst and stock values declined 80% by 1932. Headlines and stories of financial ruin and suicides amazed the general public, which was as yet untouched. Then banks began to fail and close. They too, had played the market in a gambler's type of double bet. They had invested and lost depositors' money in stocks, and made huge loans to individual market investors that now became uncollectable. As word spread that bank assets had been gambled away, depositors rushed to withdraw their savings. Banks closed by the thousands, businesses couldn't get loans for capital, and depositors lost their savings. The sharply reduced money supply led to reduced consumption followed by increasing unemployment. By 1933, at the worst point of the depression, about one-fourth the civilian labor force was out of work.

This was the national average. In some cities it was less and in others, far worse — up to eighty percent, or 8 out of 10 workers. In some of these cities desperate men began raiding food stores, rioting, and looting. In 1932, when 5,000 out of work war veterans rioted in Washington D.C., President Hoover sent Federal troops under General Douglas MacArthur to restore control. Outside these worst-case cities, many local governments employed citizens in local public works projects that offered some relief, and/or fell back on more direct aid, such as soup kitchens. By the time Franklin Roosevelt was elected, Americans raised in the Puritan ideology of hard work and self-help were now standing in line for relief. It was now clear that this national crisis required a national solution and average Americans elected a new President in 1932 to carry out that mandate.

Right after he took the oath of office, Roosevelt signed the Emergency Banking Act to restore bank solvency, and next he signed the Federal Emergency Relief Act that sent $3 billion to state and local governments for direct relief to the unemployed. In 1933, he launched the New Deal, a variety of federal programs and policies designed to pay individuals to perform jobs. The Civilian Conservation Corps (CCC) put young unmarried men to work building reservoirs and bridges, planting trees and digging ponds for $30 dollars per month, plus room and board. The Civil Works Administration (CWA) hired unemployed men to work in their communities and build parks, repair public buildings, clear brush and rake leaves for $15 per week. The Works Progress Administration (WPA), which later replaced the CWA, expanded its sphere to include art and literary projects, and ultimately employed more than 9 million Americans.[2] After these stopgap measures were taken, the Roosevelt Administration implemented a set of reforms to establish the ongoing responsibility of the federal government for the social welfare. In August 1935, Roosevelt signed the Social Security Act, a package of social programs that included unemployment insurance, old age pensions (Social Security) and poor relief, later known as "public assistance" or "welfare".[3]

The Great Depression brought an end to a remarkable seventy-year period of growth and prosperity in Worcester. According to Norton historian Charles Cheape, "textile, clothing and shoe firms, important customers for Worcester's machines" were already in decline from foreign and southern competition, when the depression "disastrously reduced all markets for the city's metal-working, machinery, and machine tool companies. Worcester's population, which had gained more than 40% per decade in the last half of the 19th century, slowed to 9% in the 1920s and decreased in 1930s."[4] Historians generally agree that Worcester's unemployment level was in line with the national average, and that by 1932, one-fourth of the city's labor force was unemployed. As with the Panic of 1873 and the Depression of 1893, the City tried to keep its workers off the dole with public works programs. Beginning in 1930, the able-bodied unemployed were hired to pave roads, paint and repair city buildings, clean up streets and parks, and prune trees at Hope Cemetery. "Three mornings each week, about 2,000 men checked in at the Boys Club Building to be assigned work.[5] A major source of real employment and stimulus was provided when the Commonwealth of Massachusetts financed the construction of the Boston and Worcester Turnpike. It was started in 1930 and employed hundreds of laborers, equipment operators, and support people. After it was completed in 1931, the Boston & Worcester trolley line was discontinued and bus, automobile and truck traffic brought commercial development to an area once dominated by farms, pastures and woodlands. Within two years gas stations, farm stands, restaurants and ice cream stands sprung up and brought commercial growth along the new highway.[6]

Even at its worst, the depression never prompted food riots or like demonstrations in Worcester. There may have been soup kitchens, and there are plenty of accounts of men selling apples on the street corners for five

236

cents apiece. As one Worcester County woman recalled many years later, the descent from prosperity to poverty seemed to have happened overnight. "Of course I went right through the Depression… to go to the bank one day and the next [day] a man would be sitting on the street selling apples."[7] Iconic scenes like this were seen in many cities around the country, but the Depression didn't affect everyone in the same way. In fact, close to forty percent of Americans never faced any real hardship during those years. Many of the very rich—those who hadn't gambled on the stock market—felt no impact at all. The very poor, mostly minorities and recent immigrants, were generally among the "last hired" before the depression and the "first fired" during it. For them, hardship and desperation continued. In between the rich and poor, most Americans were touched by the depression in some way, and in varying degrees. Many lost their bank savings, lost their jobs, or had to work fewer hours and settle for reduced wages. These families were forced to sacrifice and adapt, and many of these adaptations changed their lives in fundamental ways.

Traditional roles within the family changed. Proud men who lost skilled jobs or worked for reduced wages became dependent on their children or on their wives, who reversed tradition and went to work outside the home. Many sons and daughters who did have work delayed marriage and remained under their father's roof to support the household. Married couples moved in with their senior parents to combine family resources under one roof. And couples delayed having children, which dropped birth rates below the replacement level for the first time in American history. For most families, it was a time of pulling together and making do with a roof over their heads, enough to eat, and a few simple pleasures like gathering around the kitchen table and listening to the radio or going to a movie.[8] As another Worcester woman recalled, "I was born during the Depression so when we were kids we were kind of on the poor side. We had a neighborhood movie and you could go almost any-time—mostly I went on a Saturday. They used to give out dishes on Tuesday night and my girlfriend's mother wanted two of everything. So she would pay my way to the movies on Tuesday night and I would get to see for free whatever was playing. Twelve cents [was the price of movies]."[9]

Movies remained popular during the depression, in part by offering moviegoers a chance to acquire a free set of dishes in addition to a temporary escape from reality. In his book, "The Little Girl Who fought the Great Depression", John F. Kasson tells us how, "Shirley Temple radiated optimism and plucky good cheer that lifted the spirits of millions and shaped their collective character for generations to come." Escapist fare like this, in addition to screwball comedies, horror films like "Frankenstein", and classic films like "It Happened One Night" attracted two out of every five Americans who saw at least one movie per week.[10] The advent of commercial broadcasting in the 1920s opened a new form of entertainment that became so popular that the Great Depression is also known as the "Golden Age of Radio." In spite of their initial cost, a radio was the single luxury item that every family wanted and strove for. Once purchased, it offered a wonderful variety of free entertainment and information that could be enjoyed by everyone. In the comfort of their own living rooms parents and children alike could enjoy comedians like Jack Benny and Fred Allen, westerns like The Lone Ranger, mysteries like the Lux Radio Theater, and soap operas like "Our Gal Sunday". Radios were an expensive luxury at first, about $139 in 1929. But deflation brought the price down to about $47 by 1933 and that, plus the availability of installment buying helped the average worker to purchase one. By 1933, the worst year of the depression, 60% of U.S. households owned a radio.[11]

Throughout the depression years and beyond, President Roosevelt kept Americans informed and reassured via a series of soothing "Fireside Chats" that were broadcast on the radio. In the election year of 1936, Roosevelt made a series of "whistle-stop" tours of the country. One of these took him to Worcester on October 21, 1936, where he offered these encouraging words about the Nation's recovery: "I have found a Nation more greatly prosperous, more definitely on the highway to complete recovery than at any time in the past seven years. I have seen the record of what we have done in the faces of the people I have met. We have banished Old Man Gloom… I have seen things today even more welcome to me than your lovely autumn foliage. I have seen the smoke from factories which three and a half years ago were smokeless. I have heard the sound of mills which three and a half years ago were silent. I have seen men at work who three and a half years ago were jobless. I have seen women and children who, after long years of fear, have begun to live and hope again. Three and a half years ago we declared war on the depression. You and I know today that that war is being won."

Two years later, on September 21, 1938, disaster struck again, this time delivered by Mother Nature. Evelyn Herwitz describes it in her book *Trees at Risk*: "… a devastating hurricane with wind gusts up to 100 miles per hour smashed into New England, wreaking death and destruction as it tore through Worcester and raged up the border between New Hampshire and Vermont. By the weekend, the New England death toll from the hurricane neared 500… and Worcester was struggling to recover from an estimated $5 million in property damage. 'Buildings were partially collapsed' reported the Gazette, 'roofs ripped off, church steeples toppled, store fronts blown out, trees uprooted, chimneys leveled, signs torn down, and streets littered with glass, tree branches and other debris. There were dangling live wires in many sections. Telephone and electric service, affecting lighting and radio went out of commission.' With Worcester's trees, the hurricane was ruthless. In just three hours, the storm downed 3,931 street trees and 11,189 trees in city parks and playgrounds… Working day and night, men from the federal Works Progress Administration helped clear homes and public buildings of dangerous branches and fallen trees, but the full repairs would take years."[12]

The English working class community of South Worcester found themselves in the same sinking financial boat with others of that class who lived in Worcester, and they responded to it in the same practical ways. They didn't lose investments in the stock market, but some lost investments in banks or in property. Annie Jones, whose real estate holdings on Clay, City View, and Caro Streets were worth over $14,000 in 1923, owned only the City View property, valued at $5,500 in 1940. In 1938, she wrote that although her husband (George) had left "her well taken care of… the depression came and changed things". To which she added, "if I don't live too long I may be able to manage." To help manage, Annie went into training and became a licensed Practical Nurse, and in 1939, at the age of 66, she worked 8 weeks in that profession and earned $120. Likewise, her children and stepson made practical adaptations that got them through the depression without major hardships; they moved in together and shared resources, and those who could find work, young and old, male and female, helped support their blended families.

Annie's multi-family home on 1 City View was a not quite a three-decker, but it offered plenty of space. Above the basement, which she once used as a grocery store, was a two-story apartment building, topped by a third attic apartment that she rented out (fig 11-1).

During the depression, two of her children and their families moved into the building and shared expenses. Annie lived on the first floor apartment with her son Milton and his wife Margaret Jones, who were married November 1930, just as America was sliding into the depression. At the time of their marriage, both were employed; Margaret was a card setter at Whittalls, and Milton was working at Norton Company. In this, he was fortunate, because Norton's was well on it's way to becoming a major international manufacturer of grinding wheels and abrasives, and a primary employer in Worcester. Although production slowed during early 1930s, 50% of its workers remained on the payroll with a shorter work-week. Norton's actually expanded its Greendale facilities by 1938 and was back to full employment during World War II, thanks again to war production. Milton was among those laid off, but the duration was probably a short one. Margaret may have

Figure 11-1. The house and store at 1 City View Street as it looked in 2007. (Photo by the authors.)

worked for a while during this time but their first son, Donald, was born in 1934, and by 1936 the couple was able to move to a place of their own on Malvern Road. If they had any serious difficulties during the depression they were never spoken of. On the contrary, their memories of those years were the warm and nostalgic memories of their early family life.

Ethel Rainsford, Annie's daughter, lived upstairs with her husband Harry and their two grown sons. Harry was a weaver at Whittall's Associates, which was still hurting from the effects of the depression in 1940. Like many employers of that time, Whittall's chose to spread available work among their workers, rather than laying some of them off. As a result, Harry worked just 25 weeks in 1939, which was about the average for weavers. However, by this time their two sons had full time jobs; Vernon (23) at Howard Brothers and Gilbert (19) at Reed & Prince, and they were both able to contribute fifteen to twenty dollars per week toward family expenses. (The monthly rental for a three-decker apartment at the time was about $20-$35.)

Annie's son Roy Jones and his family appear to have made it through depression without serious financial injury. At its start, Roy had steady work as a purchasing clerk at Graton and Knight Company which made, among other things, drive belts for machines and automobiles. In addition, his wife Gladys and her sister were both working and contributing to household expenses. When domestic production slowed during the depression, Graton and Knight shifted to the production of war materials, such as leather holsters and casings for binoculars. If Roy lost time at work or wages it was probably temporary. Sometime between 1931 and 1939, Gladys quit work to stay home and raise their young son Malcolm. This may have caused some belt-tightening, especially if her sister (Dorothy White) lost her job. But she was back to work by 1939 and Roy Jones worked full time that year and made good wages for the time — $1560.

The family of Annie's stepson, Frank Jones, may have been the most squeezed by the depression, but they were not impoverished by it. His wife, Beatrice had worked as a milliner at Sherer's Department Store on Front St., across from Worcester Common, before child care kept her at home. They rented on Caro Street and then Boyden Street until 1924, when they moved into a single family house on Tracy Place, the newest South Worcester suburb to develop (fig. 11-2). By this time, the trolley went out Southbridge Street to the Auburn line (fig. 11-3), so it was an easy commute to downtown Worcester from there.

Frank lost a good job while supporting his wife and three young children. As his daughter Shirley (Jones) Mickelson later recalled: "When I was small my father had a very good job. He was treasurer of a construction company… the construction company folded a few years into the depression… then he got a job with the WPA, which President Roosevelt had instigated… It made work for a lot of people." Childhood memories of the depression rarely speak of hardship or suffering, because most parents managed to keep them fed and keep a roof over their heads. More likely, they

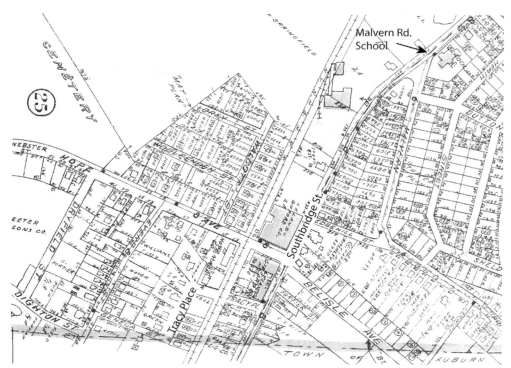

Figure 11-2. Map of the Tracy Place — Hope Avenue neighborhood published in 1922. This is at the southern edge of Worcester at the Auburn line. Richards, L.J., 1922, Plate 14. (From the collections of Clark University.)

recalled repetitious meals rather than hunger. Some remembered eating a lot of soup, but Shirley remembered, "We ate an awful lot of oatmeal in the depression." Here again, extended family members moved in and shared living space and resources. "After my grandfather died [Frederick Jarman, also a weaver at Whittall's] my grandmother [Phoebe] came to live with us. She brought a little money with her to help us out." During the dark years of the depression there were a few silver linings that brightened them. For example, the deflation that came with it brought prices down, and most families could occasionally break the monotony of repetitious meals with something special. These occasions were bright enough to remember long after. Shirley recalled, "My mother would send me down to the store, Goldstein's, on the bottom of Hope Avenue. It is now a tavern. Once my mother gave me 25

243

cents and said now get me two pounds of bottom round ground." Like most families with some yard space, they had a garden and canned many vegetables for the winter. Even in the 1950s the big cellar storage cabinet was filled with full canning jars.

Figure 11-3. The South Worcester trolley on Southbridge Street near Tracy Place. The cars were painted orange and white. (From the collections of the Worcester Historical Museum, Worcester, Massachusetts.)

Another "silver lining" was the new fields that were opening up in employment for young women, who were thus able to help support themselves and their families. Shirley Jones found work in 1938: "After high school I went to Fairchild's Business School. It was uptown in the penthouse of the Central Building. I went to the beach that summer on vacation with the family after I graduated. When I came back home I was looking for a job and Dick Wilson had the job of hiring girls for Travelers Insurance. So he called me and asked if I would like to work as a secretary with one of the agents. Travelers had the whole floor in the Central Building. Company girls worked in the inner part of the building. Agents had offices all around the perimeter."

Depression years that included vacations to the beach couldn't have been all that bad. In 1925, Shirley's parents had purchased a beach house at

244

Hamilton Beach, in Wareham. They spent many happy summers there, and managed to hang on to it through the depression. "I don't know how they kept it," Shirley wondered, "except that Grandma (Jarman) used to live with them and probably paid some of the bills. A lot of the banks went easy on people in those days. You could stall on your mortgage payment. The banks couldn't afford to be loaded with a lot of property." And, she added, "They rented the beach house for part of the summer when things got real tough."

Things never got "real tough" for the family of Matthew J. Whittall. In fact, they were among the very rich who were untouched by the depression. After his death, Textile World magazine reported that the M.J. Whittall Associates would continue the business without any change in policy. "The latter's son, Matthew P. Whittall, will head the company with his son, Matthew Whitin Whittall, and James E. Whitin as Associates.[13]

In 1930, Matthew Percival Whittall, formerly known for his fast boats and fast cars, was 55 years old, and fully settled into life as company President and community leader. By this time, the transition from father to son was fully realized. He owned his father's first home at 692 Southbridge Street and lived there with his wife Betsey and two of their three sons (fig. 7-11). The census record for 1930 put a value on the mansion at $65,000. Living under the same roof with the Whittall family are two female Swedish servants, a female Swedish cook, and a male butler from Scotland.

Matthew P. also assumed his father's place at St. Matthew's as Senior Church Warden, and he and Betsey continued to nurture and finance the church as his father did before him. The old English manor was alive and well in that little corner of South Worcester.

The two sons who then lived in the old manor with their parents were James Paget Whittall, age 26, and Matthew John Whittall II, age 12. James Paget was Superintendent at the carpet mill, and Matthew John II was still in school. A third son, Matthew Whitin Whittall, 29, had recently married and moved away with his wife, Bernice. Matthew Whitin was a handsome and dashing young man when his 21st birthday was celebrated at a huge company party attended by over 4,000 men, women and children. After the celebration, Matthew W. was treated to a pleasure cruise that lasted nearly a year and took him to Spain, Gibraltar, Italy, Constantinople, France, Great Britain, and beyond. When he returned, he was expected to settle down and prepare for a leadership role in the Company. For a while, he followed expectation. In 1930, he was an Assistant Treasurer at the carpet mill and lived in a trendy West Side neighborhood on Rittenhouse Road. But it appears he didn't fit into the corporate expectations he was supposed to follow. Just as his father once loved fast automobiles and boats, Matthew Whitin was fascinated with the exciting new adventure of flying; a fascination he shared with his with his younger brother, James P.

The story of how this fascination led to the development of Worcester's first airport is told by Albert B. Southwick: "In the 1920s, flying was an adventure. For the Whittall brothers of central Massachusetts, the years after World War I were spent testing their skill and luck by flying canvas-covered biplanes over the fields and villages of Worcester County. But the Whittalls, like other local pilots, faced a serious obstacle: there was no airport in Worcester. Farm fields provided a bumpy alternative for recreational flyers, but commercial passenger planes and mail carriers needed the improved runways available at a real airport. In 1925 an informal group of Worcester businessmen and flying enthusiasts began to scout potential sites for an airport in Worcester County. But, as often happens when committees are involved, the plans stagnated. Finally, Whitin Whittall grew impatient with the delays. He used his own money to hire engineers to survey possible sites. Inches Farm field in North Grafton came up at the top of the list. Whittall took out options to purchase the land, then drummed up excitement and support from Worcester businessmen. Within three weeks, the group had the funds to incorporate, and by October 3, 1927, two runways and two hangers were open for business. Whittall Field became Worcester's first airport. For 18 years, Whittall Field was one of the busiest spots in Worcester County. Until 1945, the field hosted airplanes such as Jennies, Robins, Wacos, Fords, Stearmans, Cubs, and Taylorcraft; special charters brought visiting performers and dignitaries, and pioneers such as Wiley Post made stopovers on around-the-world flights. In the years leading up to World War II, the field was especially busy with the Civil Pilots Training Program. World War II brought major advances in aircraft design, and it became clear that the old farm fields would soon be too small for modern aircraft. On May 4, 1946, a new Worcester Airport was dedicated; commercial service to New York City began a week later. The old Whittall Field was sold for a housing development in 1951."[14]

Perhaps Matthew W. Whittall's love of adventure and flying made him unsuited for a life behind an executive desk in a carpet mill. In 1940, he sold his home on Rittenhouse Road, and moved with his wife to Florida. They divorced that same year, and he died there in 1948 at 46 years of age. His younger brother, James Paget Whittall, grew up in the same family tradition and with the same expectations. When James Paget was 22 years old, he too, made an extensive tour of Europe, after which he was supposed to return to the family fold and enter the carpet business. It appears that he at least went through the motions; after starting in the mill as a weaver, he worked his way to Superintendent and then Vice President in 1930. But he shared his brother's passion for flying, and according to his obituary, he owned several planes and frequently participated in amateur flying races. In 1940, he lived in North Grafton, near the airport he founded with his brother and where he served as Treasurer. The census for that year records that he and his wife Millicent had four children, a maid, and lived in a home valued at $20,000. In addition to airport treasurer, James P. was recorded as an "unpaid family worker" at the carpet company, meaning, he was comfortable (and gracious) enough to take no salary from the family firm in the lean years. He retired from Whittall Associates as Vice President, having never reached the top spot. When he died in 1976, he left four children and nine grandchildren, none of whom lived in Worcester.

Matthew John Whittall II may have been more suited for the family destiny than his brothers, but he was born too late (1917) to fulfill it. He joined the company in 1938 and worked in various departments in his apprenticeship for later leadership. At the time of the 1940 Census, he was 22 years old and owned a home on the west side of Worcester off Salisbury Street. According to the census his occupation was "rug finisher" and he worked 50 weeks at the mill in 1939 and earned $850. No doubt, this was his concession to the company's financial straits. Yet his home was 3,779 square feet, with five bedrooms, and valued at $15,000. Living in the home with Matthew were his wife Mary, their year old daughter, and two female servants. Not bad on a rug finisher's salary! Matthew John served in the U.S. Air Force as cryptographer during the Second World War and was later elected Vice President in 1949. He was President of Whittall Associates from 1954 to 1956, the year it was sold. After closing the family firm, he moved to New Hampshire, where he became President of Cornwallis Boat Company, a boat-building firm that participated in races on Lake Quinsigamond. When he died he left two sons, two daughters, and a stepson. They were all living outside the State of Massachusetts.

Edgeworth (Daisy) Whitin, beloved daughter of company founder Matthew J. Whittall, lived her adult life in the manner and style in which she was raised. In 1940, her husband, James E. Whitin was a trustee and Treasurer at Whittall's and also had the position of General Manager of the Uxbridge Cotton Mill in that city. They lived in North Uxbridge where they were tended to by a lady's maid, a laundress, a maid and a butler whose salary for the year 1939 was $1,200. That was about twice the amount the average weaver earned that year at Whittall's!

According to an article in "America's Textile Reporter", Matthew J. Whittall left his entire estate to his wife Gertrude Clarke Whittall, his son

Matthew P. Whittall, and his daughter, Mrs. James E. Whitin. The value of the estate was said to have amounted to several million dollars.[15] Gertrude's share alone must have been a fortune for that time, and she not only held on to it through the financial collapse, but she thrived on it throughout the rest of a long lifetime and second career as a wealthy patron of the arts. It may have helped that she and her husband had been investing in the arts, rather than in stocks. Sometime after their marriage, she began collecting fine musical instruments, manuscripts, autographs, and other documents of the classical European composers like Mozart, Beethoven, and Brahms. After her husband's death, she went on a collecting spree, and during the six years between 1923 and 1930 she made at least eight recorded trips to Europe that included England, Monaco, France, Italy, and the Netherlands. In 1927, Mrs. Whittall deeded her Juniper Hall mansion in Shrewsbury to the Grand Lodge of the Masons in memory of her husband, and moved to Boston. At this point, it seems she severed forever any and all ties to the Whittall Company, the Whittall family, and to Worcester.

She remained in Boston for about five years, during which she made several more trips to Europe and prepared for her future as benefactor of the fine arts. Since her collections focused on classical music and poetry, she decided to center her patronage on the Library of Congress in Washington D.C. She moved to that city in 1935, and settled in a pricey apartment building (now the luxurious Omni Shoreham Hotel). Her monthly rent there was $300 per month according to the 1940 census. (Compare this to $20-$35 per month for an apartment in a three-decker.) Her career as an arts patron began in 1935 with the donation of the first of five Stradivari string instruments to the Library. She also established the Gertrude Clarke Whittall Foundation for their maintenance, and the "Whittall Pavilion" for their use in live concerts. She followed this with donations of additional musical instruments and autographs, manuscripts and memorabilia of the major classical composers.[16] This done, she turned to poetry. She gave the

Library her extensive collection of manuscripts by contemporary poets, and established a poetry room on the 3rd floor that enabled the library to "present poets reading their works, actors interpreting Shakespeare, and critics lecturing on literature."[17]

Wealthy and haughty benefactors must be appeased by those who seek their favors. A biography of Edward N. Waters, then Chief of the Library's Music Division says that he was especially valued for his "skill and diplomacy in handling Mrs. Gertrude Clarke Whittall." "Although the facts of her beneficence are well known, Mrs. Whittall required care and nurture from Library personnel. She could be quite difficult at times, awfully, awfully obstreperous if something displeased her."[18] The esteemed American poet Robert Frost, a "dear friend to Mrs. Whittall", managed her with an exaggerated flattery that is truly embarrassing. In one letter, he told her that, "Having you there in Washington is like having seeds of fire on the hearth that only needs a scrap of manuscript for tinder to burst into flame with the first passing breath of inspiration."[19] Indeed, Matthew Whittall had left his wife "well taken care of". She lived a life of noblesse oblige and grandeur for thirty years in Washington D.C., where she died at 93 years of age.

With the approach of the Second World War, defense spending sparked an economic rebound and brought new life to Worcester's factories as they turned to the manufacture of war materials. Jobs became plentiful again, and, as young men left for the service, women and unemployed men came into the workforce to replace them. After Pearl Harbor, as Margaret Erskine writes, "Defense-related factories stepped up production to their utmost capacity. Other companies, forbidden to produce what were considered to be luxury products, found work for their employees by subcontracting from larger firms. Worcester was once again a town full of energy and optimism, with plenty of work to be had and fortunes to be made."[20]

That last statement may be a bit too cheerful, because the restraints and anxieties of the depression were to some extent replaced by the restraints and anxieties of the war. Americans on the home front had to conserve or recycle items that were needed as war materials, and privately controlled consumption during the depression morphed quickly into federally mandated rationing. Gas was hard to get, and tires couldn't be replaced, so family automobiles lay idle, or were sold. New cars were hard to get because tanks were being made instead. Butter was replaced by margarine, a white, pasty product that came in a plastic bag that took on a yellowish color when a red solution in the package was pressed and released. No one complained, and everyone wanted to do his or her part. "Victory Gardens" for the private production of vegetables sprouted up in the back yards of American neighborhoods. Yet, in spite of the war's great financial costs and shortages, the standard of living on the home front actually improved. More Americans were able to buy consumer goods like vacuum cleaners, washing machines, electric record players and modern radios. And it was during those years, that many families were able to realize the American dream and buy a home of their own. In April 1941, Milton and Margaret Jones purchased a two-story (single family) Cape on Glade Street, and two years later, Harry and Ethel Rainsford moved to a pretty bungalow-style home on West Hampton Street. These were the "upsides" of the war.

The downside of the war, of course, was shouldered by those who served in the military, and the families who worried for them. On September 16, 1940, Selective Service began drafting men between the ages of 21 and 36. By November 1942, the age range expanded to men 18 to 37. Blacks were bypassed at first, but were called in 1943 and later integrated to fight during the Battle of the Bulge. And many young women volunteered and served in a variety of important non-combat service roles. Not everyone called would serve because of health or other circumstances, but almost every family had a loved one in the service or knew a family that did. By the war's end, about 34 million men had registered, and 16.1 million military personnel had served.

After she came to Worcester and until she died, Annie Jones kept up a written correspondence with her siblings in England, and a few of her letters remain in the family. Through them, we have a glimpse of the war years as she saw them. In a letter dated March 23, 1942, she worries that, "it does seem the allies should be able to clean them [the enemy] up but the way the news goes it might be some time. We were caught unprepared so they seem to have the best of it just now. I'll be 70 years old the 8ᵗʰ of June but I keep very well and busy. I was away eleven months taking care of a lady who was very ill [and] I have done a lot of nursing since my husband died, but now I feel rather lazy and want to stay home so if possible shall get into some defense work." In a later letter, May 1943, she was more confident of the war's outcome: "… it was good to hear you are all safe for there are many who cannot say that today. But the way things are going it won't last long and that will be the day when we can live in peace. My family are all well, some of the boys [have been] called and others waiting and ready to beat off the Japs and Nazis."

She also mentions conditions at home and on the home front: "Of course this war has made a difference [here]. We will not be able to do much traveling on account of gas and tire rationing [but] everybody is glad and willing to do all possible to beat these sneaking Japs — lets hope the worst is over and they can get a good dose." As usual, in spite of "feeling lazy", Annie kept busy. "I still work for the British Relief, we knit, mend and raise money by concerts and sales, which enables us to buy goods to send to Britain. So let's keep our thumbs and chins up and get this over." Having that out of her system, she concludes her letter on more nostalgic tone: "we just received a radio [broadcast] from London. To hear the nightingales singing in the woods, it was so clear and the birds sang lovely. What a wonderful thing the Radio is, it brings so much into our homes I wonder sometimes how we ever managed without it."

As mentioned in her letters, a number of Annie's grandchildren did go off to war against the Japanese and Nazis—grandsons Gilbert and Vernon Rainsford, Malcolm, the son of Roy Jones, and Robert and Gordon, sons of Frank Jones.

Another letter in our possession is dated September 7, 1943 that was written by Annie's daughter, Ethel Rainsford. "Dear Uncle Albert, I am sorry to have to write this sad news telling you mother passed away at 9:45 Monday evening after being sick only a few hours after suffering a heart attack. She will surely be missed by all, as she has many friends. Hoping you are all in good health. I remain, Ethel Rainsford."

By the mid-1940s, many of the English immigrants who came to South Worcester in the 19th century had passed on or were retired. Very few of them remained in the core neighborhood near the mill, having moved either to the College Hill/Malvern Road neighborhood, or to the newer one that opened in the 1920s farther south near Tracy Place that included Hope Avenue, Dighton and Evers Streets, and Hope Place (fig. 11-2). By this time, the College Hill/Malvern Road area on Pakachoag Hill was fully developed and hemmed in by the Auburn line on its southern border, Holy Cross College on the northern border and Cookson Park in between. Named for Mayor Walter Cookson, the park site was sold to the City of Worcester in June 1936 by real estate developer Herbert E. Howe. Consisting of 26.5 acres, the park straddles Clay Street from Kendig Street to Malvern Road (fig. 10-11). Howe was probably happy to unload the property, as in all likelihood this area was saved from development by the decline in home building during the depression.[21]

The English immigrant population that lived in these newer neighborhoods was aging but still plentiful, and the young boy who delivered their newspapers was accustomed to the sound of English accents as he made his rounds. But make no mistake; these neighborhoods were quintessentially American in character. Most of the children of these elders were American born, owned their homes, and had American children of their own. A few, like Alfred Giles, a weaver, William Green, accountant, and John Green, a foreman, worked at Whittalls as their fathers had before them, but most worked elsewhere or married someone who did. This led to further dispersal as some of them moved closer to their work. Annie Jones' daughter Ada, moved with her husband Frank Daly to the north side of the city, and her stepdaughter Emeline moved with her husband Raymond Lees to California where they and their ten children became known as the California branch of the family.

Most of these first generation Americans married first generation Americans of English heritage like themselves. But their children had more exposure to people from outside the English community, and marriages between them were becoming more common. Shirley Jones married Melvin Mickelson, and Vernon Rainsford married Dessideria Schonbeck, both of Finnish or Swedish heritage. However, although their ethnic backgrounds differed, their religious (Protestant) backgrounds were the same. For reasons we discuss below, intermarriage between Protestants and Catholics was still a bridge too far, and was unusual even by the third generation.

The original core neighborhood around the carpet mill took in the biggest share of the English immigrants who came in the 20th century, and they replaced their predecessors who had moved to the new neighborhoods. For a time, this kept the area refreshed with younger English workers and their cultural habits. But after 1925, English weavers stopped immigrating to Whittalls. The lengthy weaver's strike that crippled the carpet company in 1921, the hiring of locals to replace the strikers, the depressed years that followed, and then, the Great Depression, put an end to the flow. Eventually, they too moved into the newer neighborhoods to the south, and like them, this aging mill neighborhood gradually lost its English character.

In the heart of these neighborhoods, the Catholic College of the Holy Cross continued to expand. It came through the depression years in fine shape. In fact, it was during those years that the college built a large and costly dining hall, (Kimball Hall) and in 1940 it opened a new dormitory with a capacity for 240 students. The financing that made these buildings possible was accomplished through a combination of cuts in the salaries of faculty and staff, and a modest increase in basic room a board fees. However, the year 1932 brought an end to active farming on the campus, as it was no longer profitable. But they kept the old Red Barn, remodeled it as an exercise center, and converted the house where the farm laborers lived to a dormitory they named "Campion" that housed 48 students. The next threat to full dorms and financial stability came after the Fall of 1940, when the draft began taking potential students into the military. Here again, the college managed its options well. Although most schools saw a drop in enrollment of 10-18%, Holy Cross managed to keep all its dormitories filled except Campion. College historian Anthony Kuzniewski said that the college accomplished this by admitting a "goodly number of 'slow coaches', people who would normally never have been admitted."[22]

After the Japanese attack on Pearl Harbor, enrollments declined in many of the nation's colleges and universities, as prospective students went into military service. Holy Cross was one of many that took advantage of the Navy's V-12 Program to keep its dormitories full and its finances healthy during the war. Because the Navy required that its commissioned officers be college graduates, the V-12 Navy College Training Program was initiated in 1943 by the federal government to meet the need for qualified officers. Eventually, V-12 screened and selected about 125,000 young men who attended regular college classes at 131 colleges and universities. While in class, they were on active duty status, in uniform, and under military discipline. Those who successfully completed the curriculum went on to receive commissions as Navy ensigns or Marine Corps second lieutenants. The program was a perfect match for the government and educational institutions like Holy Cross, where loss of enrollment meant financial loss. It's no wonder that in the mid-1940s, the baseball and football bleachers at Holy Cross suddenly blossomed with squads of Midshipmen in coats of navy blue, white caps, and gold buttons. (The neighborhood locals affectionately called them "Middies".) Author Kuzniewski says that 3,900 alumni served in World War II (not all were "Middies"), and 109 were killed.

During this time, Holy Cross sports events became a major draw, not just for middies and students, but for the general population of Worcester as well. Baseball games were well attended, and in 1934 the Holy Cross "Crusaders" began a series of annual exhibition games against the Boston Red Sox, and later with the Boston Braves, giving the locals a chance to see their favorite professional ball players in person. In fact, according to the Evening Gazette of April 15, 1939, famed Red Sox slugger Ted Williams had hit his first rookie-year home run at Fitton Field on April 14—a grand slam in the first inning!

But football was becoming even more popular, thanks in part to the Boston College—Holy Cross "Holy War" that pitted two Jesuit Colleges against each other in one of the biggest rivalries in New England, and packed Fitton Field on Thanksgiving weekends. A Boston writer recalls this rivalry at its height:

"In 1942 came perhaps the most famous game in the history of the rivalry. Boston College was looking to close a perfect season and was already destined for an Orange Bowl date with Alabama. A post game victory party was already scheduled for the Coconut Grove in Boston. The Eagles forgot to focus on football and the Crusaders came and buried their unbeaten season hopes with a 55-12 thrashing. But if a loss was ever a good thing, this was it—the party at Coconut Grove was canceled, and a tragic fire broke out at the club on Saturday night, resulting in the death of 500 people."[23]

The post war years introduced a period of rapid change in Worcester. The burgeoning middle class could now afford a home in the suburbs and an automobile to carry them to work. But the city's infrastructure was aging, and it needed those years to catch up with the changing needs of its businesses and private communities. The transition from rail to automobile and truck traffic required better highways, streets and bridges. According to Erskine, as the veterans returned, the city's housing shortage was acute, and starting in 1946 the Worcester Housing Authority built apartments at Lakeside, followed by the Curtis Apartments and Great Brook Valley. Another new sewage treatment plant was begun that year, new sewers and water mains were laid, and "one after another modern structure replaced the old buildings."[24]

After the war ended, most veterans returned home and resumed their interrupted lives. Not all of them returned to the homes they left behind. Some like brothers George E. and Raymond F. Pugh, returned to places they first saw and became attached to while in uniform. They were the sons of an English immigrant named Edward A. Pugh, a weaver who lived on Boyden Street. Both brothers were young mail carriers in 1940, and lived there with their parents. After the war, they married and found work as mail carriers in Pasadena, California where they made their homes. However, most Worcester veterans returned to the city and took up the jobs they left behind. Shirley (Jones) Mickelson wrote this about her returning brothers: "Gordon was working for Howard Brothers before he went into the service. Bob started off with Mass Electric. When they came back from the service they got their jobs back. They never worked for anyone else." To the outsider, it seemed as though the re-assimilation of the veterans was effortless, although surely, there were private exceptions to this appearance. Likewise, the conversion from war to commercial production in Worcester's factories seemed trouble free. Business was booming again, and prosperity was back, not just in Worcester, but in cities across America. As with Gordon and Bob Jones, men took up jobs that supported a family and lasted a lifetime. This was the dawn of the halcyon years of the middle class; years that offered security backed by the Federal government, and private sector jobs with pensions and health insurance, vacations, and a 40-hour work week.

As the men returned home, some women receded to their tradition roles as housewife and mother. All over America, neighborhood family life took on the aspects that were later characterized as typically American in television shows of the 1950s like "Leave it to Beaver". Husbands went off to work on a strict daily schedule; on weekends, they did home repairs, maintenance, mowed lawns and played golf. Their wives spent their daytimes in the kitchen preparing meals, or house cleaning, and child raising. A husband's pride in being the family breadwinner was matched equally by his wife's pride in a well-kept home and a well-cooked meal. Characterization notwithstanding, this is much like it was in suburban South Worcester, although many households had 2 wage earners. By that time, the community was as American as apple pie, with only a hint of England in the homes of grandparents. For this grandson, these hints came mostly from Grandmother Mary (Brewerton) Dodsworth, who lived on the corner of Southbridge Street and College Street. Her modest apartment resembled what might be described as aging Victorian; a cast-iron stove and a worn ornate carpet in the kitchen/living area, a pantry separated by curtains, a wall mounted toilet tank with pull-chain in the bathroom, and what might have been one of the last ice-boxes still in use in Worcester. Pictures of a young Queen Elizabeth and Bonnie Prince Charles decorated the walls, along with a picture of Jesus with eyes that seemed to follow one's every move. Her apartment was the first stop on the paper route, and it started there with a cup of tea and toast, or a slice of bread spread with butter and topped with sugar.

The children of the community were raised in the "free range" style, and the playground was anywhere outdoors. Reverting to memory: Our mothers let us outside to play with our neighborhood friends, and we came back home whenever we were tired, cold, or hungry. We had plenty of places to play in our ample backyards or the nearby woods. We hit baseballs at Cookson Park, or caught frogs in Stillwater pond, which was unfit for swimming. But we could hop on our bikes or take a bus and swim in the blue waters of Camp Gleason, in Auburn. In addition to sleds, skis, skates and bicycles, our playthings included BB guns, bows and arrows and jackknives; all of which, in our unsupervised freedom tempted danger and caused untold numbers of cuts, bruises and broken bones. In fact, one of the authors remembers being shot in the leg at a very young age with a pellet gun while playing "cops and robber".

But neither we, nor our parents, thought about the unknown dangers that strike fear in our modern neighborhoods, and somehow we survived the dangers we made for ourselves. Grownup friendships, leisure and entertainment increasingly centered on the neighborhood and less on the church, although the two were still intertwined. There were backyard parties (fig. 11-4) on holidays that featured buckets of clams and melted butter, corn on the cob, hamburgers and hot dogs. On summer Saturday nights, the men played badminton on a well-lit backyard court while the women watched and their children played games that kept them busy and out of the way.

Figure 11-4. A backyard party at the Margaret and Milton Jones yard at 10 Glade Street. The 3-decker in the background is on Boyden St. (From the Jones Family collection.)

As was the case elsewhere, these South Worcester neighborhoods eventually added local commercial developments as befitted their needs. On Southbridge Street at College Square the neighborhood had a gas station, the Union Public grocery market, Dominic's (Schiavone) hardware store, Farrell Cleaners, and Thompson's Lunch (drug store/soda and ice cream counter), a barbershop and the Purple Diner (fig 11-5).

Figure 11-5. The Purple Diner was located on the west side of Southbridge Street at College Square and in the authors' youth was owned by "Twisty" Bent. Whittall Mill buildings are in the background. (From the collections of the Worcester Historical Museum, Worcester, Massachusetts.)

Dining out was not common among the families that lived there. Women were responsible for feeding the family, and they did—breakfast, lunch, and dinner. At home, meals were what can best be called "American"; cereals and porridge or bacon and eggs for breakfast, soups and sandwiches for lunch; pork chops, beef, and chicken with mashed potatoes or French fries and peas for dinner. Vestiges of English heritage were sometimes served, like fish & chips, ox tail soup, and beef and kidney pie with a heavy crust on top. There were plenty of restaurants in downtown Worcester, mostly in hotels, but they weren't frequented by the working classes and only rarely by middle class suburbanites, except for special occasions. When on downtown errands to pay telephone and electric bills (in cash), one might stop at a cafeteria or lunch counter at Woolworth's or Kresge's for a quick bite to eat. In addition to lunch counters and cafeterias, diners were entering the peak of their popularity. These iconic American eating establishments evolved from horse drawn lunch wagons that once roamed city streets and served simple meals and coffee to night shift workers (fig. 11-6).

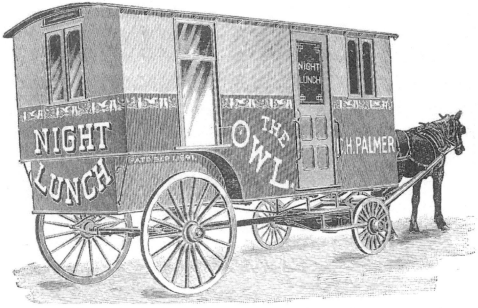

Figure 11-6. "The Night Owl", a new concept in traveling night restaurants that was patented in 1891. The company eventually became the Worcester Lunch Car Company and made diners that were shipped all over eastern U.S. It sat up to 16 people and served meals during the night, probably mostly to factory workers leaving or arriving at late shifts. (Worcester Board of Trade, 1893, p. 97.)

"Around the beginning of the 20th century", according to diner historian Gutman, "Worcester was a city of lunch wagons [with] no fewer than 14
men guiding their horses through the streets at dusk, parking their wagons
at designated spots, and serving food at the wee hours."[25] In 1906, an enterprising insurance and real estate agent named Philip Duprey established
the Worcester Lunch Car and Carriage Company that quickly became one
of the most successful manufacturers of diners in America. It was located at
the corner of Southbridge Street and Quinsigamond Ave. By the mid-1920s,
lunch cars had become known as diners and were open 24 hours, serving
breakfast, lunch, and dinner. To soften their image, and to invite female patronage, many diners added the prefix "Miss" to their names, as in the "Miss
Worcester Diner".

By the 1940s, most suburban neighborhoods had their own local lunch
counter, soda shop, or diner. (South Worcester neighborhoods had their Y-D
Diner and the Purple Diner.) These neighborhoods were very self-contained,
as if they had some invisible boundary. The people of South Worcester rarely
ventured out into other neighborhoods in search of ethnic foods like Italian,
Jewish, or Middle Eastern, not because they feared the people, but because
their food was too exotic for their tastes. South Worcester had at least one
"ethnic" restaurant of its own: a fish & chip shop, which, ironically, became
popular with the local Irish Catholics (who faithfully ate fish on Fridays), as
well as the English community. As recalled by Alice (Chew) Jones, wife of
Gordon Jones, her father opened the first shop in 1925:

"He started out on Canterbury Street and didn't make a go of it. It just
wasn't a very good area. So he moved over near Maloney's Field [fig. 10-12]
on Douglas Street and within a month he paid my grandfather back the
money he had borrowed from him. That was a Catholic neighborhood. The
Irish went to Sacred Heart and the French went to Notre Dame in the West
Main neighborhood. He did a very good business. People used to come in
on Friday and the line would be way back to the door. He was open from 9

in the morning till 11 at night. My mum cooked the chips, my dad cooked the fish and some chips, and my sister and I were waitresses and served the counter too, when we got old enough. We wrapped the fish and chips with paper. There was some eat-in but mostly take-out. My brother and I used to take fish and chips up to Crompton & Knowles for their dinners and we also went to Whittall's with a wagonload of fish and chips. We just sold the fish and chips and also had haddock by the pound. It was $.39 a pound at that time."

Later in the decade, as the number of two car families increased and their more adventuresome driving age children were dating, this inward neighborhood focus began to change. More mobility, leisure, vacation and Sunday drives invited the growth of roadside eateries, and drive-ins and drive-throughs came to typify American roadways and neighborhoods. In South Worcester, a taste for Italian sandwiches ("grinders") first acquired through their sale at Holy Cross games attracted its young people to Turo's and Toscano's markets on Shrewsbury Street or Maury's Deli in Webster Square. Sometime in the late 1940s or early 1950s, pizza was introduced to Worcester as "tomato pies." Two decades later, when the craze for ethnic foods began, pizza shops were already competing with American hamburgers and hot dogs and the diners that served them.

In response to a request for a brief history of the Whittall Carpet Company, an employee of the Worcester Historical Museum concluded with this succinct description of the Company's demise: "The depression of the 30s, changing styles, and the war years brought changes, but it was the 1955 flood, which caused great damage to the mill complex, that really ended the era there."[26] Figure 11-7 shows the river in flood at College Square in 1955.

As we have seen, at the time of the 1940 census, Whittall's was still reeling from the depression, with most employees on part time hours, and senior executives taking pay cuts or no wages. In time, as prosperity returned, the company might have recovered, if America's tastes in floor coverings had remained the same, but, as the responder said, styles had changed. In the 1940s, consumers were decorating their floors with inexpensive linoleum, or monotone carpeting. A book published in 1941, "A History of American Carpet Manufacture" asked this prescient question about the future of Whittall's: can a carpet company that continues to make intricate, high quality, but expensive machine made Orientals (fig. 11-8) survive in an age of inexpensive monotones?[27]

And, another change, more serious than style preference, was looming. The textile industry was moving to the South, where non-union mill workers were willing to work more hours for much lower wages. When hurricane Diane drowned the Whittall's complex in the great flood of August 1955, it delivered the last blow after two decades of struggle.

Figure 11-7. College Square in the 1955 flood. One of the Whittall mill buildings is in the background behind Diamond T truck sales. From left to right are Alan Jones, Gordon Jones, Mel Mickelson, and son David peeking from behind. The entrance to Fitton Field is behind them. (From the Jones Family collections.)

Figure 11-8. Whittall's specialized in ornate, multi-colored Anglo-Persian carpets of excellent quality. This is pattern 304.

Five years earlier, in October 1950, the 600 to 650 remaining employees of Whittall's shut down their machines and walked off their workstations. It was called a "Wildcat Strike" because it was unauthorized by the Textile Union. By that time, even the Union recognized that weavers in the Northeast were on thin ice and losing out to low-wage competition in the South. Just months before the flood, Whittall's was undergoing an expensive modernization process, and its leaders were talking about taking in an "allied line" in order to remain competitive and stay in Worcester. At that time, Whittall's was the last remaining carpet company in the area, and had only about 400 employees. The flood's damage destroyed this last hopeful outlook. In 1956, The Roxbury Carpet Company turned the tables and acquired Whittalls Associates. A portion of the company remained as the Whittall Division until 1964, when it closed. By that time, it employed 195 workers, down from its peak of 1500 before WWI.

Although the English community was now dispersed in three separate South Worcester neighborhoods, (with some even further beyond) St. Matthew's Church remained as its common center through the 1940s. The depression and war years were difficult times for the church, which felt their impact in diminished pledges and attendance. In 1934, a shortfall in the budget prompted the church to make "drastic reductions, including salary cuts for Rector, Organist, and Sexton" and put tight restrictions on all expenditures. The decline in pledges was a sign of the depression, but the drop in attendance signaled something more fundamental; a community that was becoming less cohesive, less like their predecessors, and more widely scattered. In response, the church sent out volunteers who "visited 170 families in and effort to stimulate more active interest in attendance."[28] Still, a core group of the devout remained strong in their attendance at worship services in church sponsored events.

Many of the faithful still carried a lingering sense of their "Englishness", especially when Britain entered the war against Germany and stood alone. The Ladies Parish Aid Society hosted English Plum Cake tea parties, and Lilian Smith, the wife of the Rector, sold half a ton of homemade English mincemeat to raise money for the British War Relief Fund. The slogan on the jars read, "Every Jar Sold Will Jar Germany."[29] The Rector, William Smith and his wife were themselves immigrants from England. In the Parish Hall, the women of the church made surgical dressings for the Red Cross, knitted afghans, sweaters and mittens and collected care packages of other useful items for shipment to the embattled English homeland. An active social calendar still engaged parishioners in events like Ladies Night, Men and Boys Night, Mother and Daughter Banquet, Strawberry Festival, Military Whist, Turkey Supper and the Annual Bazaar. Radio broadcasts of St. Matthew's church services began in the summer of 1947 and continued for the remainder of the decade, which helped to keep the more distant and infirm in touch with their church. But times were changing; the younger generations were disconnecting and fewer children were attending church school. The new Rector, Father McKenzie, called for, "Less birth control and more religion" and urged the parents to take more interest in their children's attendance: "Please parents, begin to realize the seriousness of your neglect. Delinquent parents cause juvenile delinquency."[30]

At the time, the issue of birth control was highly controversial. In 1944, Hudson Hoagland and Gregory Pincus of Clark University formed the Worcester Foundation for Experimental Biology, which developed the world's first oral contraceptive. In 1948, the Anglican Bishops announced a Church doctrine that stressed abstinence but approved the use of birth control in limited circumstances. According to Paula Buonomo, Father McKenzie (who once called for less birth control), felt that "citizens had allowed the Roman Catholic minority view to dominate, and that citizens should remember, 'we have freedom to choose, by the gift of almighty God himself.'" The Anglican announcement came with another resolution that warned its membership against "contracting marriages with Roman Catholics… especially as these conditions involve, among other things, a promise to have their children brought up in a religious system which they cannot themselves accept." In Worcester, Father McKenzie advised his congregation to "give serious thought before you are too much in love [and to] see the Rector before you get in too deep."[31] Both of the present authors remember hearing those warnings when we were entering our teenage years.

In these issues of dogma we see the specific "lines in the sand" that kept ordinary Protestants and Catholics separate and apart. On a broader scale, leaders on both sides had already concluded that modern American society was too liberal and accepting of views outside their own parochial boundaries. As early as 1899, Pope Leo issued a warning to Irish liberals to refrain from efforts to mold their church to American culture and reconcile with American Protestants. As we've seen, Irish Catholics had already gained political power in cities like Boston and Worcester, and by the 20th century, Americans of Irish descent were climbing the economic ladder, and seeking acceptance and accommodation within their communities. But this was not to be. As Irish historian Timothy Meagher tells it, a super patriotism inspired by World War I, and the post-war depression that followed, led to a resurgence of Protestant nativist resentment and the re-birth of a Ku Klux Klan (KKK) that was especially virulent towards Catholicism.

By 1924, there were about 5,000 KKK in Worcester. When the Catholic New York Governor Alfred E. Smith was nominated to oppose Herbert Hoover as President, Catholicism became the primary national election issue. In Worcester, the 1928 election campaign became a fevered contest between Catholic Democrats and Swedish-Yankee Republican businessmen. Each side held parades. The Republicans organized their 1928 procession by manufacturing companies: workers and managers from Norton Company, Heald Machine, Whittall Carpet Mills, and other firms, all marched behind their company banners.[32] This rebirth of nativism and anti-Irish sentiment in the mid to late 1920s spelled the end of Irish accommodation efforts and gave way to a new era of "defiant separatism."[33] By the 1950s, Catholic churches, schools, hospitals and charities were springing up with nuns and priests everywhere. Catholic Americans would go their own way and live alongside their Protestant neighbors as separate but equal Americans. In this light, it is no wonder that intermarriages between them were uncommon.

At the base of Pakachoag Hill, just a short walk from the Catholic College of the Holy Cross, St. Matthew's Episcopal Church held on to its own orthodoxy while the world changed around it. The signature mainstay of the church was the Men's and Boys Choir (fig 11-9).

Based on a centuries old Anglican Church choir tradition, St. Matthew's choir had become something of a right of passage for generations of young boys, many of whom remained with the choir as they aged. In the opinion of these ex-choir boys, it was the choir, with soloists like George Wilson and El-liot Lassey, backed by organist "Jimmie" Gow's pipe organ, that grounded the English character of the church and kept its pews full into the 1950s. St. Matthew's Church continued to hang on, and still does, but by the mid twentieth century, it was no longer the neighborhood church for an English community.

Figure 11-9. The St. Matthew's choir in the early 1950s. (From St. Matthew's Episcopal Church collection, copying by Robert Townsend.)

269

Notes:

1. Southwick, Albert B.: "Stock market crash in 1929 took a while to hit Page One" online at: http://www.thefreelibrary.com/Stock+market+crash+in+1929+took+a+while+to+hit+Page+One.-a0192248393

2. Independence Hall Association, Philadelphia 2008-2014, online at ushistory.org.

3. Marx, J.D. *American social policy in the Great Depression and World War II* 2011. <http://www.socialwelfarehistory.com/eras/american-social-policy-in-the-great-depression-and-wwii/> Retrieved May 5 2015.

4. Cheape, Charles W. *Family Firm to Modern Multinational*, p. 1535.

5. Erskine, Heart of the Commonwealth p. 123.

6. Online at: www.The Westboro Patch. Patch.com, accessed May 1, 2015.

7. May White interview, Worcester Women's Oral History Project, July 28, 2011: http://www.wwhp.org/activities-exhibits/oral-history-project accessed May 5 2015.

8. America in the Great War, online at www.eyewithnesstohistory.com, 2000.

9. "A 73 year old woman" posted March 7. 2013, http://voicesofworcesterwomen. blogspot

10. "Social and Cultural Effects of the Depression" online at http://www.ushistory.org/us/48e.asp, accessed May 21 2015.

11. "Radio in the 1930s" on line at: http://www.radiostratosphere.com/zsite/behind-the-dial/radio-in-1930.html, accessed April 20, 2015.

12. Herwitz *Trees At Risk*, p. 147.

13. Textile World Magazine, November 11, 1922.

14. Southwick, Albert, *"Once Told Tales of Worcester County" Worcester Telegram and Gazette*, 1985. The city eventually chose a site on Tatnuck Hill, an area that straddles the borders of Worcester, Leicester, and Paxton. This airport was ceremoniously opened in May 1946, and started regular passenger service one week later on 10 May 1946. The Grafton airport remained in operation until 1951, when it was sold by the owners due to the dwindling traffic.

15. American Wool and Cotton Reporter, November 23, 1922, p. 61.

16. "Gertrude Clarke Whittall" Performing Arts Encyclopedia, Library of Congress, Music Division.

17. "Mrs. Matthew J. Whittall" obituary. New York Times, June 30, 1965.

18. Bradley, Carol June: "Edward N. Waters: notes of a career". The Free library by Farlex. Dec 1, 1993.

19. "Gertrude Clarke Whittall" Library of Congress Special Collections, Music Division.

20. Erskine, *Heart of the Commonwealth*, p. 127.

21. "Cookson Field" online at www.WorcesterMA.gov. In 1936, the Works Progress Administration (WPA) performed a site clean-up to improve the landscape and use of the park. In 1981 the City's Open Space Plans, stated that the facility was largely undeveloped, lacked suitable access and contained amenities in poor condition. The field, like other areas of the park, has since further deteriorated, becoming overgrown and unusable.

22. Kuzniewski, *Thy Honored Name*, p. 277-278.

23. boston.sportsthenandnow.com, Boston College Holy Cross Thanksgiving, Nov., 24, 2011.

24. Erskine, *Heart of the Commonwealth*, p.132.

25. Gutman, *Worcester Lunch Car Company*, p. 19.

26. Worcester Historical Museum, email June 16, 2000.

27. Cole and Williamson, *The American Carpet Manufacture*

28. Buonomo, Paula, *Forward Through the Ages*, p. 35.

29. Ibid, p. 39.

30. Ibid, p. 51.

31. Ibid, p. 53.

32. Meagher, *Inventing Irish America*, p. 307-319.

33. Ibid, p. 373.

— Chapter 12 —
Epilogue:
Change and Renewal

My co-author, David Mickelson, and I are cousins. We grew up across the street from each other on Glade Street, where it ended at the edge of the woods that bordered our yards on the northwest side of Pakachoag Hill. Ours was one of three streets that climbed up the hill from Southbridge Street. The others were Boyden and Kendig. These, plus three lateral streets, Clay, Heath and Caro, were our neighborhood, and its outer boundaries were College Hill and Malvern Road. The homes on these streets were a mix of multiple story tenements (many were 3-deckers) and single story capes built during the first three decades of the 20th century, a time of optimism, when even the working classes might own a home of their own. Regardless of style, most were impeccably maintained, which, together with their well-kept lawns and gardens, reflected a pride of ownership.

My boyhood covered the war years of the 1940s and the early postwar years of the 1950s. David Mickelson, seven years younger, would later share the same neighborhood and experiences. Within the boundaries of our neighborhood, we had woods to explore, trees to climb, hills for sliding and skiing, and at the lower end of our street, we could skate or hunt frogs at Stillwater Pond. Cookson Park was just a short walk from our homes. It was almost superfluous as an outdoor experience, but it did have slides, swings, and a relatively level field for intra-neighborhood baseball games.

Holy Cross, a few blocks away, offered college football and baseball, and pre-season baseball games with the Boston Red Sox and the Boston Braves. We could pay to watch them if we had to, but it was more fun to sneak in, if we could.

Within the span of our boyhood years, the residents of our neighborhood remained a mix of three generations - grand parents, and married couples with children. A scant few of the elders worked at Whittall's, and most of the men were employed in a variety of white collar or blue collar jobs that supported home and family. The typical family provider worked a reasonable 40 hour week, was home for dinner, and enjoyed puttering around their houses on weekends. Their wives took pride in their cooking, housekeeping and motherhood. It was not a wealthy neighborhood, nor was it a poor one, and the families were stable. Divorce, alcoholism, scandal and unemployment were not part of our boyhood memories. The only policemen in our neighborhood had been hired to guard the gates at Holy Cross athletic events. We never thought of ourselves as city boys. The city was a distinct experience. We could get to it easily enough on the 10 South Worcester bus from Boyden Street, if we needed to shop for a new Easter suit or, on Saturdays, catch the latest Westerns or horror movies at one of several downtown theaters.

By all appearances, ours was a typical American suburb of the mid-twentieth century. It was White, predominantly Protestant, and the native language was English. The restraints of war time and the depression preceding it were giving way to a new age of consumerism where home ownership, a car in every garage and a television set in every home were real possibilities. Our neighborhood was at the lower end of a new middle class spectrum, and perhaps more conservative in its habits than others, so material acquisitions came more slowly, family by family, car by car, television by television. The American character of our community belied the fact that Glade Street and the two streets adjacent to it were predominantly of recent

English descent. Besides the several Jones families, there were the Parkers, Burns, Mapps, Cutters, Taylors, Townsends, Halls, Underwoods, Hemmings, Whittakers, Woolhouse, and others with English surnames. Similar neighborhoods with the same proportion of Italians, Jews, or Irish, would probably have been labeled accordingly, but no one ever referred to our neighborhood as "English". David Mickelson's family, of mixed Swedish/Finnish descent on his father's side, added a small measure of diversity to the neighborhood when the Mapps moved out and they moved across the street in the early 1950s. As paperboys, we delivered papers to a few Catholic homes within the edges of our neighborhood, which we could distinguish by the smells of fish cooking on Fridays and displays of the crucifix on their walls. Both of us had friends among the children of these families, and our parents opposed prejudice of any kind. If this was an unusual or unique stance within our neighborhood we were unaware of it. In fact, until we began researching the history of Worcester for this book, were unaware of the dark side of the history of Catholic-Protestant or Irish-English relations. Whatever prejudices our grandparents and their contemporaries may have had were either gone, or kept under wraps.

David Mickelson and I went to Malvern Road elementary school, as did the majority of our neighbors, except for the few Catholics who went to Sacred Heart School. The only glimpses here of what might now be called ethnic diversity came from the children of French Canadian descent who lived on Malvern Road. Reflecting on this now, it's apparent that we had grown up in something of a cocoon; when our grandparents moved to this (then) new suburb, they had moved away from a neighborhood that offered more diversity than ours did. Later, we attended South High School and began our journey into a broader outside world we hadn't yet experienced.

We also shared the common "rite of passage" that was the St. Matthew's Choir. The church and parish hall were the last remaining cornerstones that still connected the broader community to its immigrant beginnings and to each other. Sunday services and occasional parish events brought members of the church together who otherwise lived separate lives in separate places. As choirboys, we were drawn out of our suburbs to our ancestral neighborhood for rehearsals on Tuesday and Thursday evenings, and services on Sundays. Otherwise, the neighborhood that spawned ours was outside our daily lives. Whittall's mills were closed and we knew them only as abandoned brick buildings that we passed on our way to church. It didn't occur to us then that those buildings and the tenements nearby were once the workplace and homes of our grandparents. Perhaps because the immigration experience of our grandparents lacked the drama and desperation of other immigrant groups, it wasn't an ingrained memory they thought worthy of passing down. Or, perhaps they simply preferred to live in the present, rather than in the past. Or was it because we never asked? What was it like for them to leave home and kin, and once they did, was it worth it? Thinking back, my grandmother (Dodsworth) talked about her beloved Yorkshire dales and moors whenever she was given the chance. I have a few photos that were sent to her, like the one inscribed, "To Mary, from your loving mother and sister." These are reminders that the act of emigration, regardless of motivation, involved sacrifice and loss.

Unfortunately, their personal histories are mostly lost, and it is too late to get their memories first-hand. Most of what we know now about them comes from ancestry records and census data, a few memories, and old letters and photos. Memory suggests that they were a reserved people; not the pinched "stiff upper-lip" reserve that is supposed to be characteristic of the British upper classes, but in their restraint of outward expressions of emotion. Regarding the supposedly dry English sense of humor, we remember elders whose humor ranged from outright silly to seemingly humorless. As parents, they weren't harsh, nor were they smothering or demonstrative. They looked with disfavor at the "coddling" or spoiling of their children. They were devout, but didn't wear their religion on their sleeves. Ancestral records tell us that although they left some family behind when they emigrated, they also took a lot of family with them. Common sense tells us they were a practical people. They weren't forced to emigrate under political or religious pressures or by poverty. They had simply seized an opportunity that opened up when a new carpet mill opened up in South Worcester.

If our portrait of our boyhood years seems too idyllic, it should be remembered that we grew up in an era that was generous and promising to white Americans in general. Here is how the U.S. history site history.org summarizes the era: "The United States was the world's strongest military power. Its economy was booming, and the fruits of this prosperity—new cars, suburban houses and other consumer goods—were available to more people than ever before... Rates of unemployment and inflation were low, and wages were high. Middle-class people had more money to spend than ever—and, because the variety and availability of consumer goods expanded along with the economy, they also had more things to buy. The booming prosperity of the 1950s helped to create a widespread sense of stability, contentment and consensus in the United States."[1]

The dark cloud on this bright American dream was "The Bomb" and a Cold War that threatened to unleash it. It was a real threat, but it was beyond the grasp of young boys who assumed that, somehow, adults would resolve it as they had resolved past threats. When change did come, it didn't come with a military bang. It snuck in with more subtle, but fundamental economic shifts and the loss of manufacturing through consolidations, relocations, and closings. The closing of Whittall's was just the beginning of that trend in Worcester. According to the Worcester Historical Museum's web site, "Between 1950 and 1992, many Worcester companies closed their doors, resulting in the loss of thousands of jobs." Their graph of closings includes a number of "old mainstays of the local economy" like American Steel & Wire, the Royal Worcester Corset Company, Graton & Knight, Heywood Boot & Shoe, Pullman Standard (formerly Osgood Bradley Car Company), Reed–Prentice Corporation, U. S. Envelope, Harrington & Richardson, Heald Machine, and Crompton & Knowles. The Crompton Loom Company outlasted Whittall's through a merger in 1897 with the Knowles Loom Works, but, "in 1980 the massive Crompton & Knowles factory works, a Worcester landmark since 1897, closed its antiquated plant and relocated in the south."[2] One of the most notable survivors of this period is the Norton Company. Through most of its history, Norton's, like Whittall's, was privately and locally owned, but it was purchased in 1990 by Compagnie de Saint-Gobain of France. However, Norton Company remains a significant presence and source of employment in Worcester.

In tandem with the decline in manufacturing jobs, Worcester's inhabitants were moving to the suburbs or out of Worcester altogether. At its peak, the city's population was 203,486 in 1950. By 1990, its population declined to 169,759, a decrease of more than 34,000 people. A recent column by Albert B. Southwick described the decline of downtown retailing that paralleled the decline of Worcester's manufacturing base and population:

"Fifty or sixty years ago, downtown Worcester was a lively place. More and more automobiles rolled along the streets and jammed the available parking spaces. The street cars and then the buses brought loads of people ready to shop at the retail stores within walking distance of City Hall. The J.C. MacInness store was directly across from City Hall. C.T. Sherer was located on Front Street, Barnard's a block or two north on Main Street. Filene's with its bargain basement sat on Main Street next to the Park Building. Bargain shoppers headed for Woolworth's or Newberry's on Front Street or Kresge's on Main Street across from City Hall. There were also a clutch of more specialized stores—Richard Healy's, Ware Pratt, etc. But the grand dame of downtown stores was Denholms, originally Denholm and McKay. It was a full-service store in all respects. Women's wear, men's clothing, kitchen utensils, toys, hosiery, costume jewelry, cosmetic creams, electrical appliances, furniture, draperies, rugs and many other lines were offered over the years… Its imaginative window displays were a constant education and entertainment for passersby. Holidays were especially important. Many recall the spectacular Denholms Christmas tree, 80 feet high, emblazoned by thousands of lights over the Main Street entrance. The final days of the great store were sad. Business started to decline in the 1960s when outlying and suburban shopping malls transformed the retailing business… Denholms closed its doors on January 14, 1974."[3]

According to historian Karen M. Pierson, "the Worcester Redevelopment Authority decided in 1965 to create a new downtown to counter the loss of more than 130 stores that had left Worcester or closed forever during the 1950s. More than 90 buildings were demolished to make way for this new office and shopping centre." However well intentioned, the Galleria shopping mall, which opened in 1971, was an "act which gutted Worcester, removing the heart they had hoped to save. The modern edifice that rose in its place was never associated with such feelings of loyalty and warmth as when the original downtown was extant."[4] Another major blow came in the 1960s with the construction of Interstate 290, which permanently divided the city and cut through many of the neighborhoods that once made it home. Although the highway made travel to and from the city easier, it also prompted additional emigration out of those neighborhoods and out of the city itself.

Because the downward spiral in manufacturing jobs was decades long, most members of the second generation—our parents, uncles and older cousins, including those who came back from WWII—managed to hang on to their jobs until they had raised their families and retired or passed on. But those decades were also times of rapid and profound social change. Although we are cousins and once lived across the street from each other, David Mickelson and I didn't know each other until long after we left our homes in Worcester and raised our own families. The difference in our ages was enough to put us out of range as potential playmates, and we took separate paths when we entered adulthood. Both paths took us away from Worcester. After we graduated from college in the 1960s, we both found jobs outside the state of Massachusetts, and we return to Worcester only for occasional visits with family.

After decades of life lived and families raised elsewhere, Worcester has become an unfamiliar place. Many of the places we knew are gone or markedly changed. Old familiar streets, while still there, are lost under a highway system built in the 1960s, and finding our way around requires a period of adjustment. Life seems to move faster in Worcester and its traffic is frantic. This is best typified by Kelley Square, a horror that one Facebook entry dubbed as "the craziest intersection in the world, where the trick is to slow down, feel the FORCE then move with it." (You can actually buy bumper stickers that say, "I survived Kelley Square.") Downtown Worcester still has a familiar ring to it, thanks to City Hall, Worcester Memorial Auditorium, the U. S Post Office, and the Courthouse buildings that have (so far) escaped the wrecking ball and still provide bearings at various points of travel along Main Street. Although both of us have returned to Worcester for family visits over the years, more often than not, they seem to confirm the old saying that, "you can't go home again." This becomes abundantly apparent when we enter Worcester on I-290 from Auburn and find ourselves riding above and beyond South Worcester with barely a glimpse of it.

If we visit our old neighborhood now, as we have done while writing this book, we take the College Square/Southbridge Street exit ramp (Exit 11) to College Square. Approaching College Square, we see a park-like setting of lawn and trees on the site that was occupied by several tenement buildings that housed my grandmother Dodsworth and her neighbors in the 1940s. Another century earlier, the first South Worcester schoolhouse stood there. This property was purchased in 1998 by Holy Cross College and was returned to nature as a gateway buffer. Perhaps this is fitting, for it makes the property a part of a 174-acre campus that boasts "more than 6,000 trees, plants, and shrubs," and "ranks No. 8 in the country on Best Choice Schools' list of "The 50 Most Beautiful Urban College Campuses."[5] A right turn on College Street shows that the college has never ceased expanding since its first purchase of land in 1843. Portions of Caro, City View, and Clay Streets have also been purchased by the college and returned to nature. Recent additions that can't be seen from College Street cover much of the eastern side of the hill almost to the borders of Quinsigamond Village and Auburn. A 2015 U.S. News Report says that the college is "among the top liberal arts colleges", with an undergraduate enrollment of just under 3,000. It describes Worcester as "the second-largest city in New England and a booming college town to boot", which seems odd, because, in spite of the proximity of the college to our homes, South Worcester never had the feeling of a college town. Perhaps this has since been enhanced, as Holy Cross is now "one of 13 schools in the Worcester Consortium" which allows students to take courses at other schools and receive discounted tickets to various events around the city. [6]

Off the western side of College Street, Cookson Park, long abandoned in that purpose, has been undergoing renewal as a nature/trails preserve, thanks to the Friends of Cookson Park, a volunteer organization that brings together neighbors, college students, businesses, and city officials to clean up, preserve and maintain this "natural gem" for the enjoyment of the community. A right turn down Malvern Road to its junction with Southbridge Street takes us past the Malvern Road school building, which has been "re-purposed" for residential condominiums. The building was listed on the National Register of Historic Places in 1984. Another right turn takes us north along Southbridge Street, and back to our neighborhood, which has changed in places, but has an overall familiar look to it. Both of our boyhood homes are still there, looking much like we remember them, but apartment buildings have been added at the top of Glade and Boyden Streets, where birch and other hardwoods once stood.

Heading north again on Southbridge Street, we no longer see Stillwater Pond, which has long since been covered over. The area called Stillwater Pond on today's Google map designates a section of the Middle River, which is now back in the place where it once was, before the Boyden & White machine shop put the first dam there. There is no need to mourn the loss of this pond; in truth, it was an abomination of pollutants that helped poison the Blackstone River and everything that lived in it. Thanks to federal, state, and local efforts such as the Blackstone River Coalition, the Middle River and the entire Blackstone River watershed has been largely restored to its pre-industrial condition. The area the pond once covered at its peak is now occupied by the buildings and parking lots of National Grid, an electric utility company. Farther north, the buildings that once were Whittall's are now part of a commercial complex anchored by Rotmans furniture and carpet company. In the 1950s, Rotmans leased 10,000 square feet in the old mill and since expanded to more than 200,000 square feet. The surviving buildings of the Whittall's mills were listed on the National Register of Historic Places in 1980, and the surviving huge beams and post can be seen at Rotmans today.

The South Worcester Branch Library building at 705 Southbridge Street was built in 1913 with funds donated by philanthropist Andrew Carnegie, on land donated by M. J. Whittall. The single story Classical Revival building was listed on the National Register of Historic Places in 1980. The library closed in 1990, and the building was later converted to a duplex style condominium.

Between the library building and the corner of Southbridge and Cambridge Streets, St. Matthew's Church and parish hall look much the same as they did when we were members of the choir. This is one of the few places that belies the old adage that "you can't go home again." Once inside, the familiar beauty and serenity of the place feels like home. Yet, beyond its physical appearance, the church has changed profoundly. Its message is surely the same, but it now speaks to a very different community. According to the St. Matthew's website, "Today, the parish has begun to incorporate more recent immigrants from Africa and other parts of the globe who have added their own gifts to this increasingly exciting and diverse community… St. Matthew's parish hall has served its community well over the years by providing space for after-school programs, twelve-step groups, ethnic congregations and other outreach programs as well as the parish Sunday school, youth group, church fairs and gatherings, meetings and activities, office and chapel." St. Matthew's isn't alone in its efforts to serve the needs of this increasingly diverse neighborhood. On November 27, 1988, the church and nearby Sacred Heart Catholic Church on Cambridge Street entered into a Covenant that commits them to work together for the common good.

Another old institution that serves the common good of this neighborhood is the Cambridge Street School. The public school was closed in 1976, but the building is leased now by the Village at Cambridge Street, a social service organization that provides homeless families with a temporary place to live while they train and search for employment. Patricia Reardon, who lives near the Village, said the neighbors, area churches, and organizations such as the South Worcester Neighborhood Center welcomed and embraced the newcomers. "This interaction is what makes a community a neighborhood," she said.[7] Brosnihan Square, known also as the "four corners", is formed by the intersection of Southbridge and Cambridge Streets. The soda shop, pool hall, and other stores that once occupied the north side of the intersection are long gone. A strip mall occupies the site of the home and gardens of the M.J. Whittall family, which, to our eyes, was a poor exchange. But it seems that the shops there have become part of the neighborhood, where they are within walking distance. This is especially true of Culpeppers Bakery and Café, where young and old people gather. An article in the February 2004 edition of Worcester Magazine described how the people of this neighborhood came together to fight off a plan to widen Cambridge Street for an access highway to the airport. As the airport itself declined, the need for an access road declined with it. But, as Pat Reardon remembers, "While we were fighting it back in 2004, the threat was very real, and we were fighting to protect our homes, churches, and cemeteries."[8]

A recent report published by GoLocalWorcester.com shows that Worcester's population is growing and that this growth is again driven by immigrants. As of the 2010 census, its population was 181,045, which is an increase of nearly 20,000 residents, or 12% over the preceding three decades. During the first decade of the 21st Century, the city's African American population increased by 77 percent, the Latino population grew by 45 percent and the Asian population grew by 31 percent. The countries of origin for most of these immigrants are Ghana, Brazil, and Vietnam, respectively. These immigrants are becoming Americans as our ancestors did over 100 years ago. The brunt of this task falls on the Public School system.[9] Once again, Worcesters' schools have the daunting task of educating students who are predominantly poor and non-English speaking. This means school officials must deal with issues like homelessness, hunger, and poor health while they are being educated. There are now seven public high schools in Worcester. They all have minority student populations that exceed 50%; three have minority populations ranging from 54% to 62%, and four have minority populations of 75% to 89%. In addition, the percentages of "economically disadvantaged students align in close proximity with these minority populations. With an almost 70% low-income population, South High Community School on Apricot Street is one of the poorest schools in the Worcester Public School system."[10] Enormous doses of creativity, dedication, and community support are needed to allow these immigrant students the opportunity their parents are seeking for them in Worcester. Maureen Binienda has been called the "Angel of the Battlefield" for the work that she does as the school's principal. In a 2013 interview with GoLocalWorcester, she describes how the community and school staff have worked together to bring this opportunity to fruition:

"In 2010 with the assistance of the Family Health Center of Worcester, the school opened a food pantry on the premises for students and their families. There is a full-service health center at the school that offers free eye exams and the Lion's Club donates the eyeglasses. Andy's Attic donates clothing to meet the needs of specific students. I volunteer as an usher at Hanover Theater and all 300+ ushers are involved in donating goods to our food pantry.

A lot of our staff members take leadership roles in dealing with these issues, so it is a group effort. In addition, our teachers volunteer their time to stay after school to provide extra academic support. 26 of our staff graduated from this school and we teach kids that education is the great equalizer. One former student even came back as assistant principal. That says so much to the kids they teach and demonstrates that there is no excuse to not move forward. Worcester is considered a safe city so kids are brought here to start a new life. They see America as the land of opportunity and the chance for a new life. The look of hope on their face is so powerful when they realize they will be given a free public education."[11]

Another encouraging prospect for renewal is the South Worcester Neighborhood Improvement Corporation (SWNIC), founded in 1969 by its Executive Director Ron Charette. Also known as the South Worcester Neighborhood Center, their goal is to "improve the quality of life of residents in our neighborhood." Toward that goal, the organization has been active in bringing affordable housing and economic development to the area. In 2011, the organization announced a grant of up to $200,000 for the creation of affordable housing units in the Southgate, Armory, and Grant Street neighborhoods. Charette's organization is also enlisting political support for the revitalization of the 11-acre South Worcester Industrial Park, which lies between Southgate Street and the Norwich and Worcester Railroad, where the Adriatic Woolen Mills and other industries once provided employment for some of the area's earliest immigrants. An article in the Worcester Business Journal Online (June 23, 2014) describes the promise of the park, and the efforts made to fulfill it: "Over the years, $6.5 million in federal, state and local funding has gone into the area—to efforts that included demolishing old buildings, cleaning up hazardous waste from old industrial operations and improving the roadways, streetlights and water and electric lines. The final product?... Space for up to six parcels of land available for light industrial and commercial uses, with the potential for as much as 180,000 square feet of new buildings. New occupants will find access to Interstates 290 and 90, Route 146, and downtown Worcester, as well as both the Providence & Worcester and CSX railroads."[12]

There are other reasons to believe that Worcester will make a comeback. Preservation Worcester, a private, non-profit organization is working to preserve the buildings, sites, and neighborhoods that represent the culture and history of the city. A good example is their efforts on behalf of the Blackstone Canal district and their maps for a self-guided walking tour. Since 2003, Worcester boosters and investors, much like the ones that brought the canal to Worcester in late 1820s, have been working toward the reopening the canal as a tourist attraction. Their initial talks led to the formation of the Canal District Business Association and later secured $7.6 million in federal stimulus funding to improve the streetscapes on Millbury, Water, Green, and Harding Streets.

Ten years later, on April 1, 2015, the Worcester Business Journal Online claimed that, "The Canal District is one area many point to as an up-and-coming place... The area, mostly Water and Green Streets, comes alive with bar and restaurant patrons on Thursday, Friday or Saturday nights. It's an image community leaders embrace, organizing events like the Mardi Gras festival Carnaval de Canal, which features food, drinks and entertainment." Plans for the area also include the addition of more housing and retail. These plans were slowed by the recent recession, but they got a big boost from a study published in 2015 that "found that reopening the canal from Harding from Union Station to Kelley Square… would mean a huge return on investment for the city. John Giangregorio, a local business owner, is one of those boosters and visionary dreamers behind the canal project. In response to the report, he said, "There's a real compelling case for why we should open up the canal… It would expand the tax base, create a larger demand for the existing hotels and encourage new ones, and the city itself would realize a benefit in terms of fees and taxes." Giangregorio also said the projected 100,000 visitors per year would also be a big win for not only the businesses within the Canal District, but also the city's attractions and restaurants.[13]

With all the ups and downs that Worcester has seen over the years, we wouldn't dare predict its future. The one thing we know for certain is that Pakachoag Hill still looks out over the city as it always has. When we lived there, one of its "pleasant springs" ran down the hill between Glade and Boyden Streets. No doubt, it still does.

Notes:

1. Online at: http://www.history.com/topics/1950s, accessed October 3, 2015.

2. Worcester Historical Museum: http://www.worcesterhistory.org/enter-prise-4c5-looms.html, accessed Sept. 28 2015.

3. Southwick, Albert B., online at http://www.telegram.com, posted Jan. 12, 2012 at 6:00 AM.

4. Pierson, *A Tale of Two Worcesters*, p. 92.

5. College of Holy Cross in the News: http://news.holycross.edu, 2015.

6. U.S. News and World Report, http://collegesusnew.rankinsand reviews.com/best-colleges, 2015.

7. Kush, Bronislaus B. "It Takes A Village", Posted Mar. 12, 2014, telegram.com, Worcester, Ma.

8. Patricia Reardon to David Jones, email, Oct. 5, 2015.

9. Drici, Joseph, "Minorities Driving Worcester's Population Growth", golocalworcester.com, Feb. 12, 2013.

10. The South High School we attended is no more. The buildings that housed it on 14 Richards Street are now used by the Goddard School of Science and Technology, grades PK–6.

11. Wagner, Susan, "Women Leading in Central Ma", golocalworcester.com accessed October 3 2015.

12. Gershon, Livia, "South Worcester Industrial Park", wbjournal.com, June 23, 2014.

13. Corcoran, Lindsay "Study Shows Blackstone Canal Opening Could Deliver Huge Return", masslive.com, January 17, 2015.

(From the collections of the Worcester Historical Museum, Worcester, Massachusetts.)

References

Books and Periodicals:
(Maps and other sources are listed after this section)

A Century of Carpet and Rug Making in America. Bigelow–Hartford Carpet Company, New York, NY, 142 p., 1925.

America's Textile Reporter, For the Combined Textile Industries, vol. 16, 1902.

Bacon, Leonard, D., *A Historical Discourse Delivered at Worcester in the Old South Meetinghouse, September 22, 1863; the Hundredth Anniversary of its Erection.* Printed by Edward R. Fiske, Worcester, MA, 1863.

Bancroft, James H., *The Merrifield Fire of 1854.* Proceedings of the Worcester Society of Antiquity for the Year 1900, no. LV., p. 142-161.

Barkan, Robert Elliott, ed., *Immigrants in American History; Arrival, Adaptation, and Integration.* eBook. ABC-CLIO LLC, Santa Barbara, CA, 2013.

Berthelson, Robert L., *An Alarm from Lexington.* Sons of the American Revolution, Connecticut. Online at http://connecticutsar.org/articles/

Biron, Heidi, *The Flame That Keeps on Burning.* The New Worcester Spy, 2015. Online at: http://newworcesterspy.net/the-flame-that-keeps-on-burning/

Bishop, Sande P., *The Story Behind Worcester's Poor Farm.* On line at: http://www.worcesterma.gov/city-clerk/history/general/poor-farm.

Blewett, Mary H., *The Yankee Yorkshireman; Migration Lived and Imagined.* University of Illinois Press, Urbana and Chicago, 232 p., 2009.

Breen, T. H., *American Insurgents, American Patriots: The Revolution of the People.* Hill and Wang, New York, NY, 337 p., 2010.

Breisch, Kenneth A. and Hoagland, Alison K., *Building Environments: Perspectives in Vernacular Architecture.* University of Tennessee Press, Knoxville, TN, 2006.

Buonomo, Paula Rowse, *Forward Through the Ages: A History of St. Matthew's Episcopal Church 1871–1995*. Worcester, MA, 118 p.,1995.

Bullock, Chandler, *John Chandler and a Few of His Descendents.* Paper read before the Worcester Historical Society, November 14, 1922.

Caranci, Paul F., *North Providence, A History and the People Who Shaped It*. The History Press, Charleston, SC, 128 p., 2012.

Cheape, Charles W., *Family Firm to Modern Multinational: Norton Company*. Harvard University Press, Cambridge, MA, 424 p., 1985.

Chenoweth, Caroline Van Dusen, *The School History of Worcester*. Oliver B. Wood, Worcester, MA, 167 p., 1899.

Cole, Arthur Harrison and Williamson, Harald Francis, *The American Carpet Manufacture, a History and Analysis.* Harvard University Press, Cambridge, MA, 281 p., 1941.

Colvin, Kenneth, *Worcester Hero of the Revolution Died — in Jail!* Copyright 1998, Bigelow Society, Inc. Online at: http://bigelowsociety.com/Col._Timothy_Bigelow_Hero.html

Connecticut History, *Combined Rail- and Water-System Makes Norwich a Key Travel Hub in Mid 1800s.* Online at: http://connecticuthistory.org/combined-rail-and-water-system-makes-norwich-a-key-travel-hub-in-mid-1800s, May 2014.

Commercialized Leisure, Digital History 2014, http://www.digitalhistory.uh.edu/disp_textbook.cfm?smtID=2&psid=3316.

Connole, Dennis A., *The Indians of the Nipmuck Country in Southern New England, 1630–1750 An Historical Geography.* McFarland & Company, Inc., Publishers, Jefferson, NC, 303 p., 2001.

Connolly, James J., *The Triumph of Ethnic Progressivism; Urban Political Culture in Boston, 1900-1925*. Harvard University Press, Cambridge, MA, 272 p., 1998

Crane, Ellery Bicknell, *Historic Homes and Institutions and Genealogical and Personal Memoirs of Worcester County Massachusetts.* The Lewis Publishing Co., New York, NY, vol. 1-3, 912 p., 1907.

Crompton, William and Crompton, George, *The Crompton Loom,* Davis Press, Worcester, MA, 101 p., 1949.

Crompton, George, *Mariemont*. Davis Press, Worcester, MA, 88 p., 1952.

Cronon, William, *Changes in the Land: Indians, Colonists, and the Ecology of New England*. Hill and Wang, New York, NY, 252 p., 1989.

Cudmore, Bob, *Stories from the Mohawk Valley: The Painted Rocks, the Good Benedict Arnold & More*. The History Press, Charleston, SC, 144 p., 2011.

Cutter, William Richard, *New England Families, Genealogical and Memorial*, vols.1-4, 1913–1915.

Daniels, Bruce C., *New England Nation; the Country the Puritans Built*. Palgrave Macmillan, New York, NY, 256 p., 2012.

Dempsey, James, *Cool, Clear Water*. Holy Cross College Magazine, vol. 44, no. 2, Spring, 2010.

Doherty, Joe, *The Poison Stream, Our River Series*. Online at: http://www.blackstone-daily.com/ourriver.htm

Earle, Alice Morse, *The Sabbath in Puritan New England*. Charles Scribner's Sons, New York, NY, 335 p., 1891.

Elliott, Emory, *The Legacy of Puritanism; Divining America*. Online at: http://nationalhumanitiescenter.org/tserve/eighteen/ekeyinfo/legacy.htm, 2013.

Emerson, William A., *Incidents, Anecdotes, Reminiscences, Etc. Connected with the Early History of Worcester, Mass. and Vicinity*. Denholm & McKay Co., Worcester, MA, 78 p., 1905.

Erskine, Margaret, *Heart of the Commonwealth: Worcester, An Illustrated History*. Windsor Publications, Woodland Hills, CA, 208 p., 1981.

Exercises Held at the Dedication of a Memorial to Major Jonas Rice, the First Permanent Settler of Worcester, Mass. Press of C. Hamilton, Worcester, MA, 174 p., 1903.

Farley, James J., *Making Arms in the Machine Age — Philadelphia's Frankford Arsenal, 1816-1870*. Pennsylvania State University Press, University Park, PA, 158 p., 1994.

Fisher, Ericka J., *Educating the Urban Race: The Evolution of an American High School*. Lexington Books, Lanham, MD, 2015.

Foty, Geraldine R., *Worcester's Own Timothy Bigelow Dies in City Jail*. Worcester Sunday Telegram, April 13, 1986.

Gookin, Frederick William, *Daniel Gookin, 1612–1687, Assistant and Major General of the Massachusetts Bay Colony.* Privately printed, Chicago, IL, 1912. Online at: https://archive.org/details/danielgookin161201gook

Greene, George Washington, *History of Worcester, Massachusetts.* J.W. Lewis & Co., Philadelphia, PA, 1889.

Greenwood, Janette Thomas, *First Fruits of Freedom: The Migration of Former Slaves and Their Search for Equality in Worcester, Massachusetts, 1862–1900.* The University of North Carolina Press, Chapel Hill, NC, 2010, 256 p.

Gutman, Richard J. S., *The Worcester Lunch Car Company.* Arcadia Publishing, MA, 2004, 128 p.

Hall, Michael G., *The Last American Puritan; The Life of Increase Mather.* Wesleyan University Press, Middletown, CT, 456 p., 1988.

Hanft, Sheldon, *English Americans; Countries and their Cultures.* Online at: http://www.everyculture.com/multi/Du-Ha/English-Americans.html

Herwitz, Evelyn, *Trees at Risk; Reclaiming an Urban Forest.* Chandler House Press, Worcester, MA, 208 p., 2001.

Hoar, George Frisbie, *1684-1884, Celebration of the Two Hundredth Anniversary of the Naming of Worcester, October 14 and 15, 1884.* Press of Chas. Hamilton, Worcester, MA, 184 p., 1885.

Howland, Henry Jenkins, *Heart of the Commonwealth, or Worcester as it is.* Henry J. Howland, Worcester, MA, 131 p., 1856.

Izard, Holly V., *Hepsibeth Hemmenway's Portrait: A Native American Story.* Old-Time New England Magazine, vol. 77, no. 267, p. 49-85, 1999.

Janzen, Carol Anne and Paine, William, *Dictionary of Canadian Biography*, vol. 6, University of Toronto/Université Laval, 2003.

Jordan, John W., ed., *Colonial and Revolutionary Families of Pennsylvania*, vol. II. The Lewis Publishing Co. , New York, NY, 1911.

Kelleher, Tom, *Father James Fitton: Missionary Catholic Priest in Early 19th Century New England.* Old Sturbridge Village Documents, May 1997.

Kingsley, Elbridge and Knab, Frederick, *Picturesque Worcester, Complete in Three Parts with 2500 Illustrations.* The W.F. Adams Company, Springfield, MA, 1895.

Kinnicutt, Lincoln N., *Historical Notes Relating to the Second Settlement of Worcester.* Worcester Society of Antiquity, Worcester, MA, 30 p., 1916.

Kush, Bronislaus B., *Prof Works to Preserve Indian Site.* Worcester Telegram & Gazette, Worcester, MA, November 24, 2005.

Kuzniewski, S.J., Anthony J., *Thy Honored Name—A History of the College of the Holy Cross 1843–1904.* The Catholic University of America Press, Washington, D.C., 516 p., 1999.

Larkin, William J., *Looking Back on a Half Century: A retrospective newspaper series published by the Worcester Evening Post*, 1935–1936, and re-published online, 2011 at Google Books, 160 p.

Lepore, Jill, King Philip's War and the Origins of American Identity. Alfred A. Knopf, New York, NY, 368 p., 1998.

Lawes, Carolyn J., *Women and Reform in a New England Community, 1815–1860.* University of Kentucky Press, Lexington, KY, 2001, 265 p., 2001.

Leach, Douglas Edward, *Flintlock and Tomahawk; New England in King Philip's War.* The Macmillan Company, New York, NY, 304 p., 1959.

Lincoln, William, *History of Worcester, Massachusetts, From its Earliest Settlement to September 1836.* Moses D. Philips and Company, Worcester, MA, 408 p., 1837.

Lincoln, William, *Worcester in 1850.* Henry J. Howland, Worcester, MA, 64 p., 1850.

Lovejoy, David S., *The Glorious Revolution in America.* University Press of New England, Hanover, NH, 423 p., 1987.

Lovell, Albert Alonzo, *Worcester in the War of Revolution: Embracing the Acts of the Town from 1765 to 1783 Inclusive.* Tyler and Seagrave, Worcester MA, 152 p., 1876.

Massachusetts Historical Reconnaissance Survey Town Report Worcester, 1984.

McCarthy, Eugene B. and Doughton, Thomas L., eds., *From Bondage to Belonging; the Worcester Slave Narratives.* University of Massachusetts Press, Amherst, MA, 325 p., 2007.

McConaghy, Mary, *The Whittaker Mill 1813–1843; A Case Study of Workers, Technology and Community in Early Industrial Philadelphia.* Pennsylvania History, vol. 51, January, p. 30-63, 1984.

Meagher, Timothy J., *Inventing Irish America; Generation, Class, and Ethnic Identity in a New England City, 1889–1928.* University of Notre Dame, IN, 523 p., 2001.

Meagher, Timothy J., *To Preserve the Flame; St. John's Parish and 150 Years of Catholicism in Worcester.* St. John's Church, Worcester, MA, 1984.

Miller, John C., *Sam Adams: Pioneer in Propaganda.* Stanford University Press, Stanford, CA, 437 p., 1936.

Miner, Sydney Roby, *Colonel Isaac Barré 1706–1802: Orator, Soldier, Statesman and Friend of the American Colonies.* Wilkes-Barre PA, Wyoming Historical and Geological Society, 1901. https://books.google.com/books?id=xfE_

Morris, Charles, *Famous Men and Great Events of the Nineteenth Century.* J.C. Winston and Company, Philadelphia, PA, 636 p., 1899.

Moynihan, Kenneth J., *A History of Worcester, 1674–1848.* The History Press, Charleston, SC, 188 p., 2007.

Murphy, Katherine, *An English Gothic for 19th-century Worcester. Worcester and Its People.* Online at: http://college.holycross.edu/projects/worcester/neighbors/stmatthews.htm

Nash, Gary B., *Red, White and Black: The Peoples of Early America.* Prentice-Hall, Inc., Englewood Cliffs, NJ, 362 p., 1974.

Nason, Elias, *A Gazetteer of the State of Massachusetts: with Numerous Illustrations.* B.B. Russell, Boston, MA, 740 p., 1890.

Nutt, Charles, *History of Worcester and its People, Vol. 1-4.* Lewis Historical Publishing Company, New York, NY, 1919.

O'Toole, James M. and Quigley, David, eds., *Boston's Histories: Essays in Honor of Thomas H. O'Connor.* Northeastern University Press, Boston, MA, 2004, 284 p.

Papazian, Bruce and Larkin, William J., *Looking Back on a Half Century: A retrospective newspaper series published by the Worcester Evening Post from August 15, 1935 to January 15, 1936.* Harvard, MA, December 25, 2011.

Putnam, Eban, *A History of the Putnam Family in England and America.* The Salem Press, Salem, MA, 1891.

Rafael, Ray, *The First American Revolution, Before Lexington and Concord.* W.W. Norton, New York, NY, 273 p., 2002.

Rafael, Ray, *Founders: The People Who Brought You a Nation*. The New Press, New York, NY, 594 p., 2009.

Rice, Franklin P., *The Worcester of Eighteen Hundred and Ninety-Eight. Fifty years a City*. F.S. Blanchard, Worcester, MA, 822 p., 1899.

Rice, Franklin P., ed., *Worcester Town Records 1822–1832*. The Worcester Society of Antiquity, Worcester, MA, 1893.

Roe, Alfred Seelye, *Light. A Journal of Social Worcester and Her Neighbors*. Worcester MA, 1890.

Rosenzweig, Roy, *Eight Hours For What We Will. Workers & Leisure in an Industrial City, 1870–1920*. Cambridge University Press, Cambridge, UK, 320 p., 1983.

Shipton, Clifford K., *The Puritan Influence in Education*. Pennsylvania History, vol. 25, no. 3, (July), p. 223-233, 1958.

Smith, L.D., *Carpet Weavers and Carpet Masters; The Hand Loom Carpet Weavers of Kidderminster 1780–1850*. Kenneth Tomkinson Limited, Kidderminster, UK, 316 p., 1986.

Stark, James Henry, *The Loyalists of Massachusetts and the Other Side of the Revolution*. James H. Stark, Boston, 505 p., 1910.

Sturgis, E. O. P., *A Sketch of the Chandler Family in Worcester, Massachusetts*. Press of Charles Hamilton, Worcester, MA, 98 p., 1903.

Thompson, Melvyn, *Woven in Kidderminster*. David Voice Associates, Kidderminster, UK, 202p., 2002.

Tulloch, Donald, *Worcester: City of Prosperity*. Commonwealth Press, Worcester MA, 324 p., 1914.

Turner, Sylvie and Parks, Roger N., *New England Cider Mills, Distilleries, and Breweries, 1790–1840*. Old Sturbridge Village Documents, 1964. Online at: https://www.osv.org/artifacts/collection-search

Van Vugt, William E., *Britain to America: Mid-Nineteenth-Century Immigrants to the United States*. University of Illinois Press, IL, 241 p., 1999.

Wall, Caleb A. Esq., *The Nipmuck Indians*. Press of O.B. Wood, Worcester, MA, 40 p., 1898.

Wall, C.A., *Reminiscences of Worcester from the earliest period, historical and genealogical: with notices of early settlers and prominent citizens, and descriptions of old landmarks and ancient dwellings, accompanied by a map and numerous illustrations.* Worcester, Tyler & Seagrave, Worcester, MA, 392 p., 1877.

Ward, Andrew Henshaw, *Genealogical History of the Rice Family.* C. Benjamin Richardson, Boston, MA, 379 p., 1858.

Washburn, Charles G., *Industrial Worcester.* The Davis Press, Worcester, MA, 348 p., 1917.

Whaples, Robert, ed., *Hours of Work in U.S. History.* Online at: https://eh.net/encyclopedia/hours-of-work-in-u-s-history/, August 14, 2001.

Whittall, M. J. and Associates, *Inside Facts About Our Whittall Rugs and Carpets.* The Whittall Press, Worcester, MA, 1922.

Wilson, Richard A., Jr.,The Blackstone Canal Historical Journal of Massachusetts, Vol. 28, no. 1, (Winter), p. 76-96, 2000.

Worcester Board of Trade, *A Tribute to the Columbian Year by the City of Worcester.* F.S. Blanchard and Company, Worcester, MA, 199 p., 1893.

Worcester Historical Museum, *Landscape of Industry: an industrial history of the Blackstone Valley.* University Press of New England, Lebanon, NH, 178 p., 2009.

Worcester Historical Museum,Worcester in the 19th Century. Online at: http://www.worcesterhistory.org/

The Worcester Magazine Devoted to Good Citizenship and Municipal Development. The Board of Trade Blanchard Press, Worcester, MA. Online at: https://archive.org/details/worcestermagazin01worc

Exercises Held at the Dedication of a Memorial to Major Jonas Rice, the First Permanent Settler of Worcester, Mass. Worcester Society of Antiquity, Proceedings, vol. 19, Worcester, MA, p. 299-306, 1903.

Yaeger, Dan, *Francis Cabot Lowell, The Brief Life of an American Entrepreneur: 1775–1817.* Harvard Magazine, September-October, 2010. Online at: http://harvardmagazine.com/2010/09/vita-francis-cabot-lowell

Maps:

Bailey, O.H. and Hazen, J.C., 1878, *The City of Worcester (Bird's-eye view)*: Boston, Bailey and Hazen. (This was reproduced by the Worcester Historical Museum in 1986.)

Baker, T.W. and Walling, H.F., 1857, *Map of Worcester County, Massachusetts*: Boston, Wm. E. Baker & Co.

Beers, F. W., Neuman, L. E., Hart, C, and Sanford, G. P., 1870, *Atlas of Worcester County, Massachusetts*: New York, F.W. Beers & Co.

Beers, F. W. and Sanford, G. P., 1870, *Atlas of the City of Worcester, Worcester County, Massachusetts*: New York, F.W. Beers & Co.

Beers, F. W. and Sanford, G. P., 1870, *Atlas of the City of Worcester, Worcester County, Massachusetts*: (Reprinted 1971.) Rutland, Vermont, C.E. Tuttle Co.

Blake, F.E, 1883, *Plan of the Town of Worcester 1795*, Copied from the original in the State Archives by John Pierce and David Andrews.

Burbank, C.W., 1871, *Plan of the central part of the City of Worcester*: Worcester, H. J. Howland.

Carleton, Osgood, 1802, *A map of Massachusetts Proper*: Boston, B. & J. Loring.

City Planning Board, 1924, *City Plan, Map of the City of Worcester Mass*: Worcester, City Planning Board.

Drew Allis Co., 1873, *Map of the City of Worcester, Worcester Co.*, Mass.: Worcester, Drew Allis & Co. (also 1889, 1890, 1891, 1892)

Drew Allis, 1910, *Map of the City of Worcester*, Mass: Worcester. Drew Allis Co. (also 1915,1919,1920)

Healy, L.B, Emery, W.B., and Howland, H.J.,1850, *A map of the City of Worcester*: Unknown, H.J. Howland.

Hopkins, G.M., 1886, *Atlas of the City of Worcester*: Philadelphia, G.M. Hopkins.

Index Publishing Co., 1901, *The Worcester Index: a bureau of information, showing in detail the official plans of real estate and maps from latest surveys*: Worcester, Index Publishing Co., 326 p.

Phelps, E.E., 1829, *Map of the village of Worcester*: Lancaster, C. Harris, Carter,

Andrews & Co.

Polk, R.L. Co., 1941, *Map of the City of Worcester*: Unknown, R.L. Polk & Co.

Polk, R.L. Co., 1960, *Map of the City of Worcester*: Unknown, R.L. Polk & Co.

Richards, L.J., 1896, *Atlas of the city of Worcester, Massachusetts*: Springfield, L.J. Richards & Co. (also in 1898)

Richards, H.H., 1922, *Richards Standard Atlas of the City of Worcester*: Springfield, Richards Map Co., Plate 14.

Sanborn Map Co., 1892, I*nsurance Maps of Worcester, Massachusetts*: New York, Sanborn-Perris Map Co.

Sampson, Murdock & Co., 1927, *Map of the City of Worcester*: Boston, Sampson, Murdock & Co.

Stebbins, H. and. Harris, C. 1833, *Map of Worcester: shire town of the county of Worcester*: Worcester, C. Harris.

Sturgis Allen, R.H., 1986, *Worcester — A Retrospect*: Worcester Preservation Society.

Triscott, H.P.R., 1874, *Map of the City of Worcester*: Worcester, Drew, Allis & Co. Directory Office. (also 1875 edition)

Triscott, S., 1877, *Map of Worcester, Mass.* IN Wall, C.A., *Reminiscences of Worcester*: Worcester, Tyler & Seagrave, Worcester, MA, 392 p., 1877.

Triscott, H.P.R., 1878, *Map of the City of Worcester*: Worcester, Geo. H. Walker & Co.

Triscott, H.P., 1885, *Map of the City of Worcester*: Worcester, Drew, Allis & Co. Directory Office.

U.S. Geological Survey, 1886, *Webster Massachusetts – Connecticut – Rhode Island 15 X 15 Quadrangle*.

U.S. Geological Survey, 1892, *Webster Massachusetts – Connecticut – Rhode Island 15 X 15 Quadrangle*.

U.S. Geological Survey, 1921, *Webster Massachusetts – Connecticut – Rhode Island 15 X 15 Quadrangle*.

U.S. Geological Survey, 1939 and subsequent, *Worcester South 7.5x7.5 Quadrangle*.

Valentine, G., 1859, *Plan of the central part of the City of Worcester*: Worcester, Henry J. Howland. (Published several editions between 1859 and 1869.)

Van Valkenburg, J.J., 1891, *Pocket map of Worcester, Masssachusetts*: Unknown, George W. Armstrong.

Walker, G.H., 1893, *Map of Worcester*: Worcester, Geo. H. Walker & Co.

Walker, O.W., 1892, *Atlas of Massachusetts*: Worcester, Geo. H. Walker & Co.

Walling, H.F. and Gray, O.W., 1871, *City of Worcester in Official Topographical Atlas of Massachusetts*: Boston and Philadelphia, Stedman, Brown, and Lyon, p. 78.

Sturgis Allen, R.H., 1986, *Worcester, Mass. A retrospect:* Worcester Preservation Society.

Newspapers:

Kidderminster Shuttle

Lawrence Journal

London Times

Nason and Varney's Massachusetts Gazetteer

The Massachusetts Spy (1775–1876)

The New York Times

The National Aegis

Worcester Daily Spy (1878–1904)

Worcester Telegram & Gazette

Primary Sources:

Federal Census Records

Worcester City Directories

Worcester City Documents

Worcester Town Records 1784–1848

Index

Made in the USA
Middletown, DE
14 October 2016